IT'S HARD TO COMB A GRASS TOUPEE

A *Spot the Frog* Collection by Mark Heath

Andrews McMeel
Publishing, LLC

Kansas City

Spot the Frog is distributed internationally by United Feature Syndicate, Inc.

It's Hard to Comb a Grass Toupee copyright © 2007 by Mark Heath. All rights reserved. Printed in China. No part of this book may be used or reproduced in any manner whatsoever without written permission except in the case of reprints in the context of reviews. For information, write Andrews McMeel Publishing, LLC, an Andrews McMeel Universal company, 4520 Main Street, Kansas City, Missouri 64111.

07 08 09 10 11 SDB 10 9 8 7 6 5 4 3 2 1

ISBN-13: 978-0-7407-6353-3
ISBN-10: 0-7407-6353-9

Library of Congress Control Number: 2006937453

www.andrewsmcmeel.com

www.spotthefrog.net

Also by Mark Heath:

For Mary

Windows and Mirrors

(A foreword by Craig Terlson)

In the Heathian universe hats fly away to Winnipeg, frogs take on the shape of what they eat, and pumpkins wax eloquent on the nature of being. And as a bonus, there's often a punch line.

Spot the Frog is more than a vaudevillian one-two punch. Each panel is a window into a world that feels larger than the daily strip. We easily imagine the stories we don't see. And because windows are mirrors in the right light, Spot the Frog reflects our world as well.

Buddy's false bravado matches our own. There are days when Lumpy feels like the perfect role model. We laugh at the speedy turtles in our lives or the loud talkers like Bull. A few of us are Karl, and many of us would like to be.

At the heart of the strip is Spot himself. He is an everyfrog, innocent but somehow worldly. He puts up with Buddy's antics in the way that Huck Finn rides along with Tom Sawyer. Through his lopsided eyes we see the beauty in a wild pond and those who live there. He reminds us that the wonder we find in nature can also be found in our friendships.

Lastly, this is a comic after all. Pushing aside the philosophical ramblings, there lies one important thing. A frog wearing a sock on his head and saying, "My hat smells funny" is hilarious and wise.

Sometimes the best mirrors are cracked.

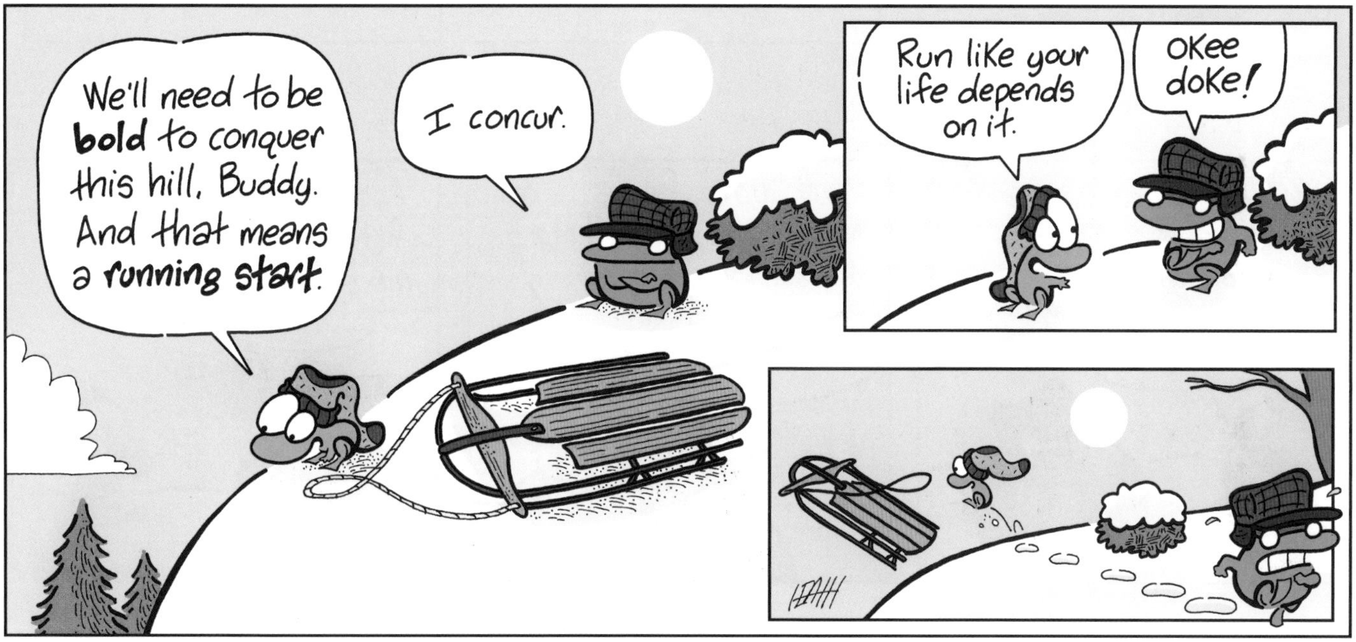
We'll need to be **bold** to conquer this hill, Buddy. And that means a **running start**.
I concur.
Run like your life depends on it.
OKee doKe!

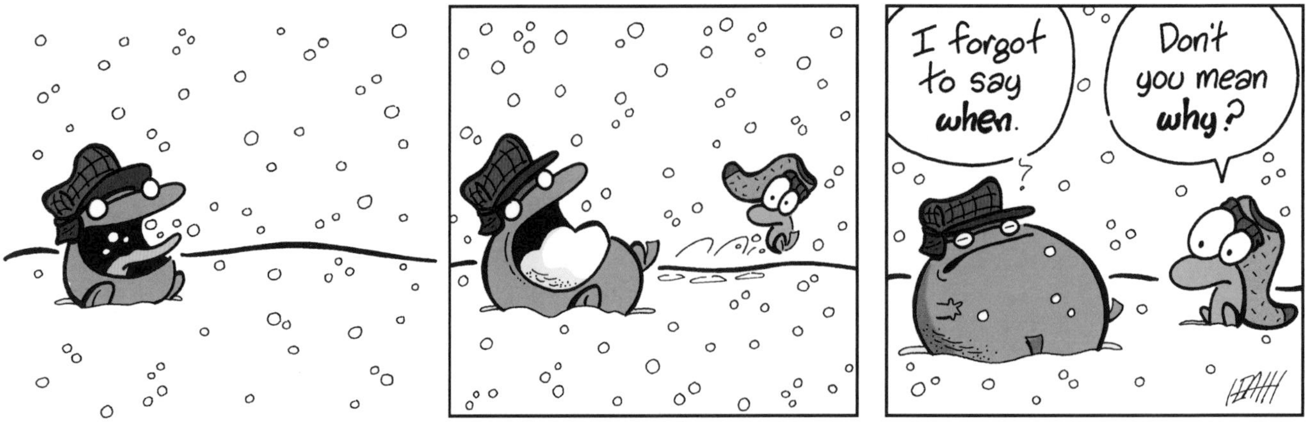

I forgot to say **when**.
Don't you mean **why**?

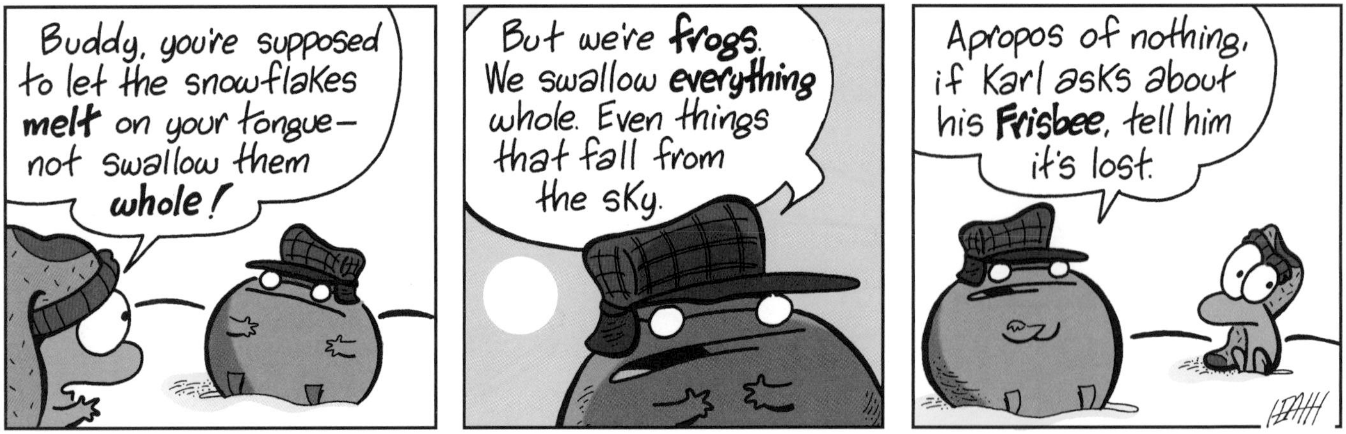

Buddy, you're supposed to let the snowflakes **melt** on your tongue— not swallow them **whole**!
But we're **frogs**. We swallow **everything** whole. Even things that fall from the sky.
Apropos of nothing, if Karl asks about his **Frisbee**, tell him it's lost.

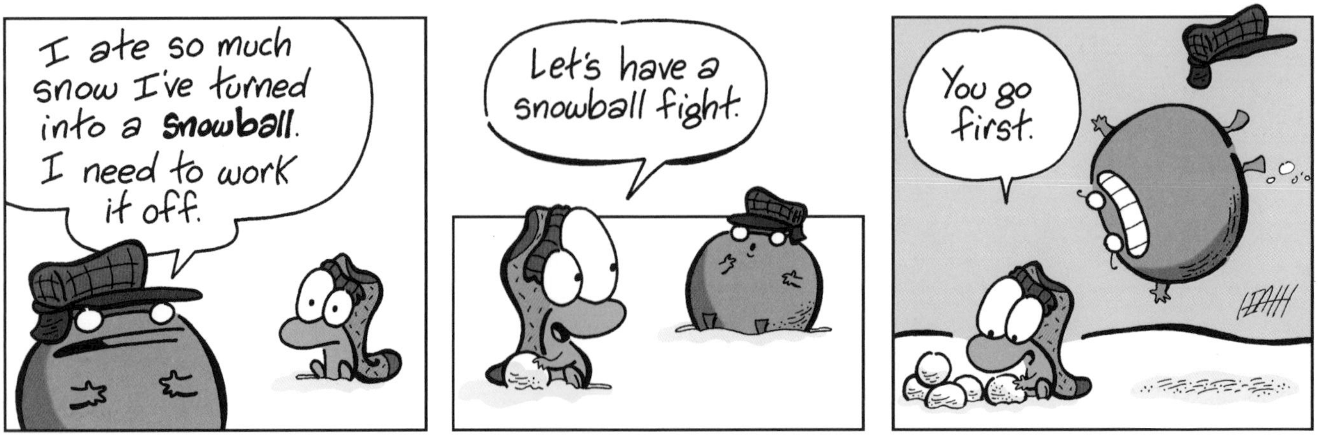

I ate so much snow I've turned into a **snowball**. I need to work it off.
Let's have a snowball fight.
You go first.

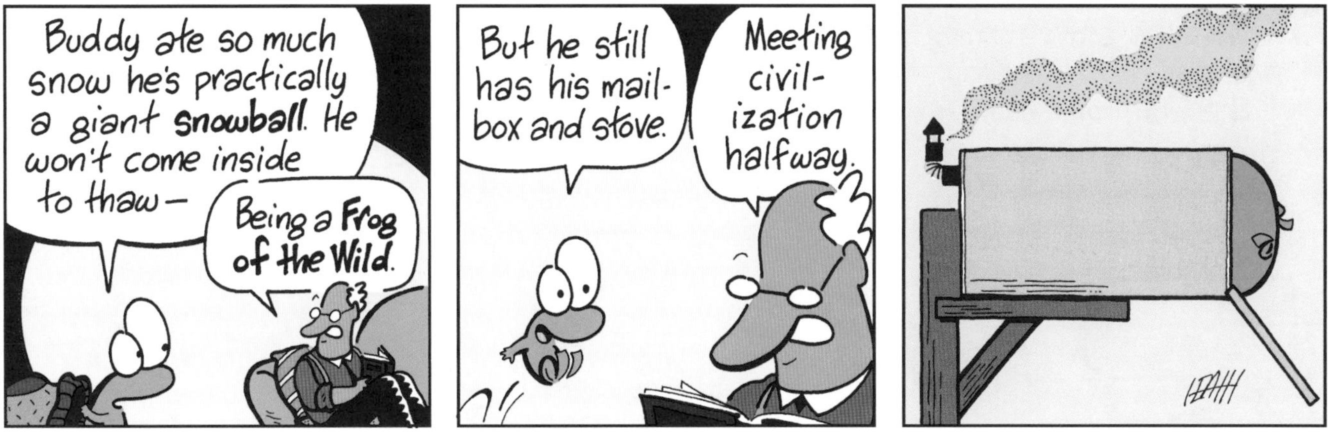
Buddy ate so much snow he's practically a giant snowball. He won't come inside to thaw—
Being a Frog of the Wild.
But he still has his mail-box and stove.
Meeting civil-ization halfway.

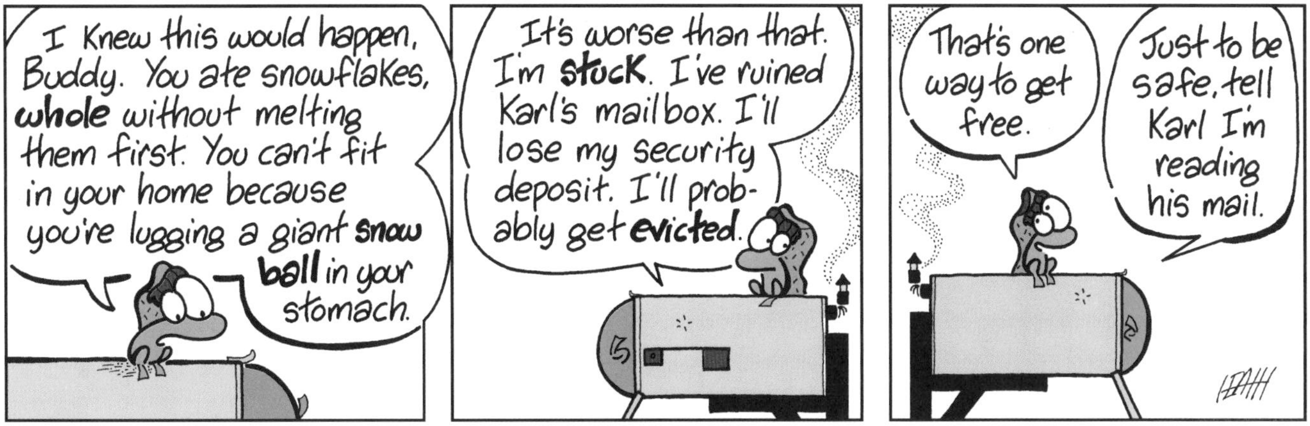
I Knew this would happen, Buddy. You ate snowflakes, whole without melting them first. You can't fit in your home because you're lugging a giant snow ball in your stomach.
It's worse than that. I'm stuck. I've ruined Karl's mailbox. I'll lose my security deposit. I'll probably get evicted.
That's one way to get free.
Just to be safe, tell Karl I'm reading his mail.

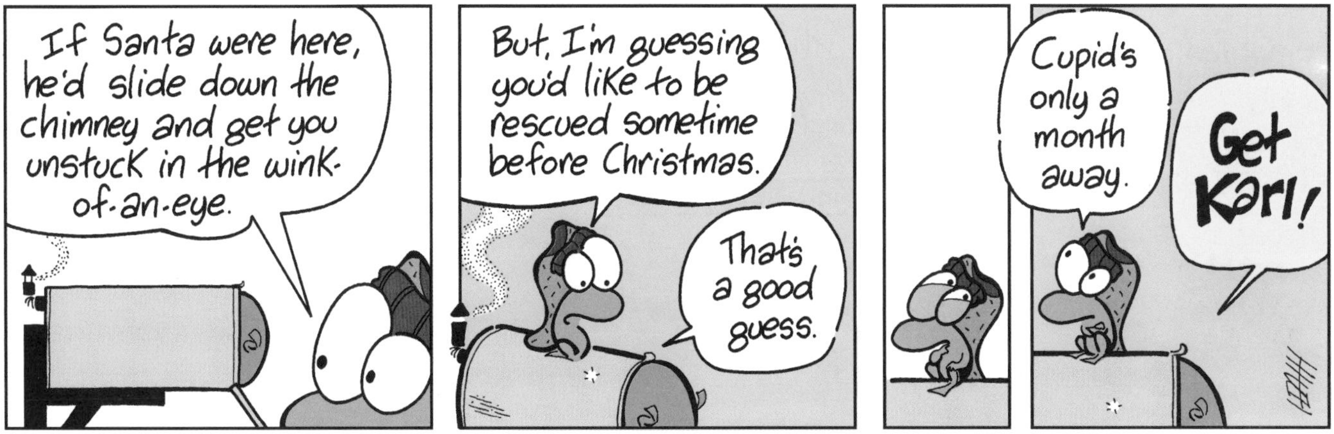
If Santa were here, he'd slide down the chimney and get you unstuck in the wink-of-an-eye.
But, I'm guessing you'd like to be rescued sometime before Christmas.
That's a good guess.
Cupid's only a month away.
Get Karl!

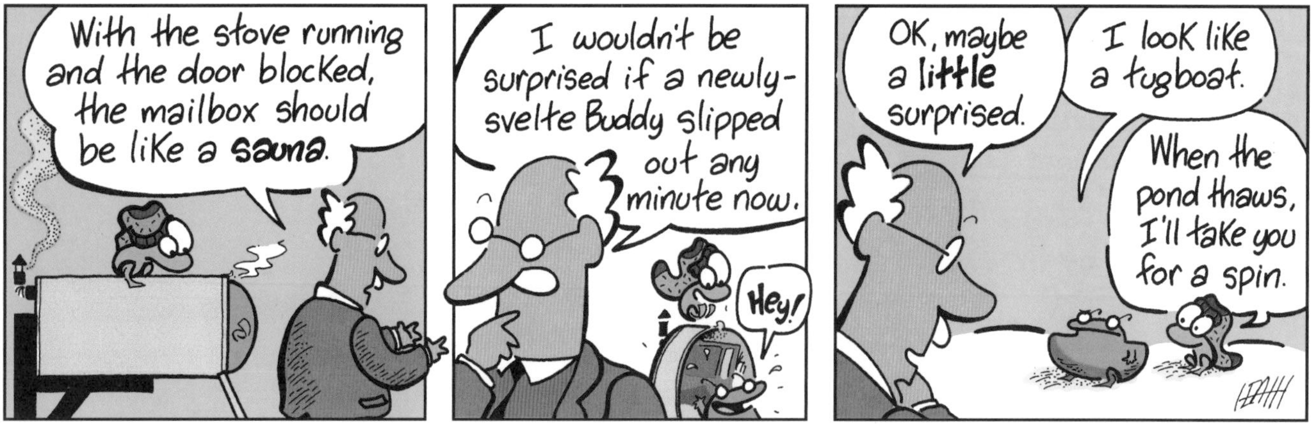
With the stove running and the door blocked, the mailbox should be like a **sauna**.
I wouldn't be surprised if a newly-svelte Buddy slipped out any minute now.
Hey!
OK, maybe a **little** surprised.
I look like a tugboat.
When the pond thaws, I'll take you for a spin.

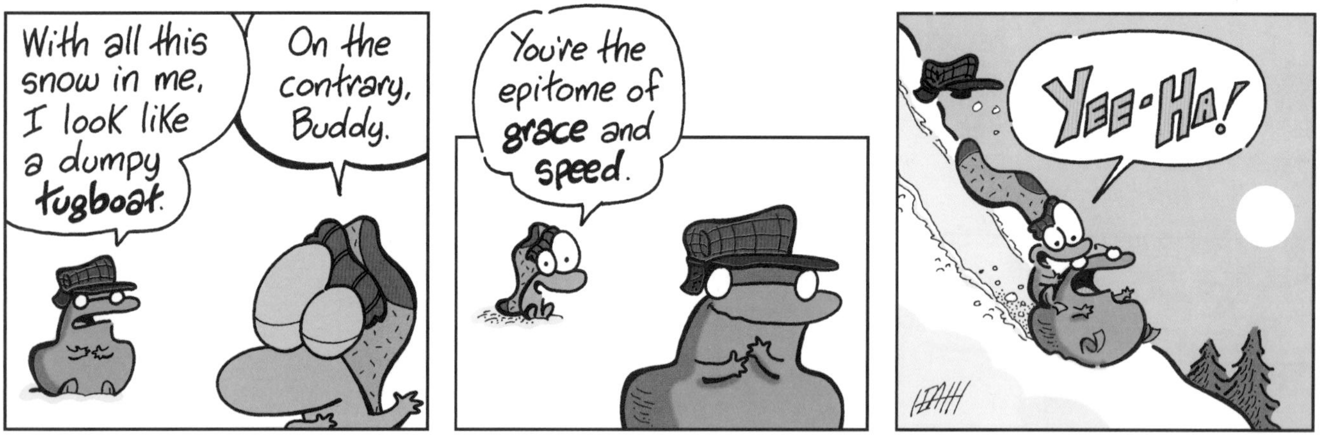
With all this snow in me, I look like a dumpy **tugboat**.
On the contrary, Buddy.
You're the epitome of **grace** and **speed**.
YEE-HA!

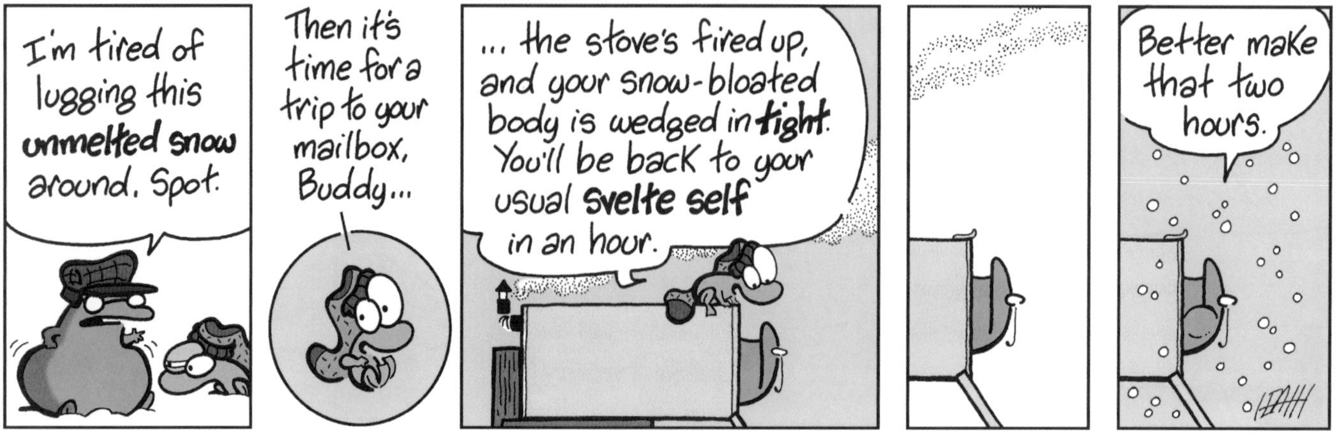
I'm tired of lugging this **unmelted snow** around, Spot.
Then it's time for a trip to your mailbox, Buddy...
... the stove's fired up, and your snow-bloated body is wedged in **tight**. You'll be back to your usual **svelte self** in an hour.
Better make that two hours.

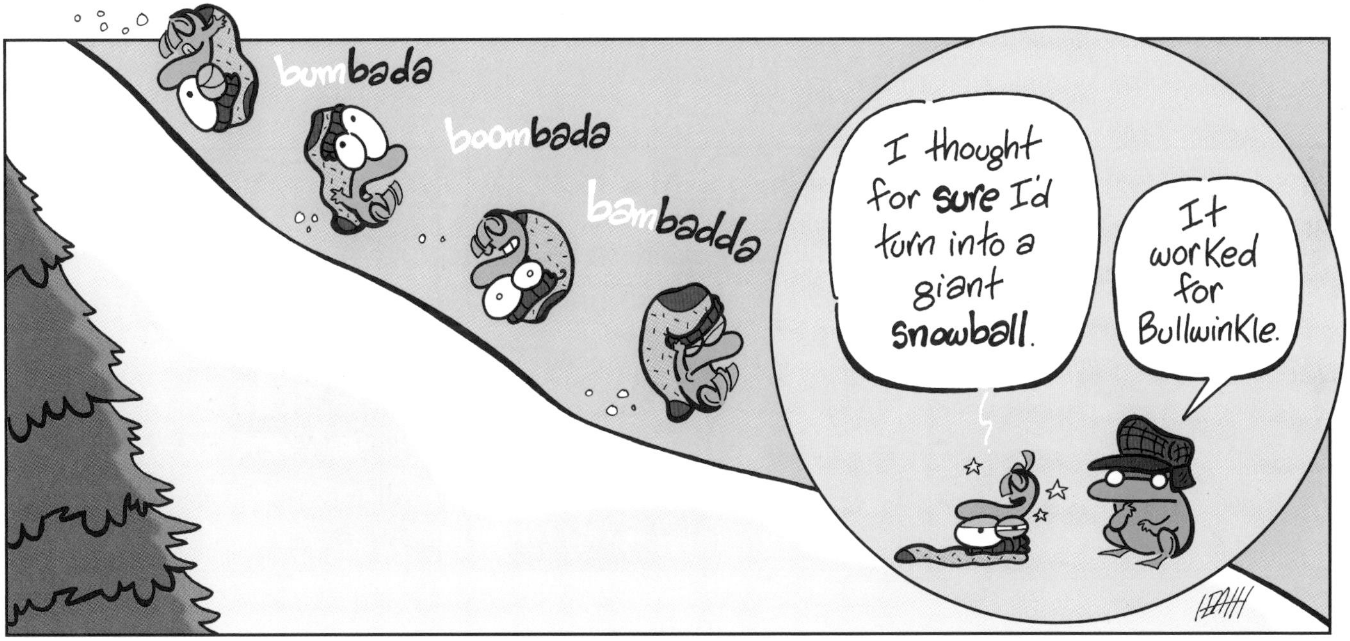
bumbada
boombada
bambadda
I thought for sure I'd turn into a giant snowball.
It worked for Bullwinkle.

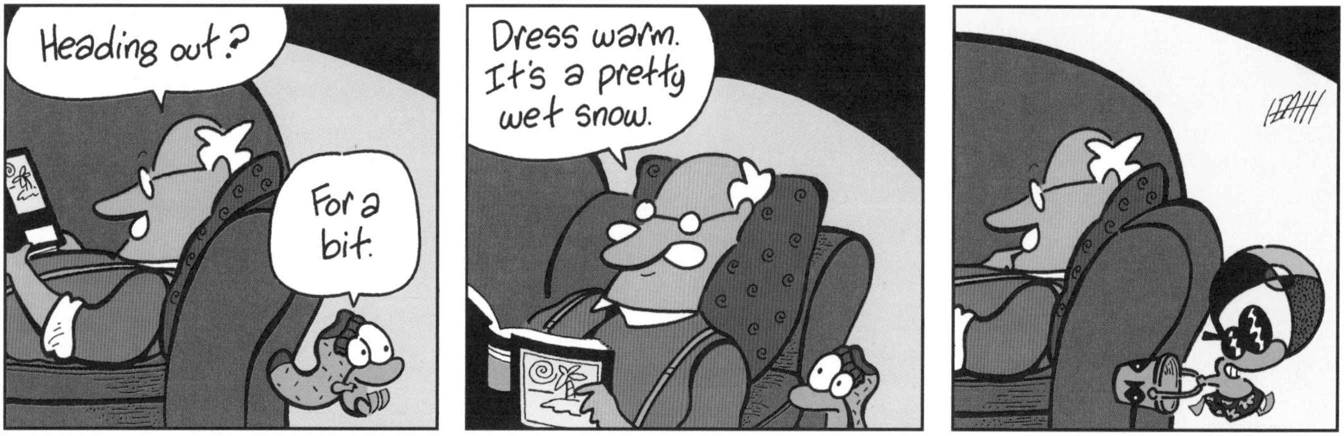
Heading out?
For a bit.
Dress warm. It's a pretty wet snow.

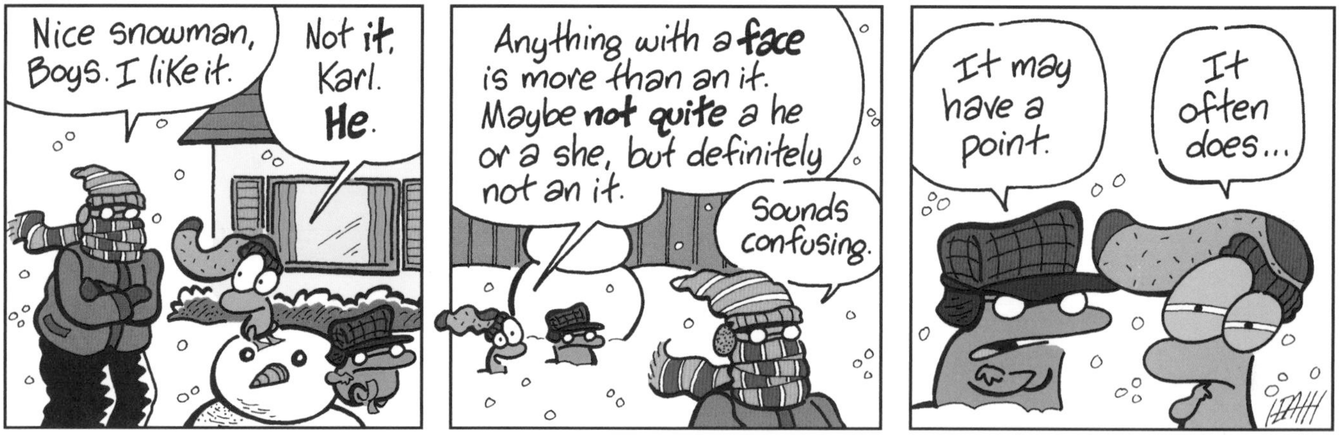
Nice snowman, Boys. I like it.
Not **it**, Karl. **He**.
Anything with a **face** is more than an it. Maybe **not quite** a he or a she, but definitely not an it.
Sounds confusing.
It may have a point.
It often does...

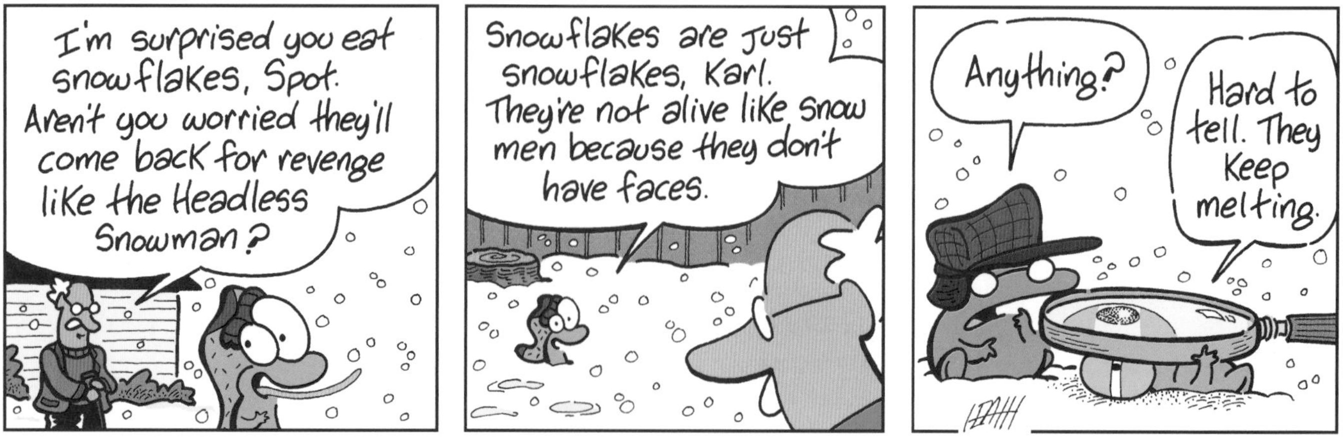
I'm surprised you eat snowflakes, Spot. Aren't you worried they'll come back for revenge like the Headless Snowman?
Snowflakes are just snowflakes, Karl. They're not alive like snow men because they don't have faces.
Anything?
Hard to tell. They keep melting.

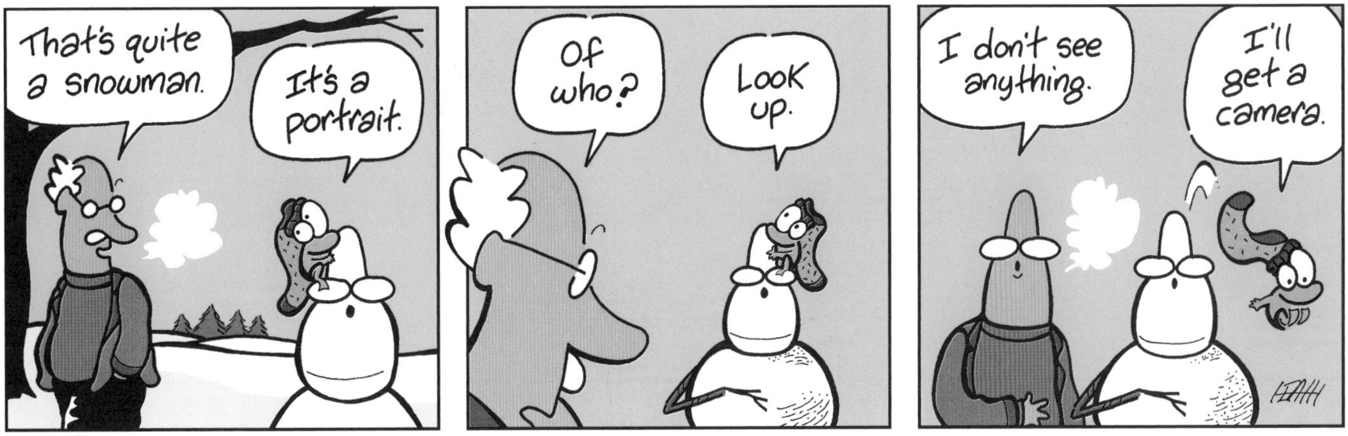
That's quite a snowman.
It's a portrait.
Of who?
Look up.
I don't see anything.
I'll get a camera.

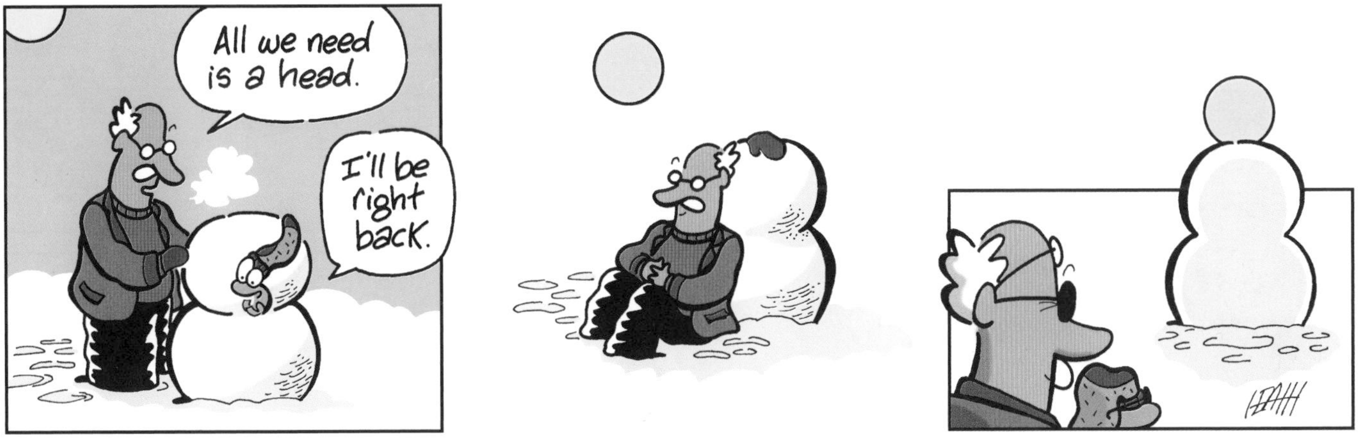
All we need is a head.
I'll be right back.

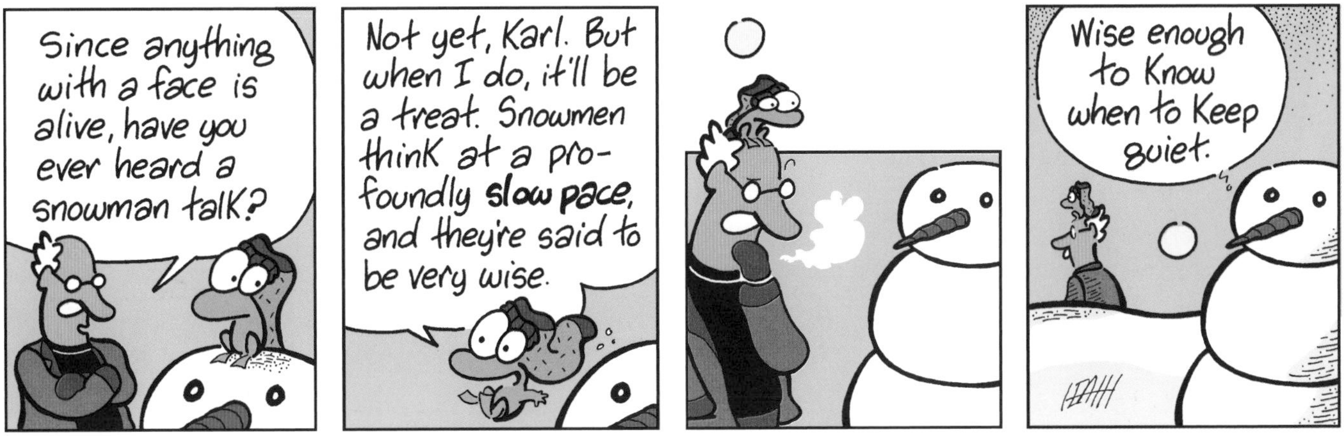
Since anything with a face is alive, have you ever heard a snowman talk?
Not yet, Karl. But when I do, it'll be a treat. Snowmen think at a profoundly **slow pace**, and they're said to be very wise.
Wise enough to Know when to Keep quiet.

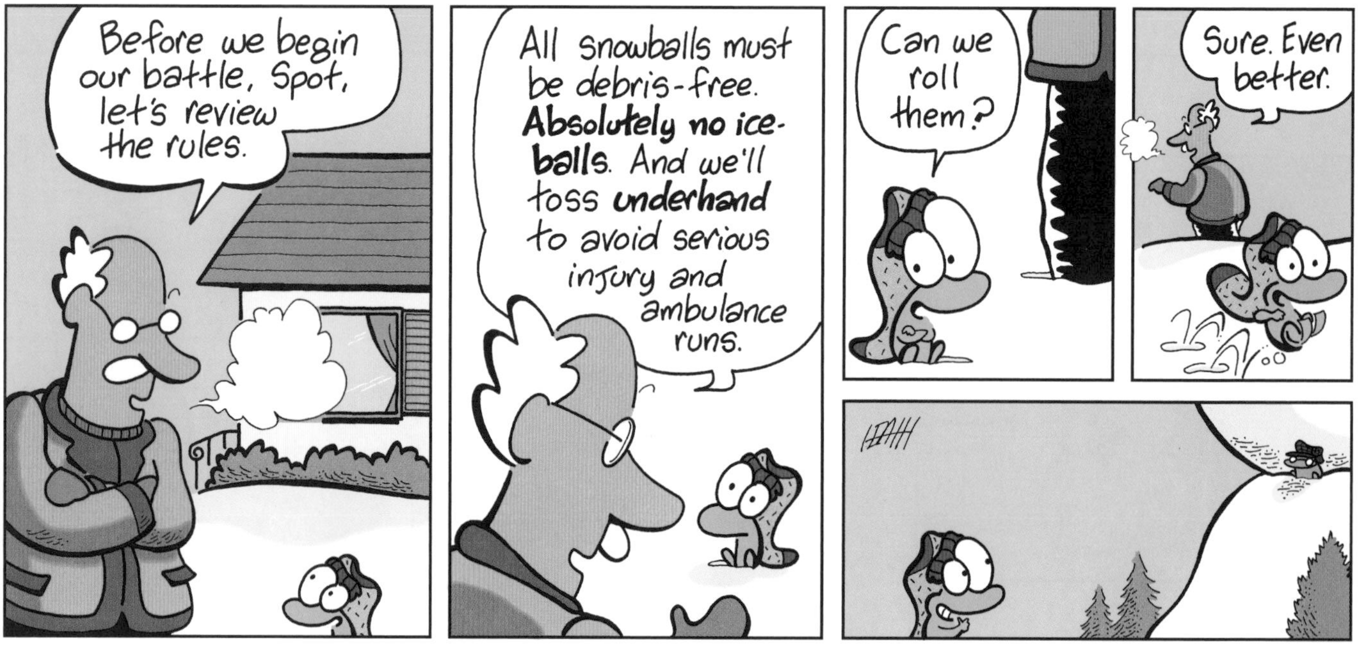
Before we begin our battle, Spot, let's review the rules.
All snowballs must be debris-free. **Absolutely no ice-balls**. And we'll toss **underhand** to avoid serious injury and ambulance runs.
Can we roll them?
Sure. Even better.

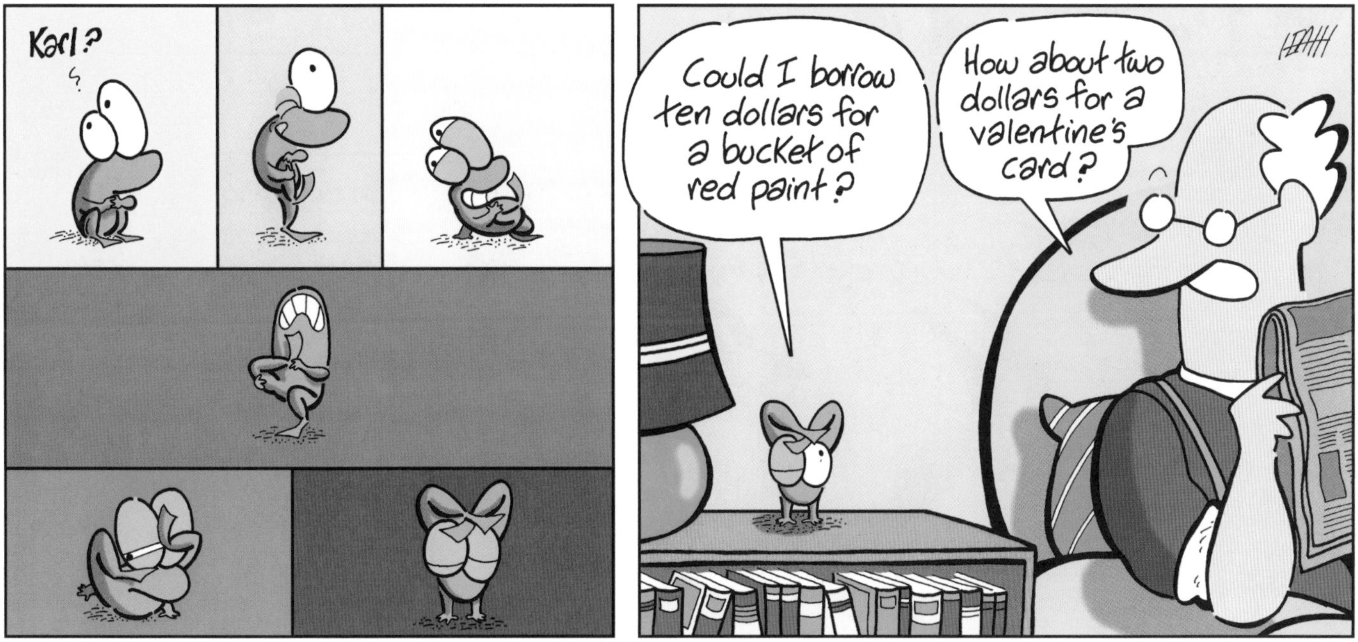
Karl?
Could I borrow ten dollars for a bucket of red paint?
How about two dollars for a valentine's card?

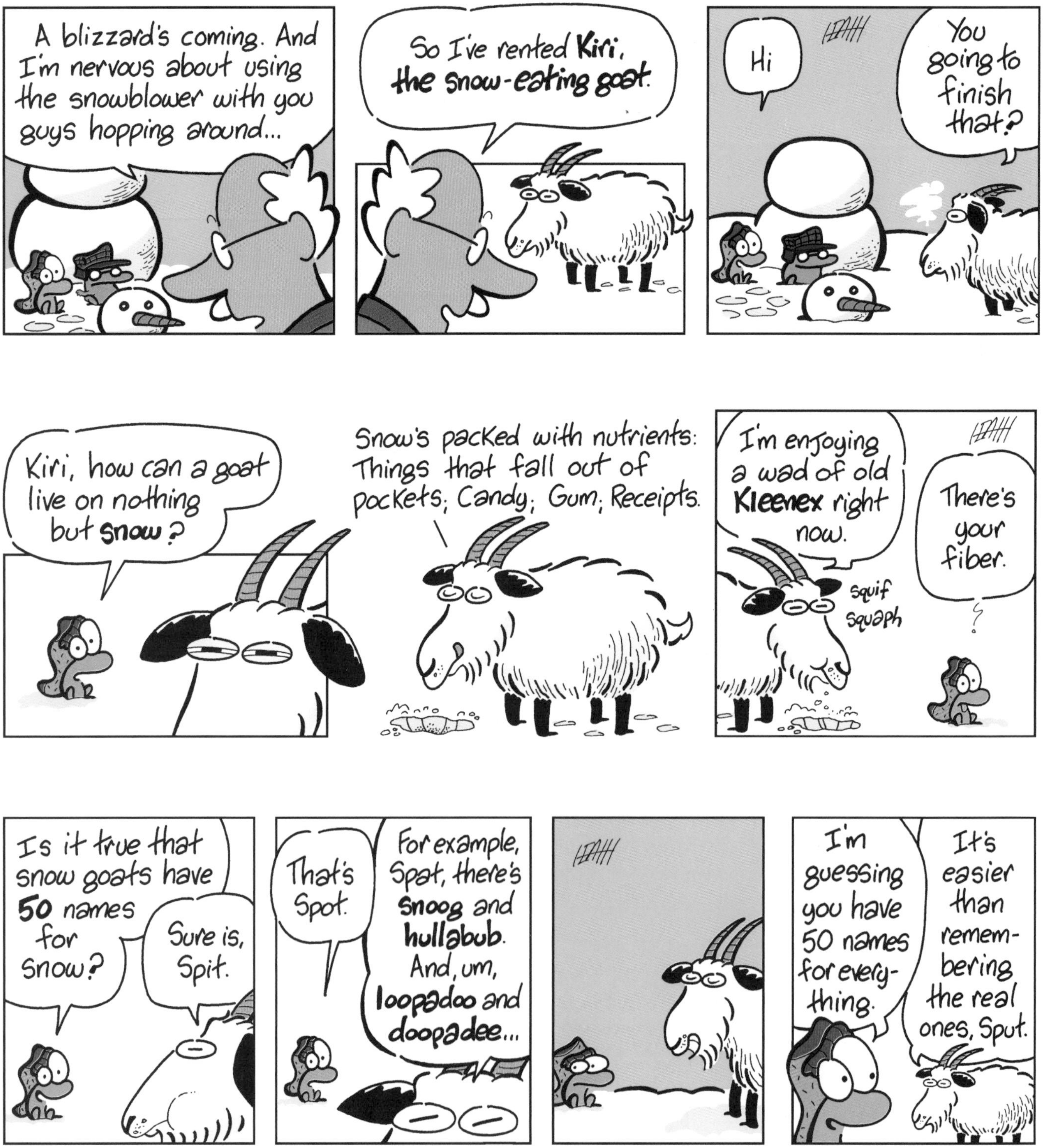
A blizzard's coming. And I'm nervous about using the snowblower with you guys hopping around...
So I've rented **Kiri, the snow-eating goat.**
Hi
You going to finish that?
Kiri, how can a goat live on nothing but **snow**?
Snow's packed with nutrients: Things that fall out of pockets; Candy; Gum; Receipts.
I'm enjoying a wad of old **Kleenex** right now.
squif
squaph
There's your fiber.
?
Is it true that snow goats have **50** names for snow?
Sure is, Spit.
That's Spot.
For example, Spat, there's **snoog** and **hullabub**. And, um, **loopadoo** and **doopadee**...
I'm guessing you have 50 names for every-thing.
It's easier than remem-bering the real ones, Sput.

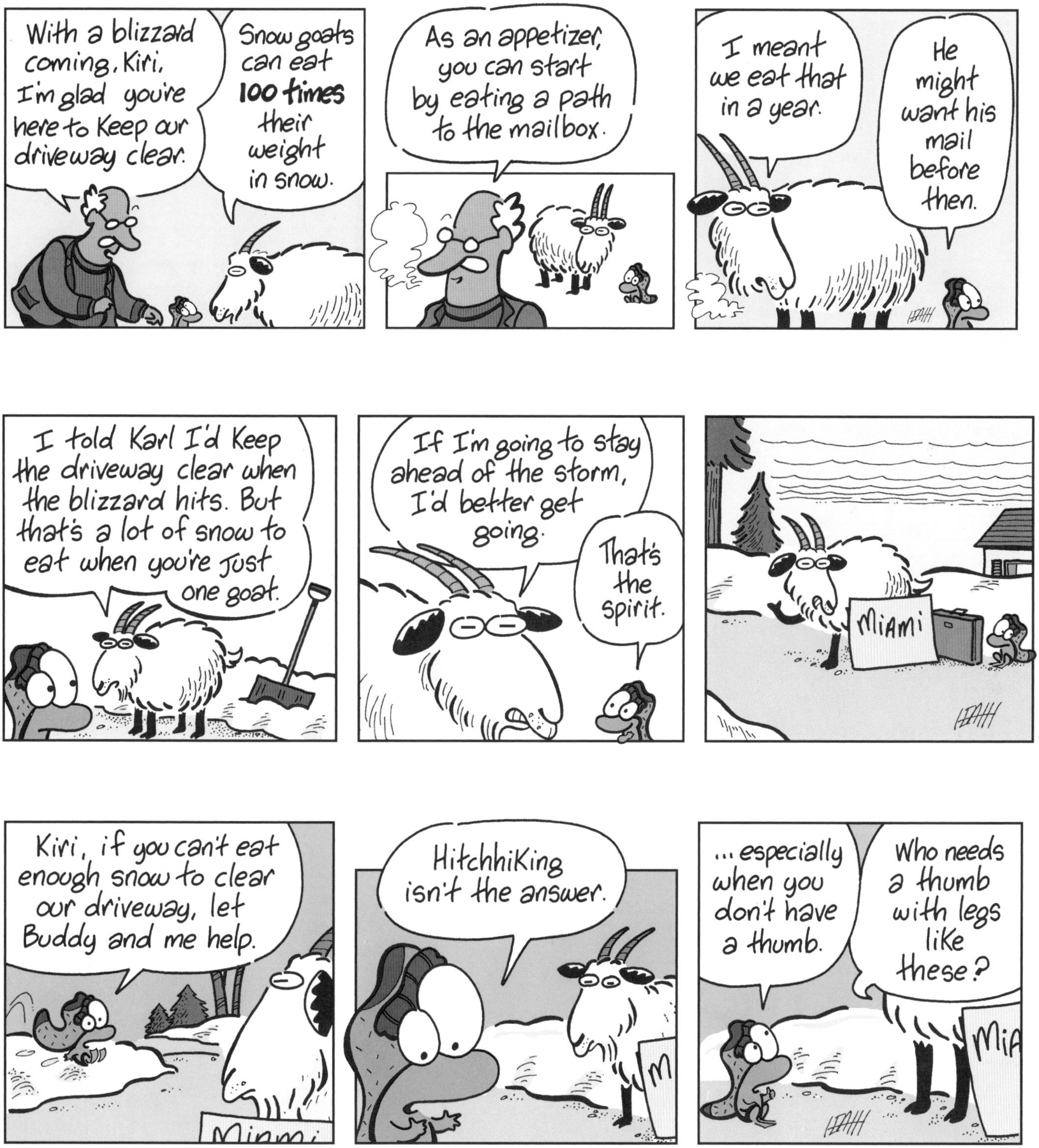
With a blizzard coming, Kiri, I'm glad you're here to Keep our driveway clear.
Snow goats can eat 100 times their weight in snow.
As an appetizer, you can start by eating a path to the mailbox.
I meant we eat that in a year.
He might want his mail before then.
I told Karl I'd Keep the driveway clear when the blizzard hits. But that's a lot of snow to eat when you're Just one goat.
If I'm going to stay ahead of the storm, I'd better get going.
That's the spirit.
MIAMI
Kiri, if you can't eat enough snow to clear our driveway, let Buddy and me help.
Hitchhiking isn't the answer.
... especially when you don't have a thumb.
Who needs a thumb with legs like these?

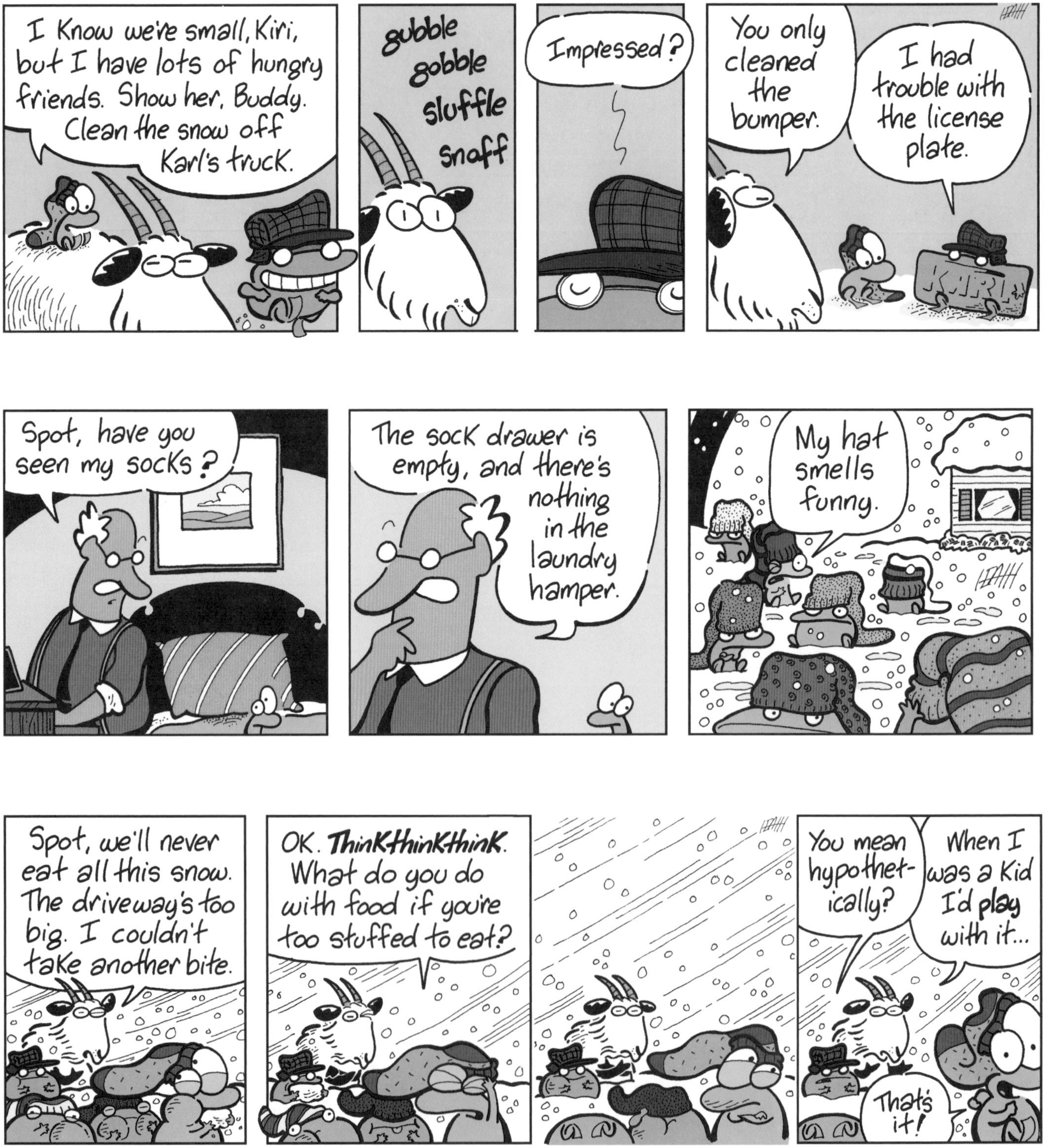
I Know we're small, Kiri, but I have lots of hungry friends. Show her, Buddy. Clean the snow off Karl's truck.
gubble
gobble
sluffle
snaff
Impressed?
You only cleaned the bumper.
I had trouble with the license plate.
KARL
Spot, have you seen my socks?
The sock drawer is empty, and there's nothing in the laundry hamper.
My hat smells funny.
Spot, we'll never eat all this snow. The driveway's too big. I couldn't take another bite.
OK. **ThinKthinKthinK.** What do you do with food if you're too stuffed to eat?
You mean hypothet-ically?
When I was a Kid I'd **play** with it...
That's it!

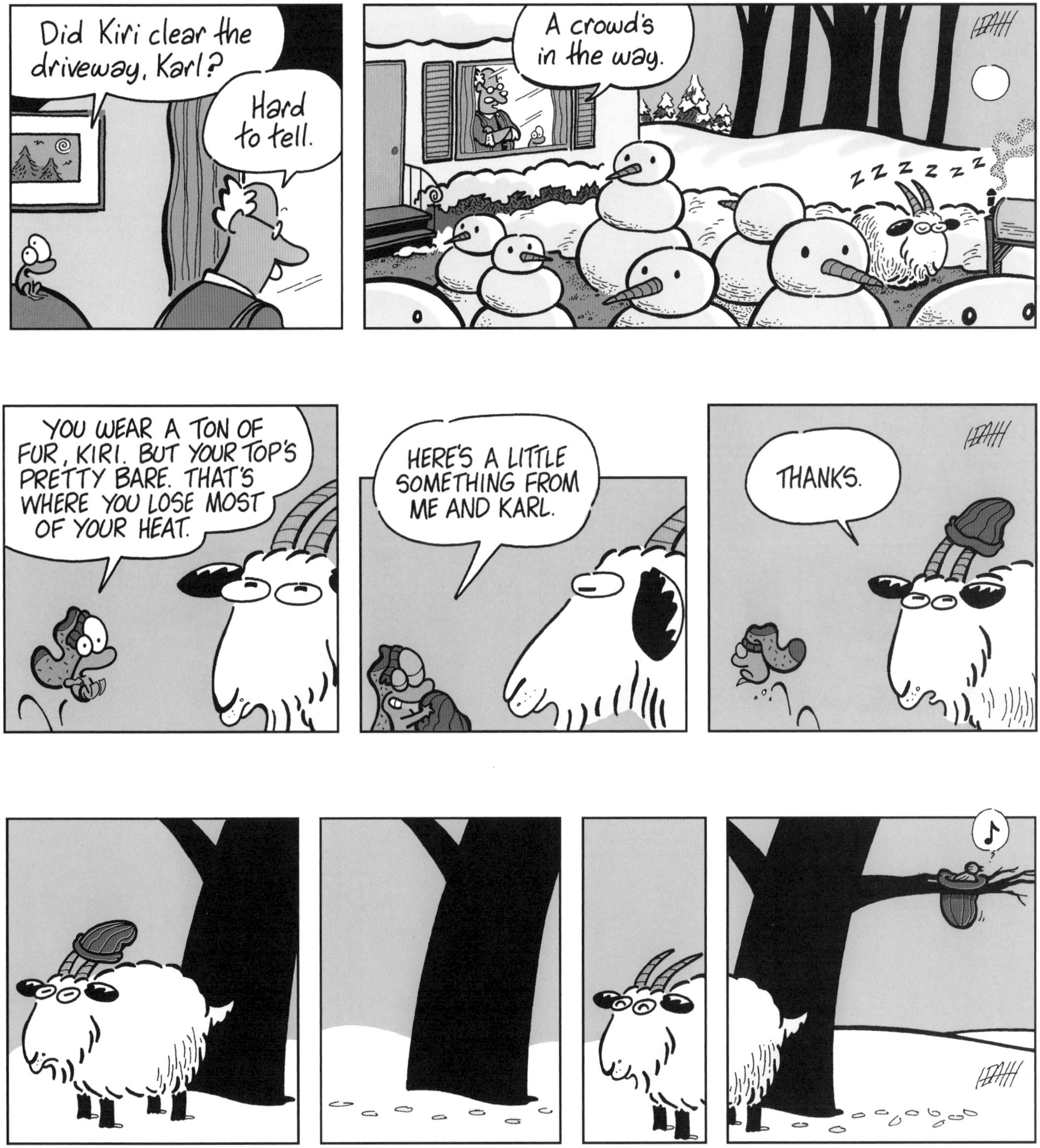

Did Kiri clear the driveway, Karl?
Hard to tell.
A crowd's in the way.
ZZZZZZZ
YOU WEAR A TON OF FUR, KIRI. BUT YOUR TOP'S PRETTY BARE. THAT'S WHERE YOU LOSE MOST OF YOUR HEAT.
HERE'S A LITTLE SOMETHING FROM ME AND KARL.
THANKS.

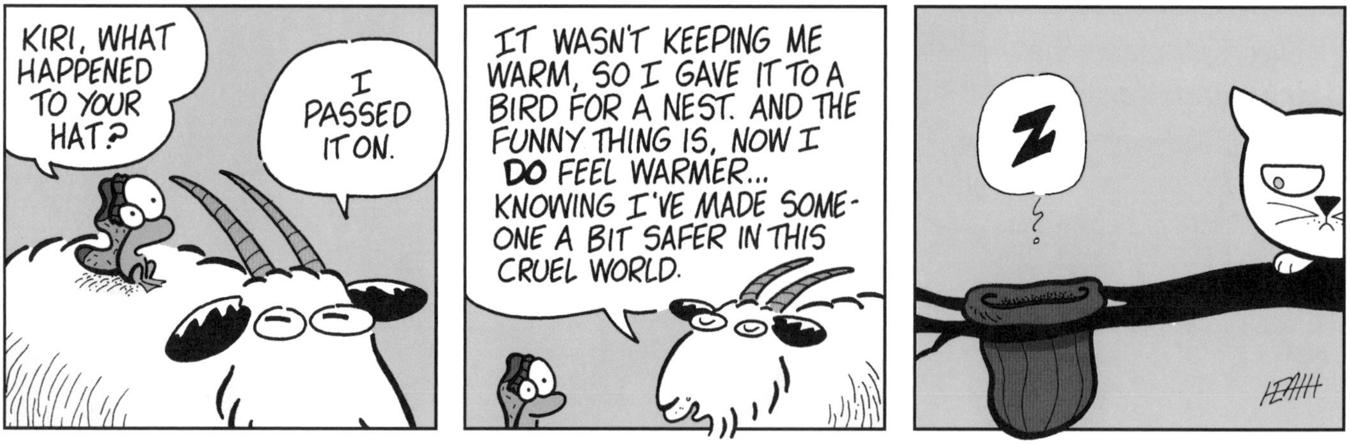
KIRI, WHAT HAPPENED TO YOUR HAT?
I PASSED IT ON.
IT WASN'T KEEPING ME WARM, SO I GAVE IT TO A BIRD FOR A NEST. AND THE FUNNY THING IS, NOW I **DO** FEEL WARMER... KNOWING I'VE MADE SOMEONE A BIT SAFER IN THIS CRUEL WORLD.
Z

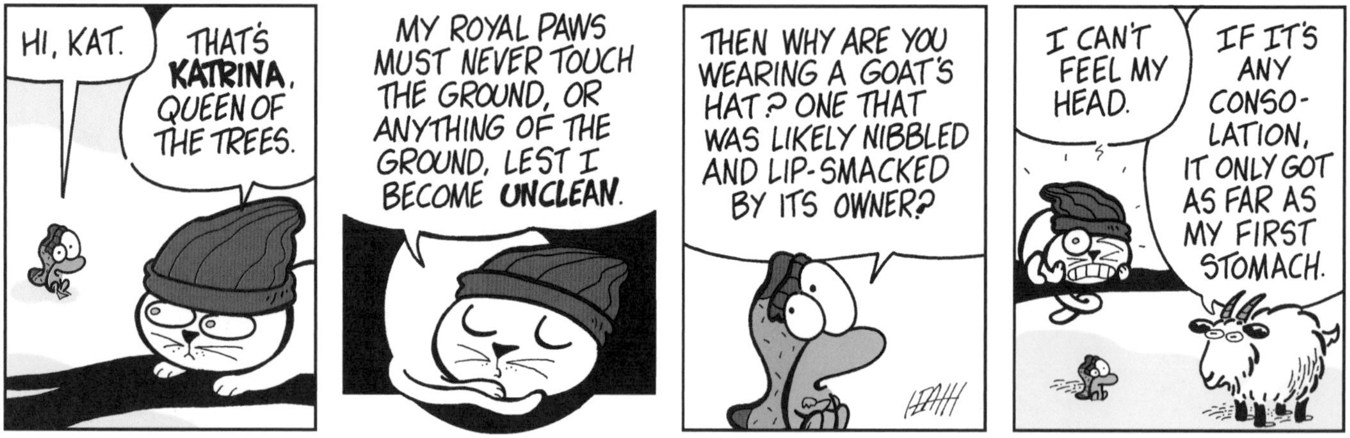
HI, KAT.
THAT'S **KATRINA**, QUEEN OF THE TREES.
MY ROYAL PAWS MUST NEVER TOUCH THE GROUND, OR ANYTHING OF THE GROUND, LEST I BECOME **UNCLEAN**.
THEN WHY ARE YOU WEARING A GOAT'S HAT? ONE THAT WAS LIKELY NIBBLED AND LIP-SMACKED BY ITS OWNER?
I CAN'T FEEL MY HEAD.
IF IT'S ANY CONSOLATION, IT ONLY GOT AS FAR AS MY FIRST STOMACH.

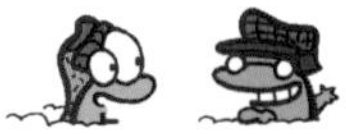

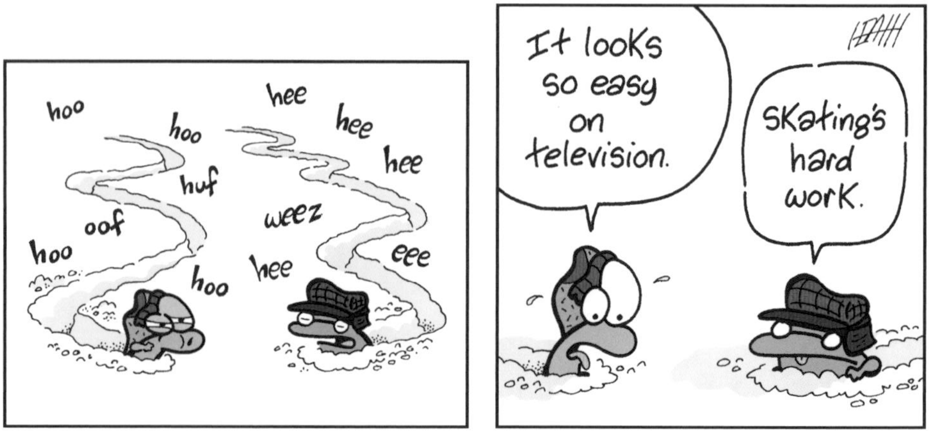
hoo
hoo
huf
oof
hoo
hoo
hee
hee
hee
weez
hee
eee
It looks so easy on television.
SKating's hard work.

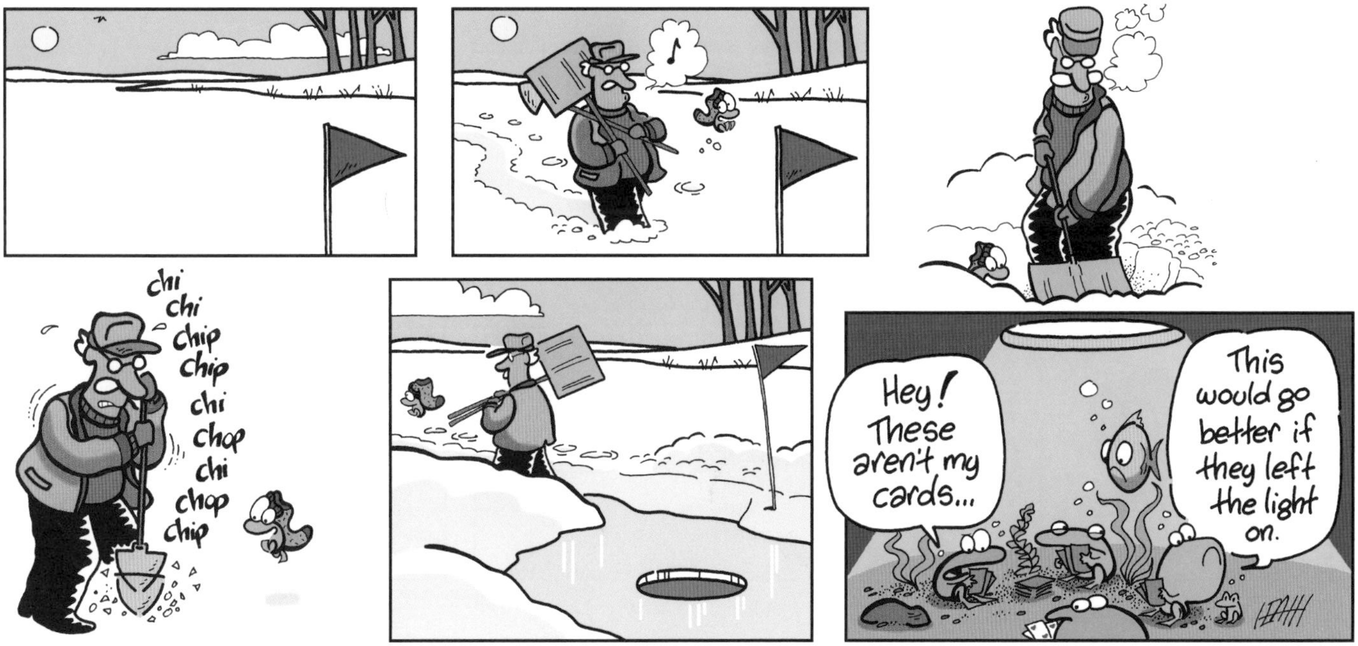
chi
chi
chip
chip
chi
chop
chi
chop
chip
Hey! These aren't my cards...
This would go better if they left the light on.

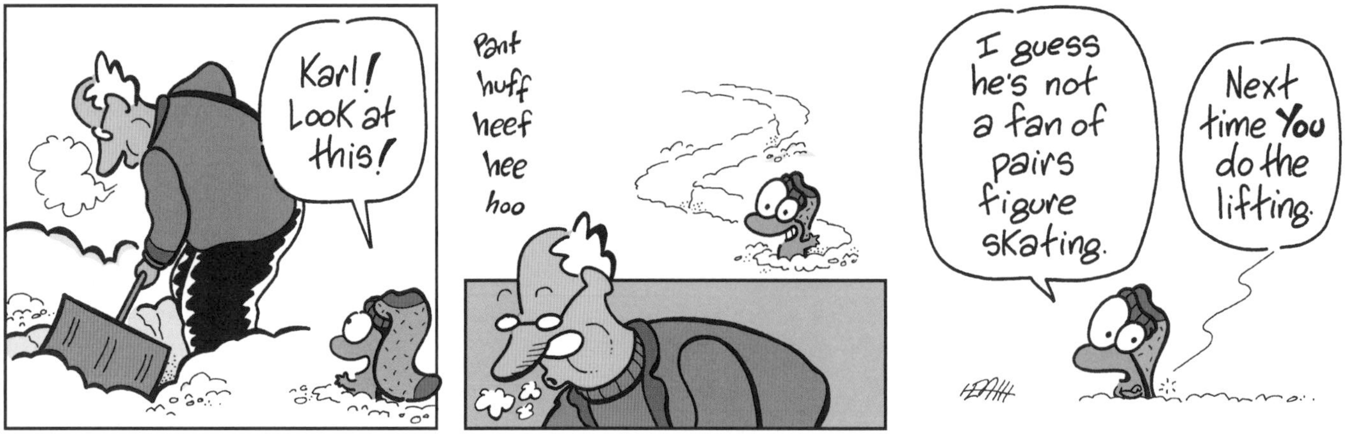
Karl! Look at this!
Pant
huff
heef
hee
hoo
I guess he's not a fan of pairs figure skating.
Next time **You** do the lifting.

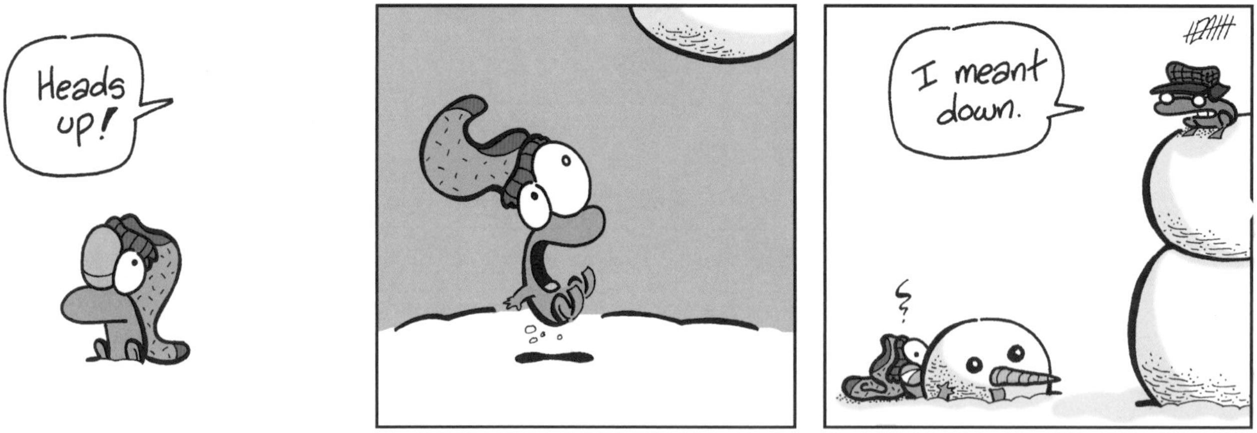
Heads up!
I meant down.

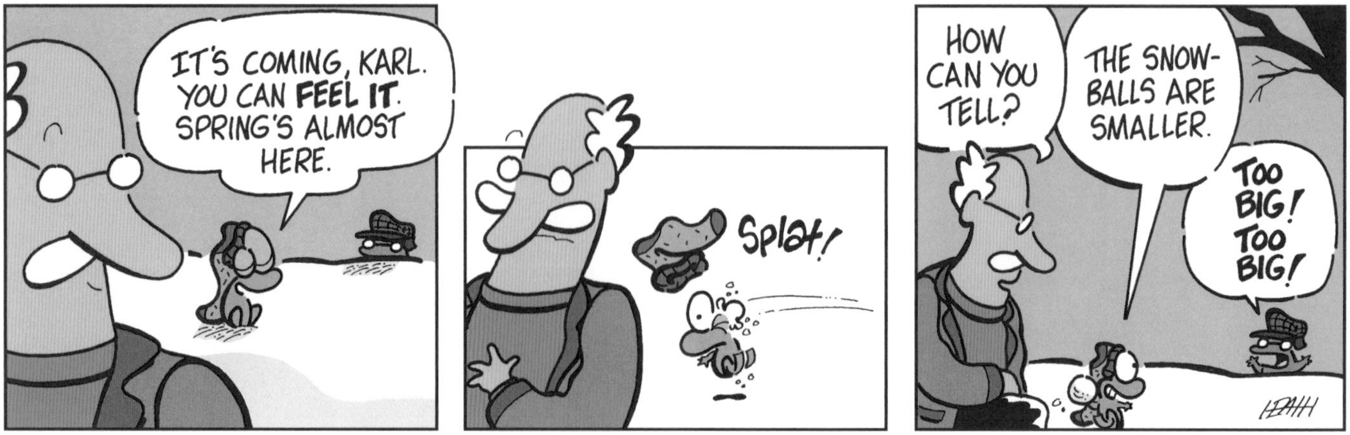
IT'S COMING, KARL. YOU CAN **FEEL IT**. SPRING'S ALMOST HERE.
Splat!
HOW CAN YOU TELL?
THE SNOW-BALLS ARE SMALLER.
TOO BIG! TOO BIG!

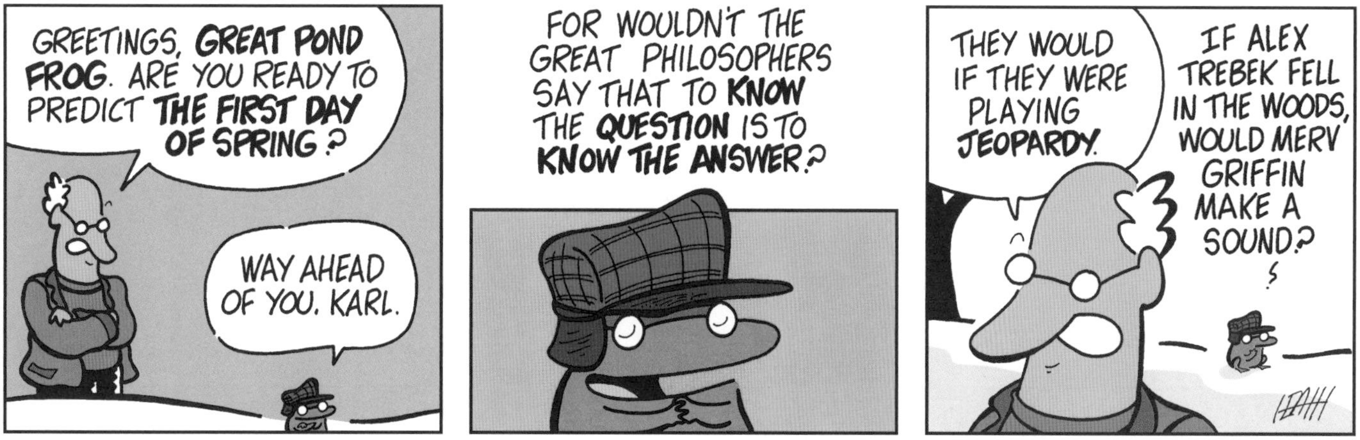
GREETINGS, GREAT POND FROG. ARE YOU READY TO PREDICT THE FIRST DAY OF SPRING?
WAY AHEAD OF YOU, KARL.
FOR WOULDN'T THE GREAT PHILOSOPHERS SAY THAT TO KNOW THE QUESTION IS TO KNOW THE ANSWER?
THEY WOULD IF THEY WERE PLAYING JEOPARDY.
IF ALEX TREBEK FELL IN THE WOODS, WOULD MERV GRIFFIN MAKE A SOUND?

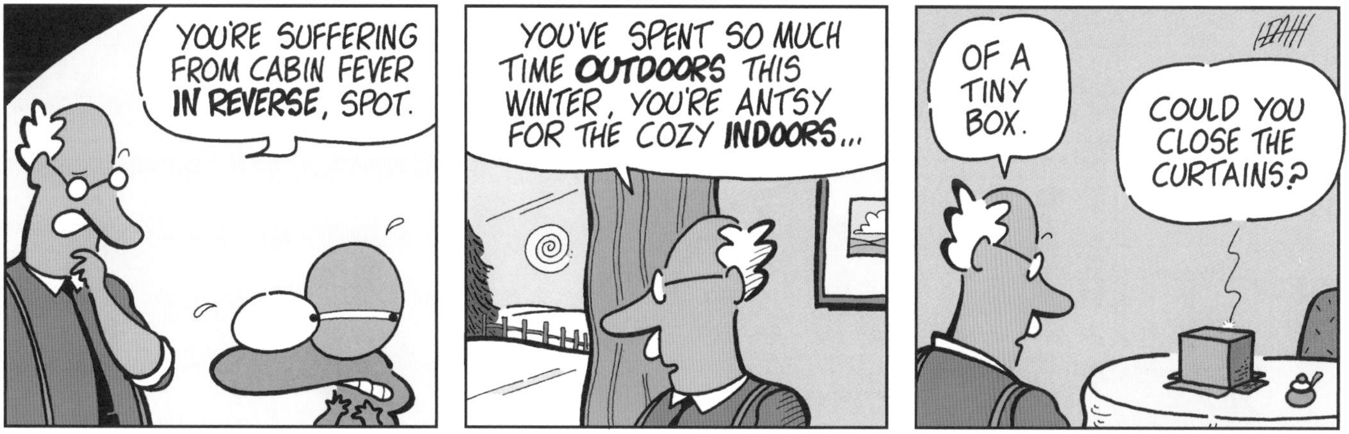
YOU'RE SUFFERING FROM CABIN FEVER IN REVERSE, SPOT.
YOU'VE SPENT SO MUCH TIME OUTDOORS THIS WINTER, YOU'RE ANTSY FOR THE COZY INDOORS...
OF A TINY BOX.
COULD YOU CLOSE THE CURTAINS?

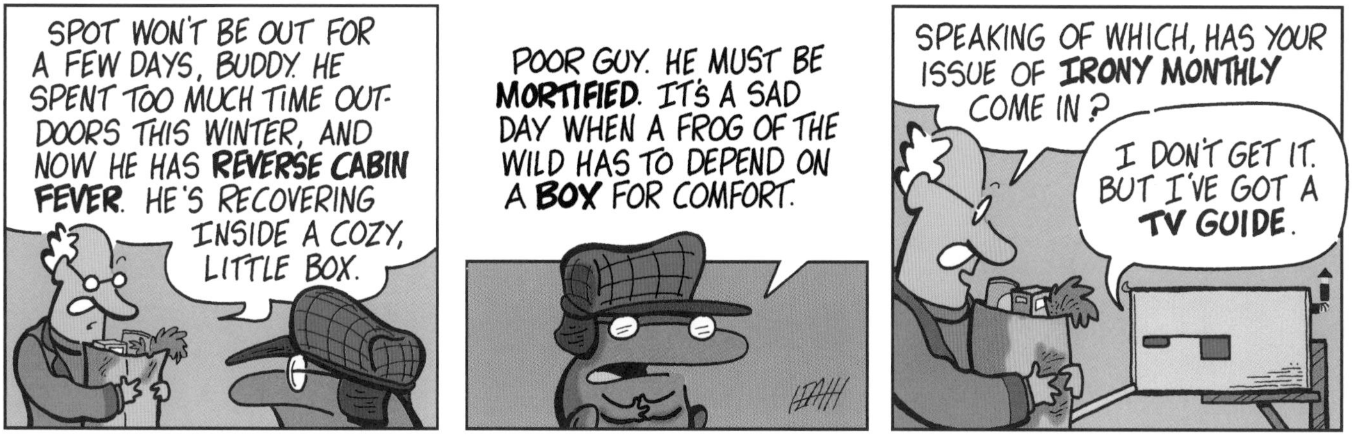
SPOT WON'T BE OUT FOR A FEW DAYS, BUDDY. HE SPENT TOO MUCH TIME OUTDOORS THIS WINTER, AND NOW HE HAS REVERSE CABIN FEVER. HE'S RECOVERING INSIDE A COZY, LITTLE BOX.
POOR GUY. HE MUST BE MORTIFIED. IT'S A SAD DAY WHEN A FROG OF THE WILD HAS TO DEPEND ON A BOX FOR COMFORT.
SPEAKING OF WHICH, HAS YOUR ISSUE OF IRONY MONTHLY COME IN?
I DON'T GET IT. BUT I'VE GOT A TV GUIDE.

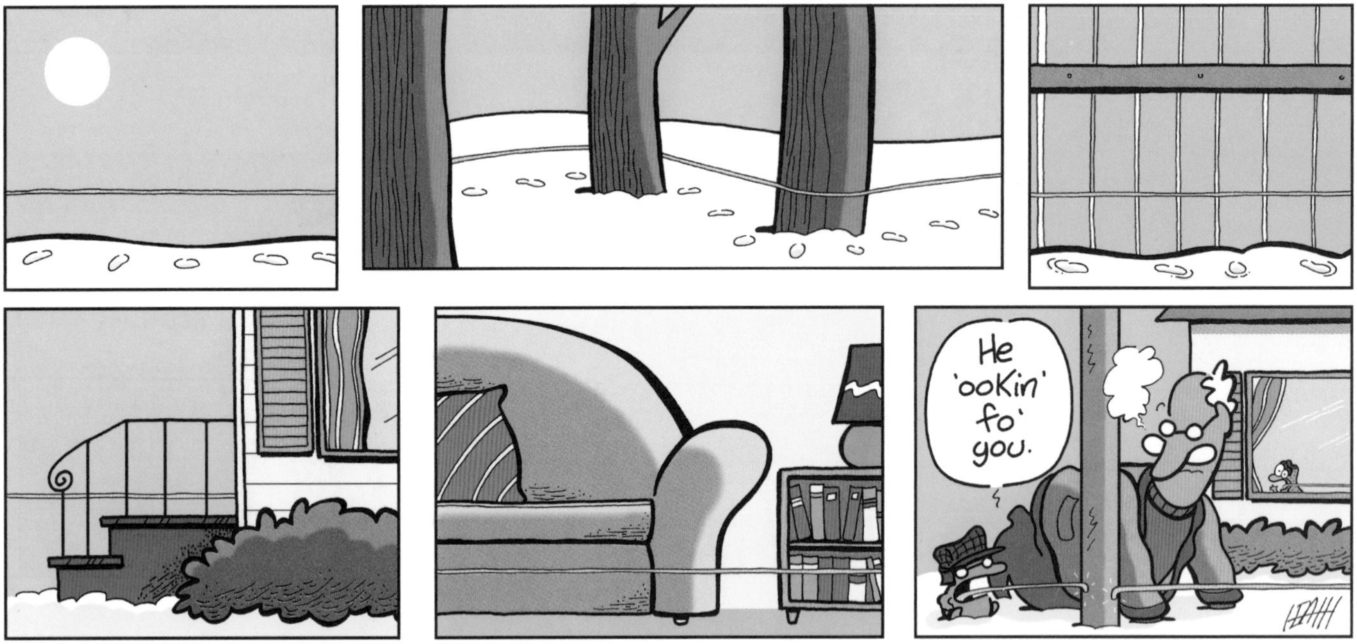
He 'ookin' fo' you.

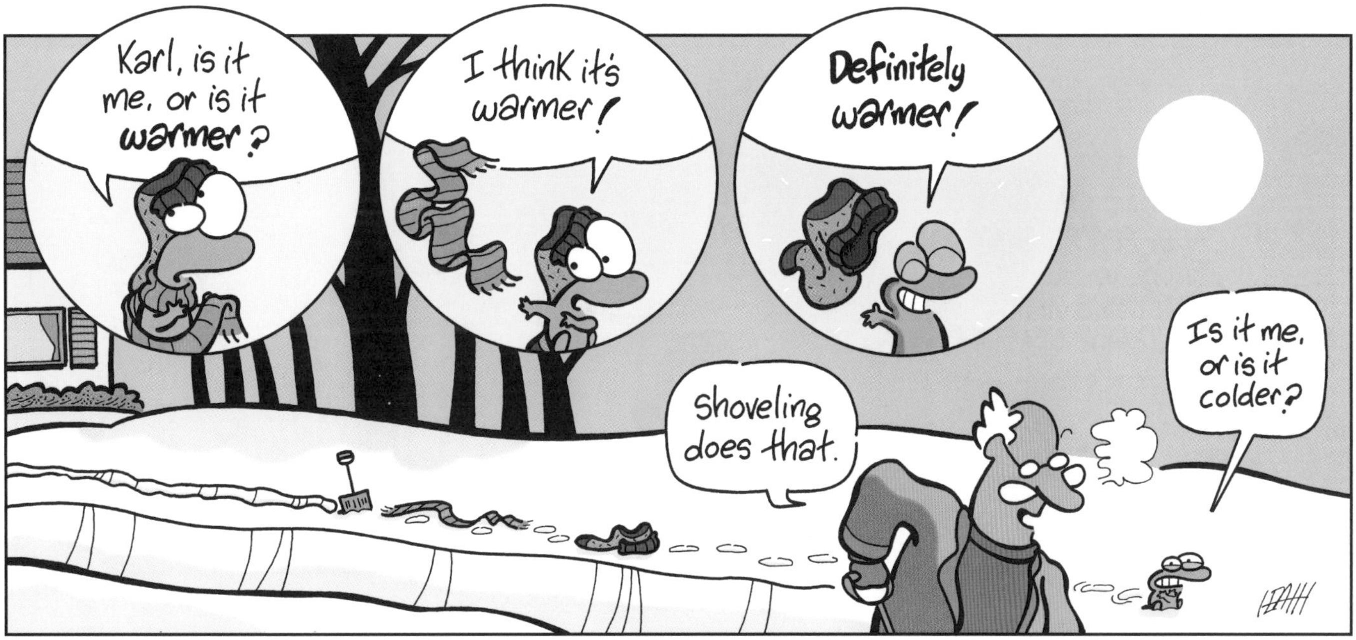
Karl, is it me, or is it **warmer**?
I think it's warmer!
Definitely warmer!
Shoveling does that.
Is it me, or is it colder?

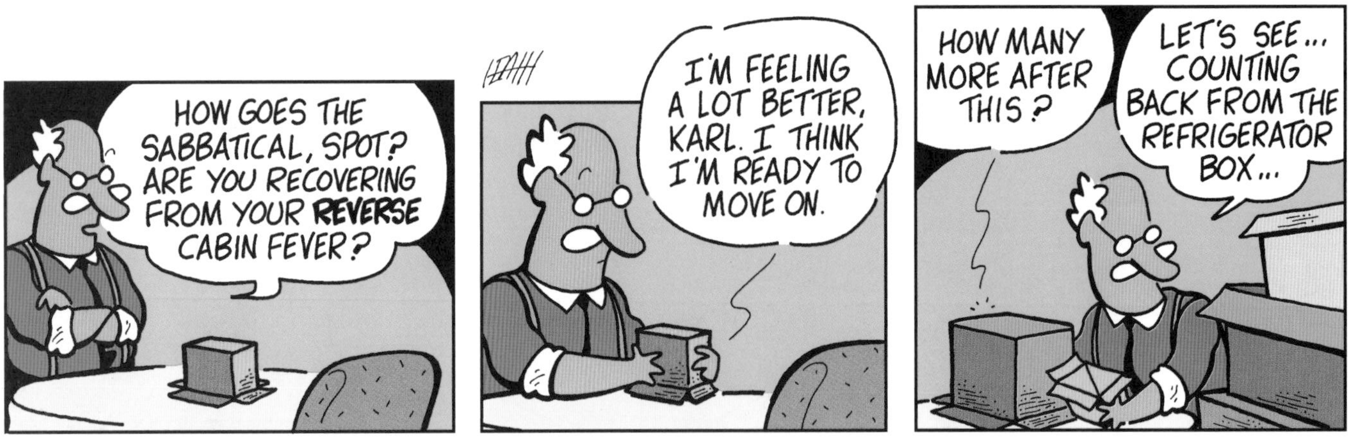
HOW GOES THE SABBATICAL, SPOT? ARE YOU RECOVERING FROM YOUR **REVERSE** CABIN FEVER?
I'M FEELING A LOT BETTER, KARL. I THINK I'M READY TO MOVE ON.
HOW MANY MORE AFTER THIS?
LET'S SEE... COUNTING BACK FROM THE REFRIGERATOR BOX...

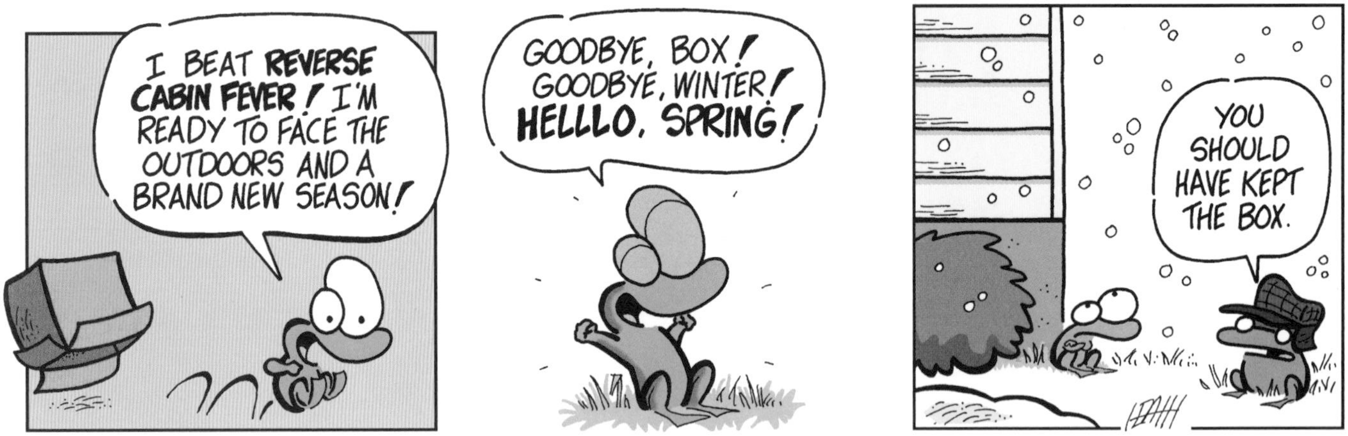
I BEAT **REVERSE CABIN FEVER!** I'M READY TO FACE THE OUTDOORS AND A BRAND NEW SEASON!
GOODBYE, BOX! GOODBYE, WINTER! **HELLLO, SPRING!**
YOU SHOULD HAVE KEPT THE BOX.

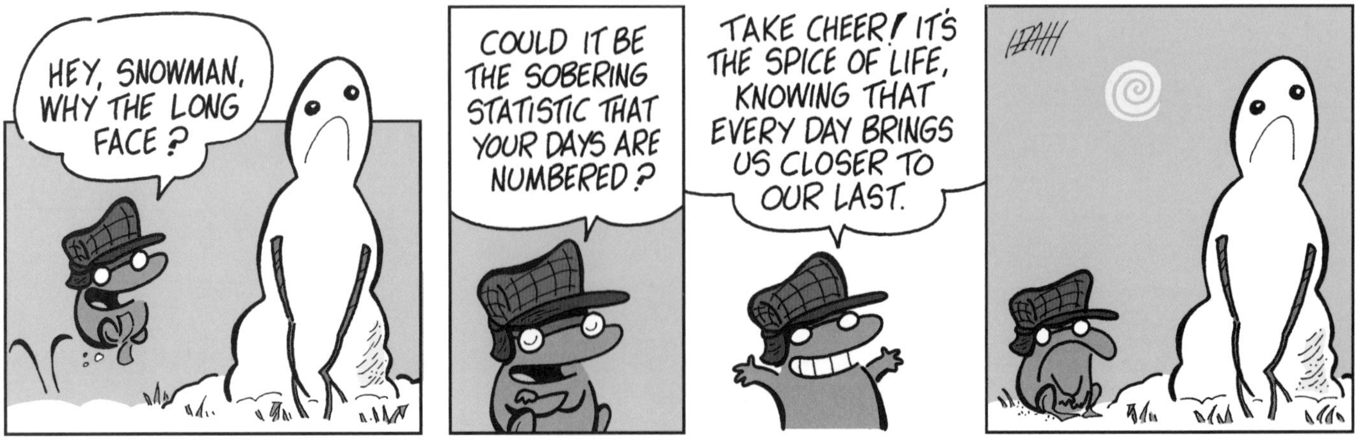
HEY, SNOWMAN, WHY THE LONG FACE?
COULD IT BE THE SOBERING STATISTIC THAT YOUR DAYS ARE NUMBERED?
TAKE CHEER! IT'S THE SPICE OF LIFE, KNOWING THAT EVERY DAY BRINGS US CLOSER TO OUR LAST.

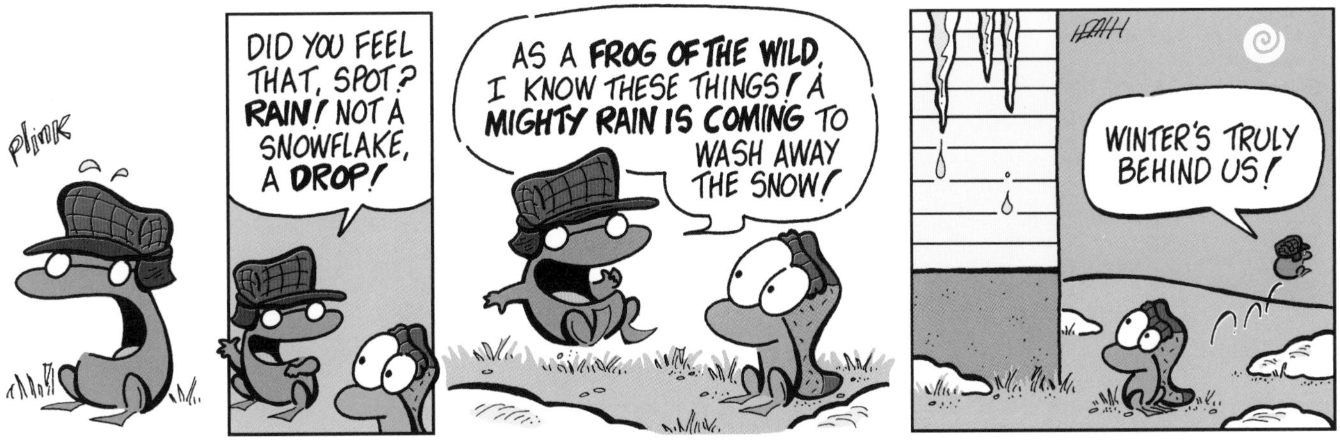
plink
DID YOU FEEL THAT, SPOT? RAIN! NOT A SNOWFLAKE, A DROP!
AS A FROG OF THE WILD, I KNOW THESE THINGS! A MIGHTY RAIN IS COMING TO WASH AWAY THE SNOW!
WINTER'S TRULY BEHIND US!

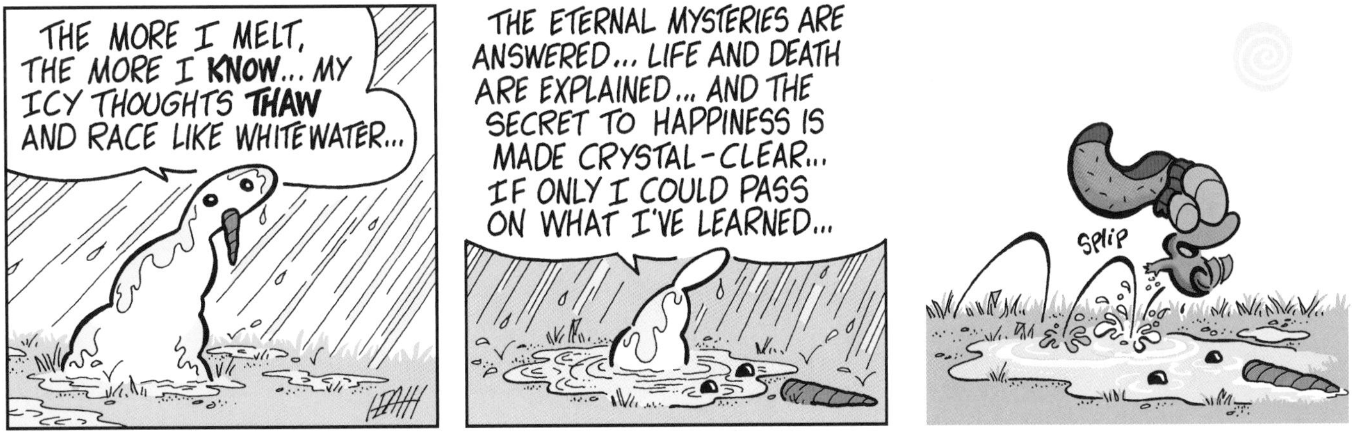
THE MORE I MELT, THE MORE I KNOW... MY ICY THOUGHTS THAW AND RACE LIKE WHITEWATER...
THE ETERNAL MYSTERIES ARE ANSWERED... LIFE AND DEATH ARE EXPLAINED... AND THE SECRET TO HAPPINESS IS MADE CRYSTAL-CLEAR... IF ONLY I COULD PASS ON WHAT I'VE LEARNED...
SPLIP

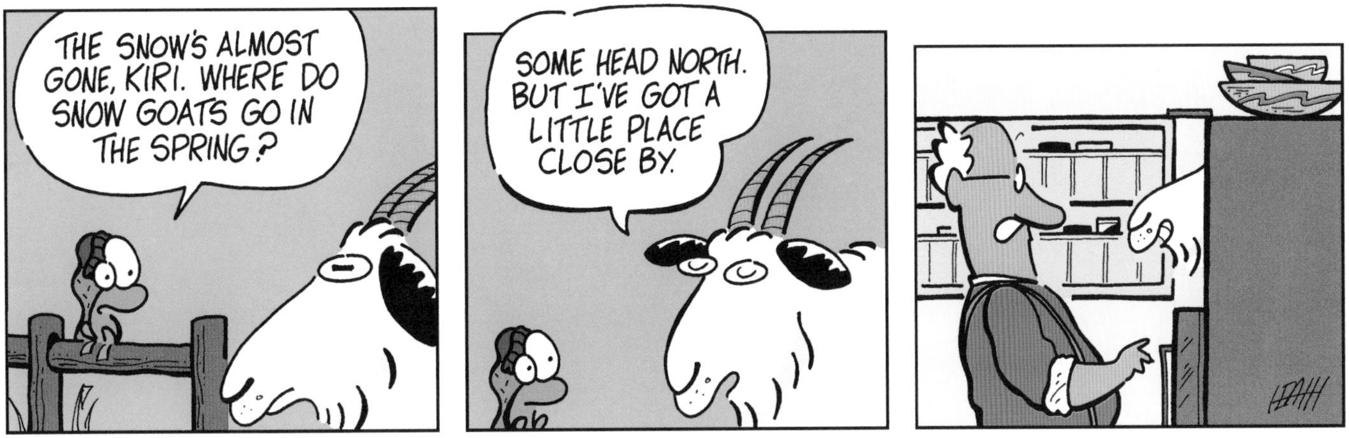
THE SNOW'S ALMOST GONE, KIRI. WHERE DO SNOW GOATS GO IN THE SPRING?
SOME HEAD NORTH. BUT I'VE GOT A LITTLE PLACE CLOSE BY.

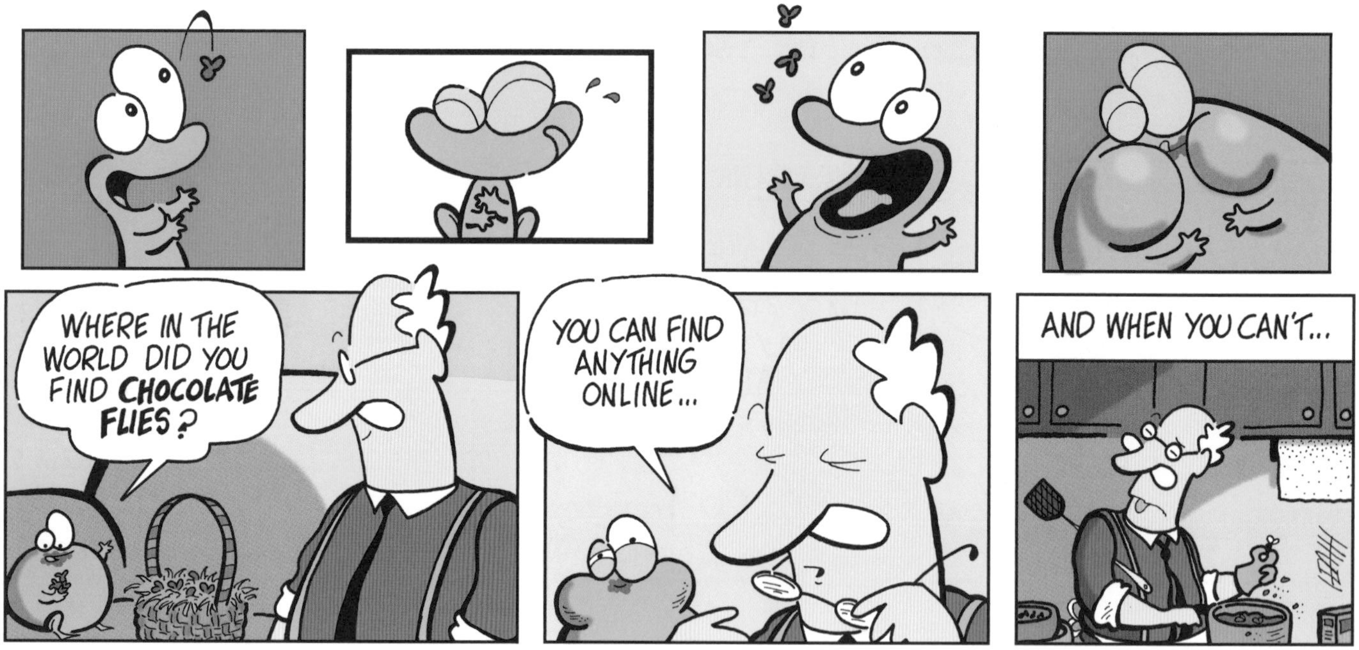
WHERE IN THE WORLD DID YOU FIND **CHOCOLATE FLIES**?
YOU CAN FIND ANYTHING ONLINE...
AND WHEN YOU CAN'T...

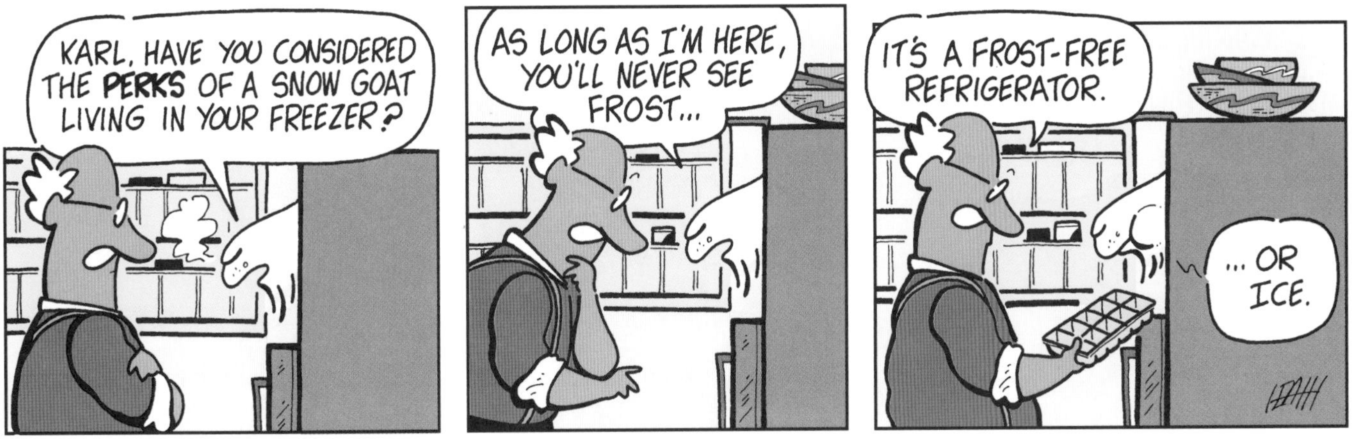
KARL, HAVE YOU CONSIDERED THE PERKS OF A SNOW GOAT LIVING IN YOUR FREEZER?
AS LONG AS I'M HERE, YOU'LL NEVER SEE FROST...
IT'S A FROST-FREE REFRIGERATOR.
...OR ICE.

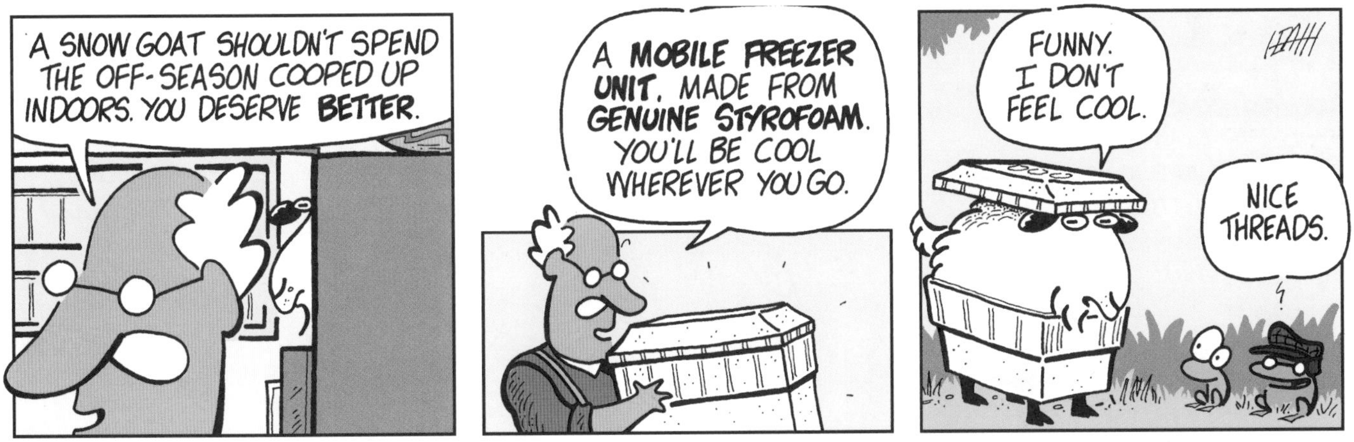
A SNOW GOAT SHOULDN'T SPEND THE OFF-SEASON COOPED UP INDOORS. YOU DESERVE BETTER.
A MOBILE FREEZER UNIT, MADE FROM GENUINE STYROFOAM. YOU'LL BE COOL WHEREVER YOU GO.
FUNNY. I DON'T FEEL COOL.
NICE THREADS.

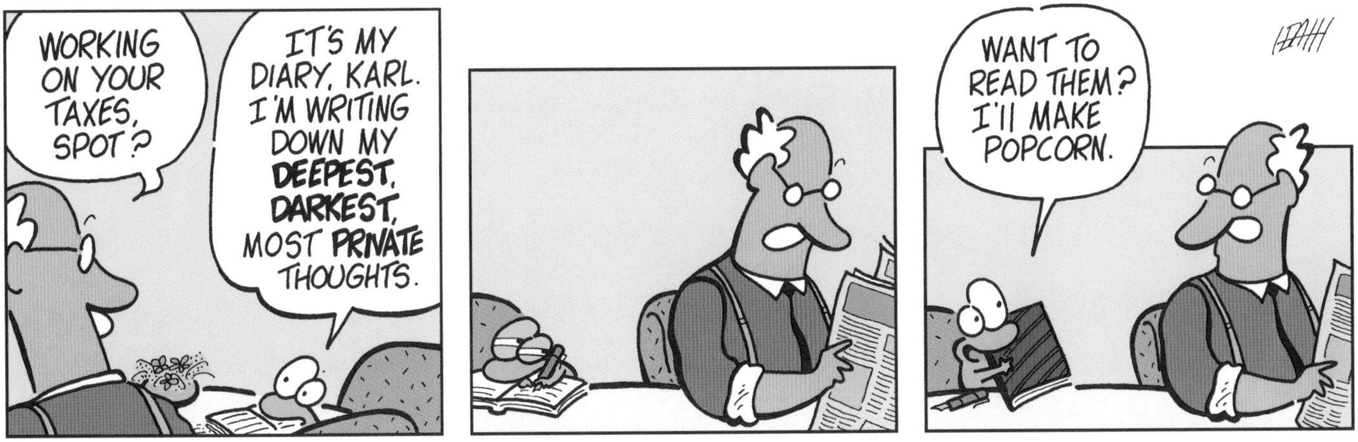
WORKING ON YOUR TAXES, SPOT?
IT'S MY DIARY, KARL. I'M WRITING DOWN MY DEEPEST, DARKEST, MOST PRIVATE THOUGHTS.
WANT TO READ THEM? I'll MAKE POPCORN.

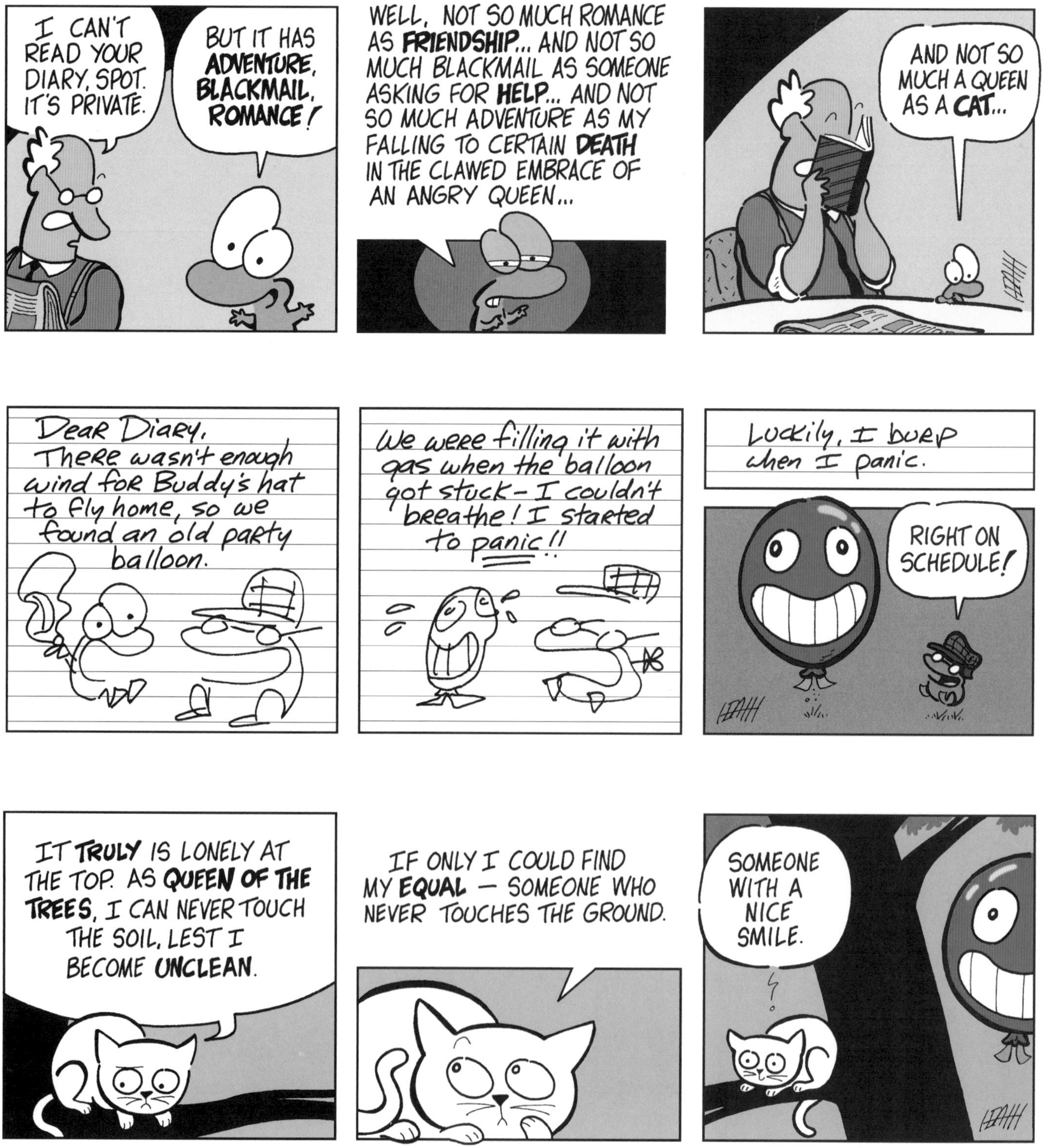
I CAN'T READ YOUR DIARY, SPOT. IT'S PRIVATE.
BUT IT HAS ADVENTURE, BLACKMAIL, ROMANCE!
WELL, NOT SO MUCH ROMANCE AS FRIENDSHIP... AND NOT SO MUCH BLACKMAIL AS SOMEONE ASKING FOR HELP... AND NOT SO MUCH ADVENTURE AS MY FALLING TO CERTAIN DEATH IN THE CLAWED EMBRACE OF AN ANGRY QUEEN...
AND NOT SO MUCH A QUEEN AS A CAT...
Dear Diary, There wasn't enough wind for Buddy's hat to fly home, so we found an old party balloon.
We were filling it with gas when the balloon got stuck - I couldn't breathe! I started to panic!!
Luckily, I burp when I panic.
RIGHT ON SCHEDULE!
IT TRULY IS LONELY AT THE TOP. AS QUEEN OF THE TREES, I CAN NEVER TOUCH THE SOIL, LEST I BECOME UNCLEAN.
IF ONLY I COULD FIND MY EQUAL — SOMEONE WHO NEVER TOUCHES THE GROUND.
SOMEONE WITH A NICE SMILE.

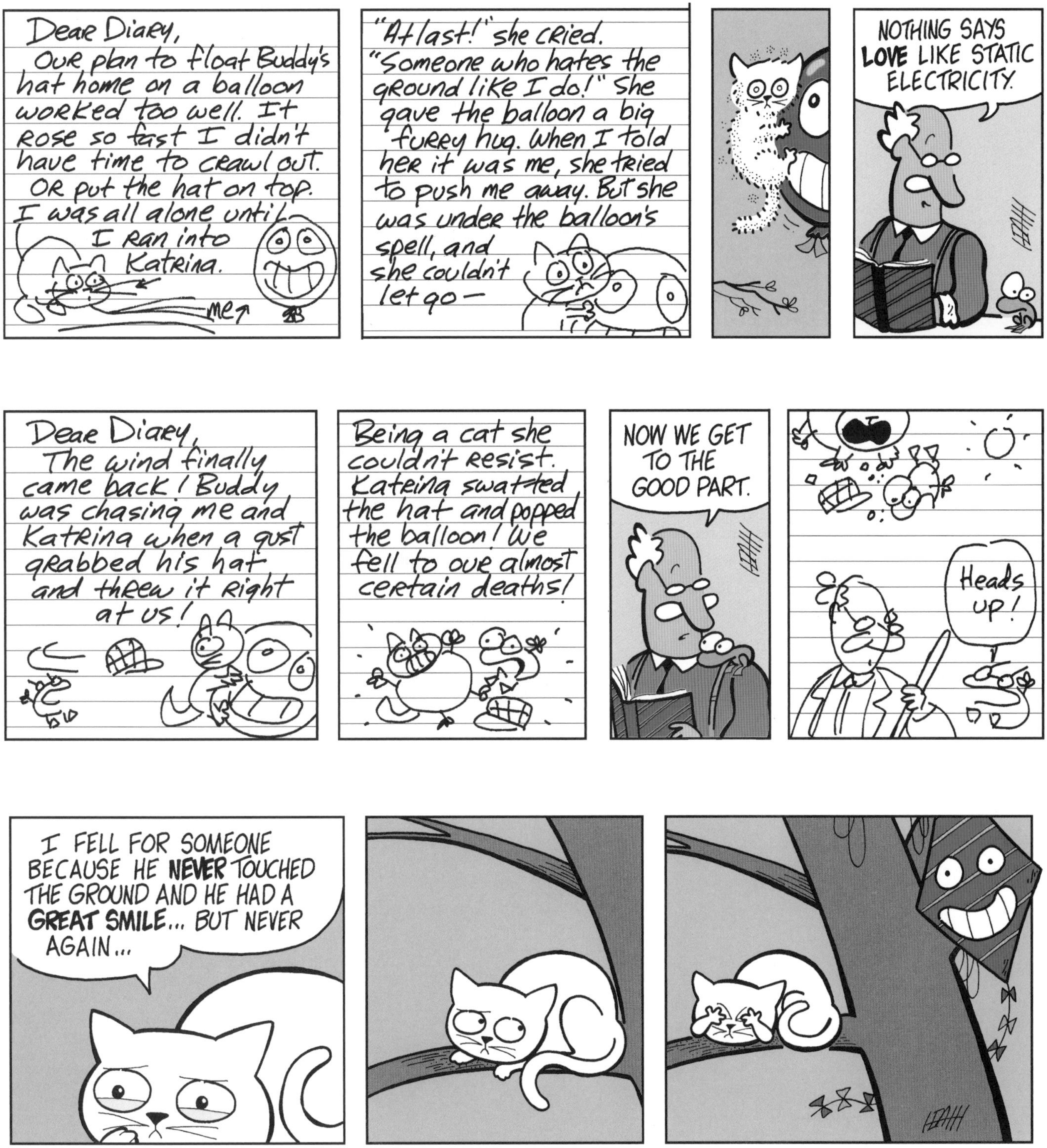
Dear Diary,
Our plan to float Buddy's hat home on a balloon worked too well. It rose so fast I didn't have time to crawl out. Or put the hat on top. I was all alone until I ran into Katrina.
me
"At last!" she cried. "Someone who hates the ground like I do!" She gave the balloon a big furry hug. When I told her it was me, she tried to push me away. But she was under the balloon's spell, and she couldn't let go—
NOTHING SAYS LOVE LIKE STATIC ELECTRICITY.
Dear Diary,
The wind finally came back! Buddy was chasing me and Katrina when a gust grabbed his hat and threw it right at us!
Being a cat she couldn't resist. Katrina swatted the hat and popped the balloon! We fell to our almost certain deaths!
NOW WE GET TO THE GOOD PART.
Heads up!
I FELL FOR SOMEONE BECAUSE HE NEVER TOUCHED THE GROUND AND HE HAD A GREAT SMILE... BUT NEVER AGAIN...

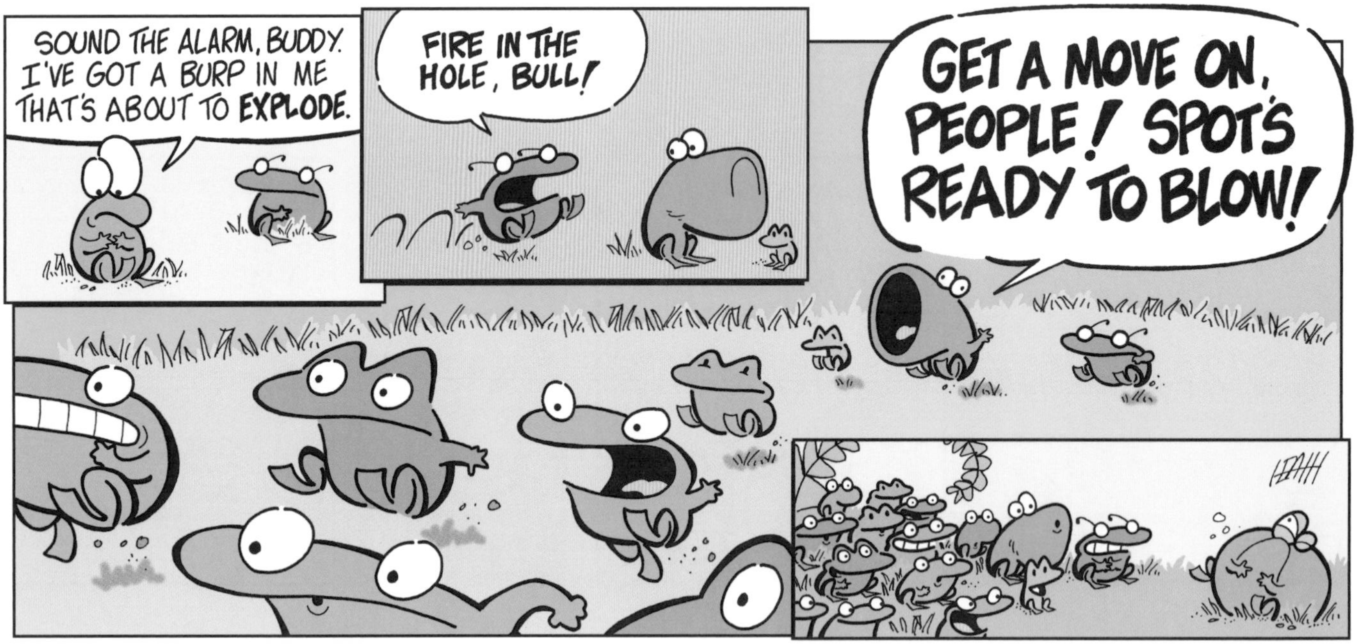
SOUND THE ALARM, BUDDY. I'VE GOT A BURP IN ME THAT'S ABOUT TO **EXPLODE**.
FIRE IN THE HOLE, BULL!
GET A MOVE ON, PEOPLE! SPOT'S READY TO BLOW!

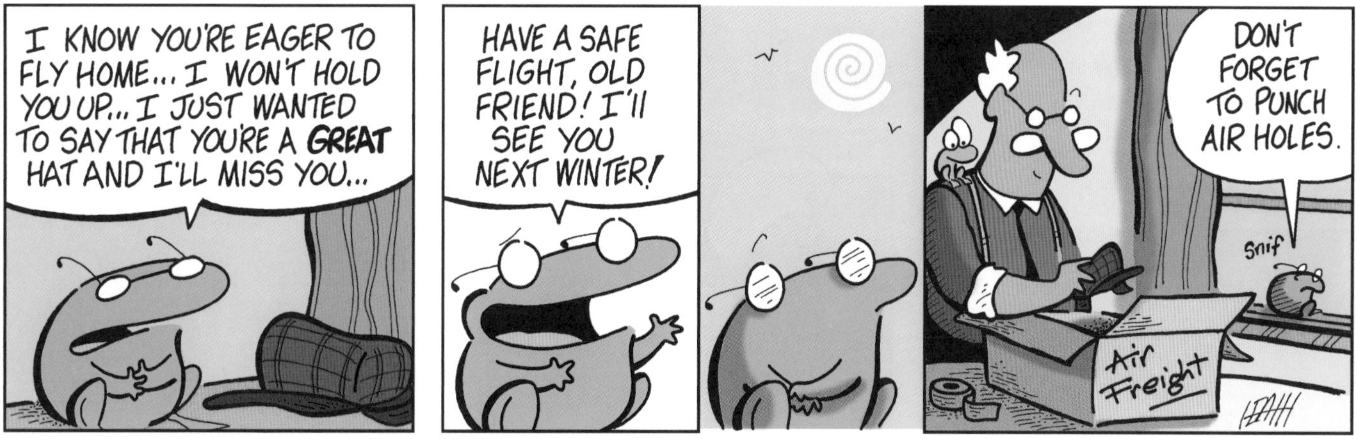
I KNOW YOU'RE EAGER TO FLY HOME... I WON'T HOLD YOU UP... I JUST WANTED TO SAY THAT YOU'RE A GREAT HAT AND I'LL MISS YOU...
HAVE A SAFE FLIGHT, OLD FRIEND! I'LL SEE YOU NEXT WINTER!
DON'T FORGET TO PUNCH AIR HOLES.
Snif
Air Freight

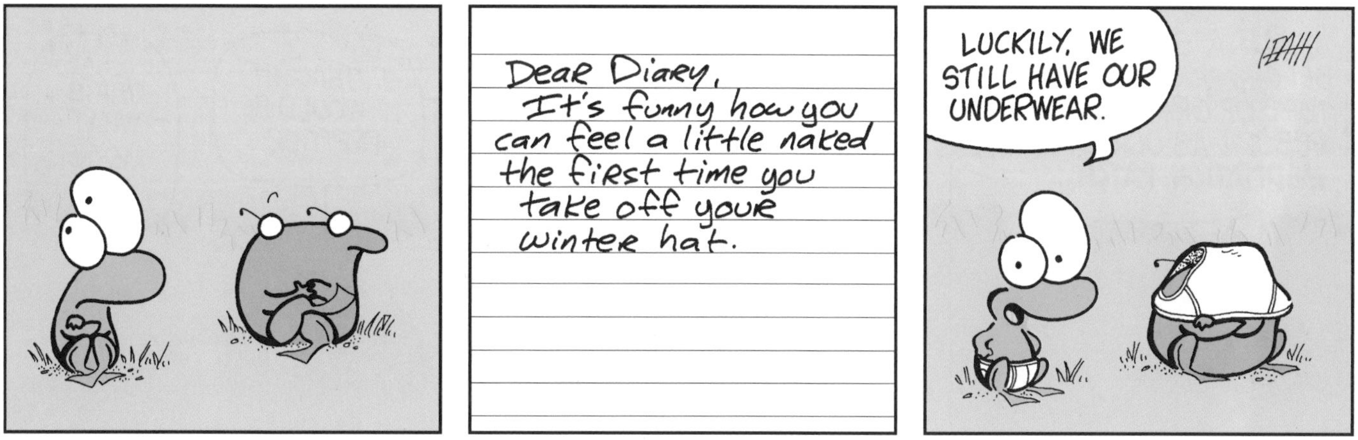
Dear Diary,
It's funny how you can feel a little naked the first time you take off your winter hat.
LUCKILY, WE STILL HAVE OUR UNDERWEAR.

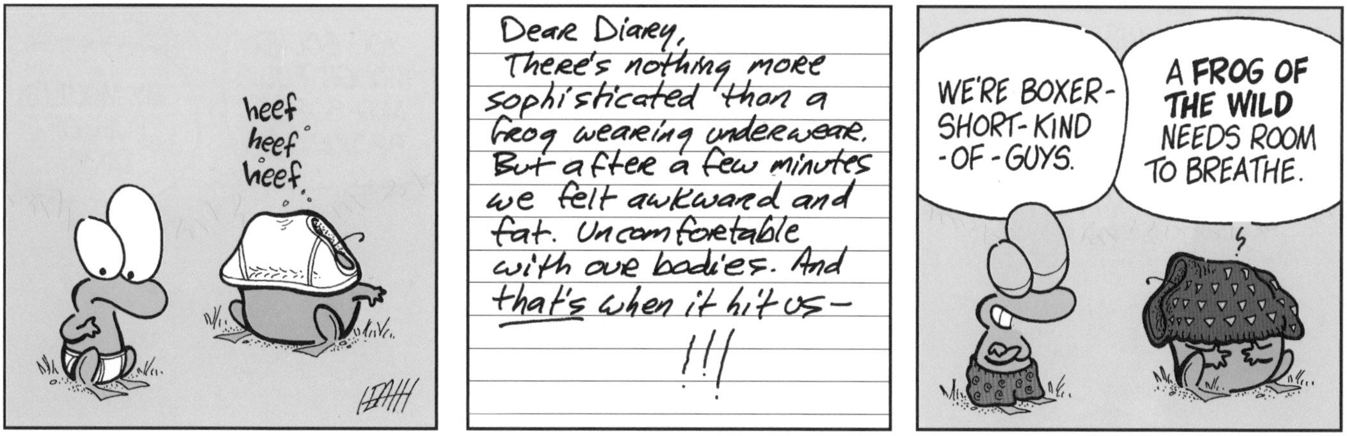
heef
heef
heef
Dear Diary,
There's nothing more sophisticated than a frog wearing underwear. But after a few minutes we felt awkward and fat. Uncomfortable with our bodies. And that's when it hit us—
!!!
WE'RE BOXER-SHORT-KIND-OF-GUYS.
A FROG OF THE WILD NEEDS ROOM TO BREATHE.

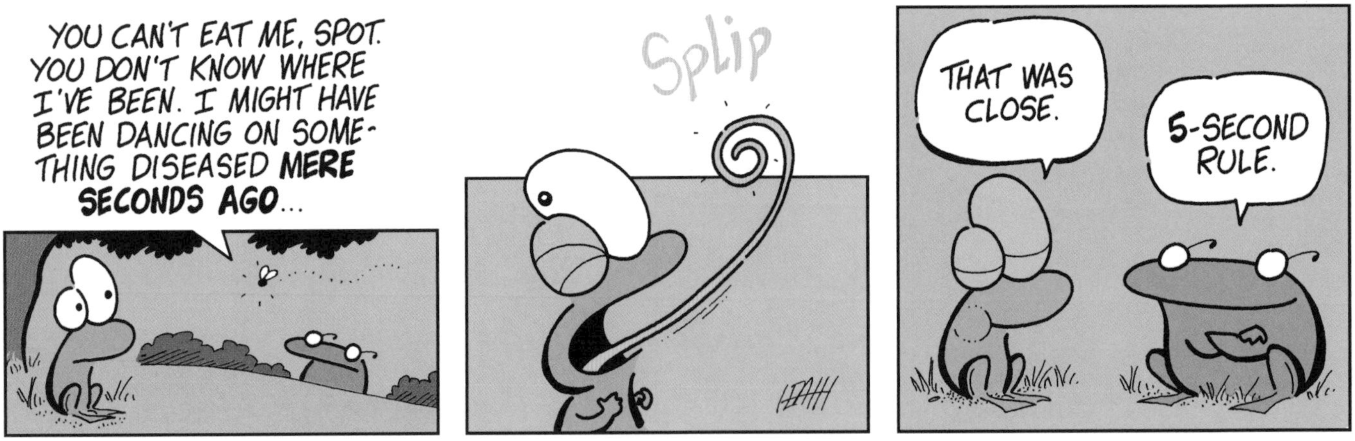
YOU CAN'T EAT ME, SPOT. YOU DON'T KNOW WHERE I'VE BEEN. I MIGHT HAVE BEEN DANCING ON SOMETHING DISEASED **MERE SECONDS AGO**...
Splip
THAT WAS CLOSE.
5-SECOND RULE.

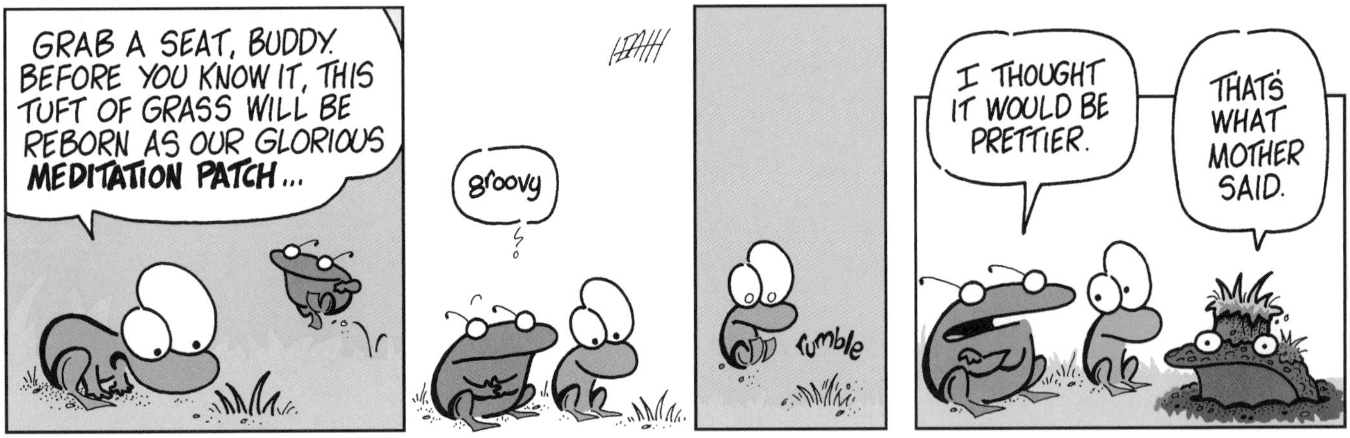
GRAB A SEAT, BUDDY. BEFORE YOU KNOW IT, THIS TUFT OF GRASS WILL BE REBORN AS OUR GLORIOUS **MEDITATION PATCH**...
groovy
rumble
I THOUGHT IT WOULD BE PRETTIER.
THAT'S WHAT MOTHER SAID.

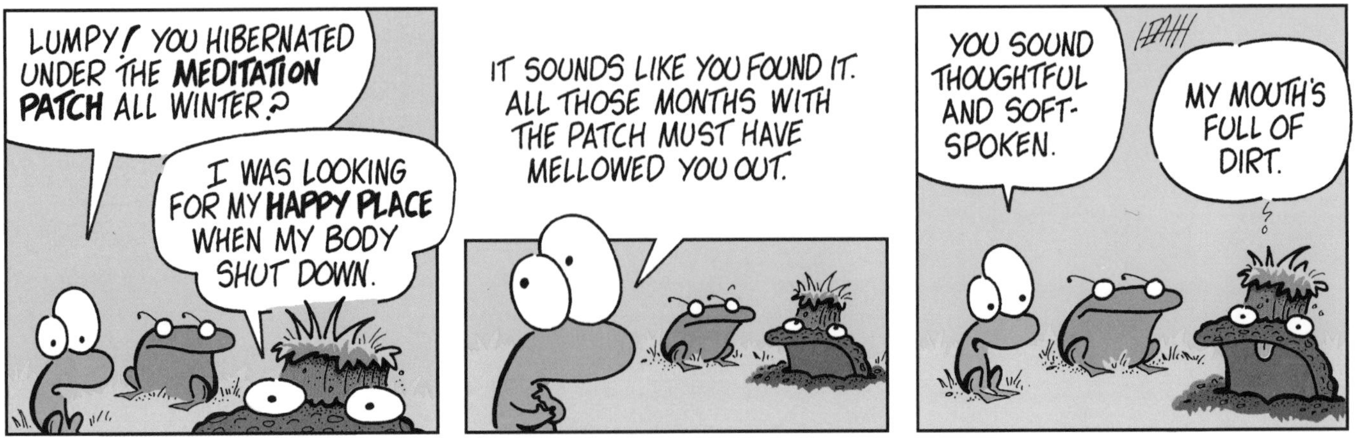
LUMPY! YOU HIBERNATED UNDER THE **MEDITATION PATCH** ALL WINTER?
I WAS LOOKING FOR MY **HAPPY PLACE** WHEN MY BODY SHUT DOWN.
IT SOUNDS LIKE YOU FOUND IT. ALL THOSE MONTHS WITH THE PATCH MUST HAVE MELLOWED YOU OUT.
YOU SOUND THOUGHTFUL AND SOFT-SPOKEN.
MY MOUTH'S FULL OF DIRT.

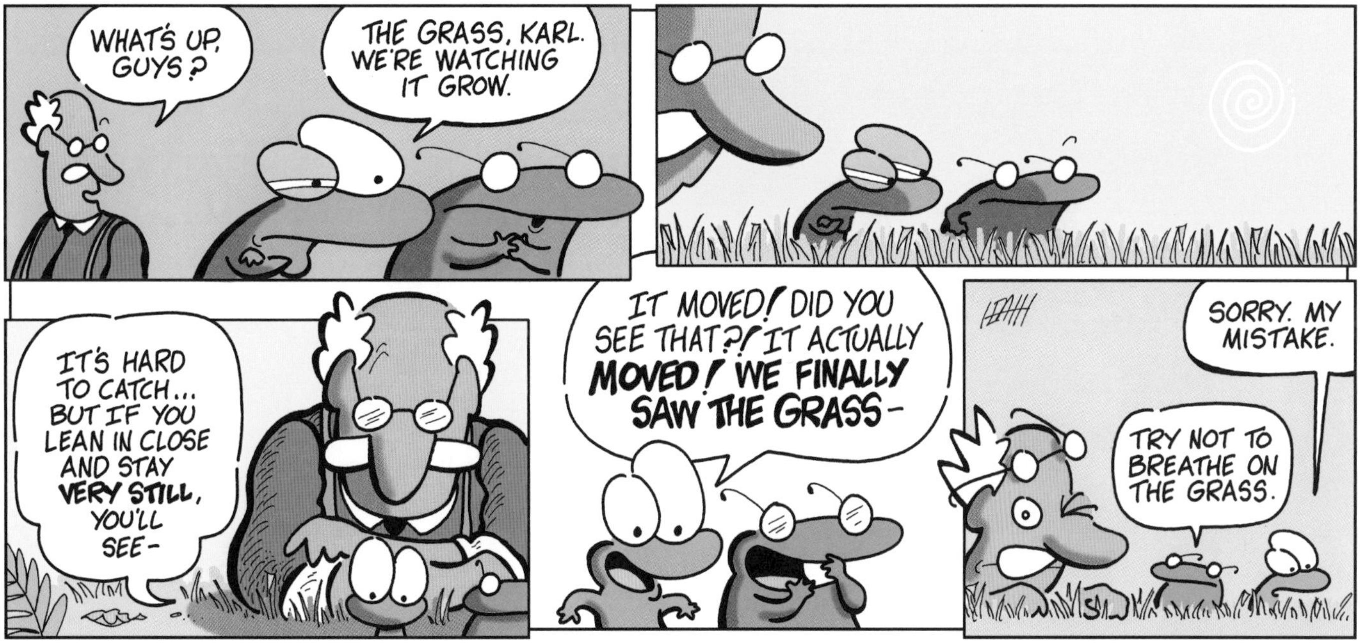
WHAT'S UP, GUYS?
THE GRASS, KARL. WE'RE WATCHING IT GROW.
IT'S HARD TO CATCH... BUT IF YOU LEAN IN CLOSE AND STAY **VERY STILL**, YOU'LL SEE-
IT MOVED! DID YOU SEE THAT?! IT ACTUALLY **MOVED! WE FINALLY SAW THE GRASS-**
SORRY. MY MISTAKE.
TRY NOT TO BREATHE ON THE GRASS.

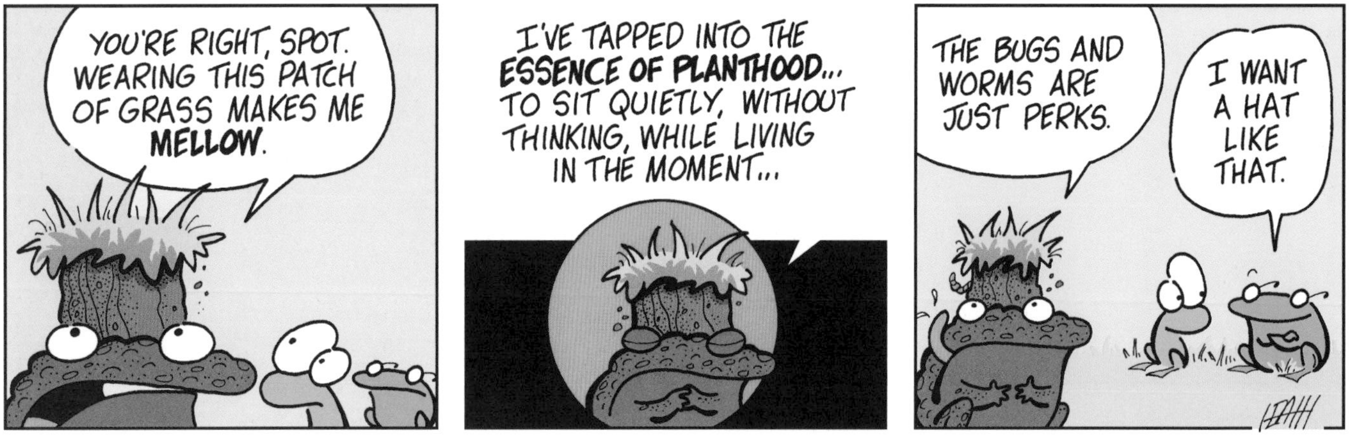
YOU'RE RIGHT, SPOT. WEARING THIS PATCH OF GRASS MAKES ME **MELLOW**.
I'VE TAPPED INTO THE **ESSENCE OF PLANTHOOD**... TO SIT QUIETLY, WITHOUT THINKING, WHILE LIVING IN THE MOMENT...
THE BUGS AND WORMS ARE JUST PERKS.
I WANT A HAT LIKE THAT.

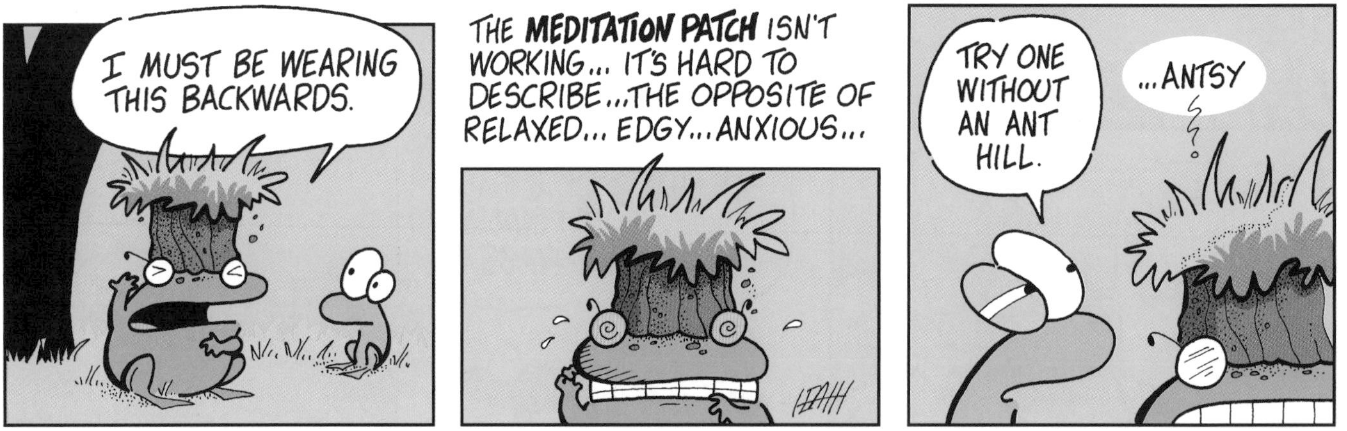
I MUST BE WEARING THIS BACKWARDS.
THE **MEDITATION PATCH** ISN'T WORKING... IT'S HARD TO DESCRIBE...THE OPPOSITE OF RELAXED... EDGY...ANXIOUS...
TRY ONE WITHOUT AN ANT HILL.
...ANTSY

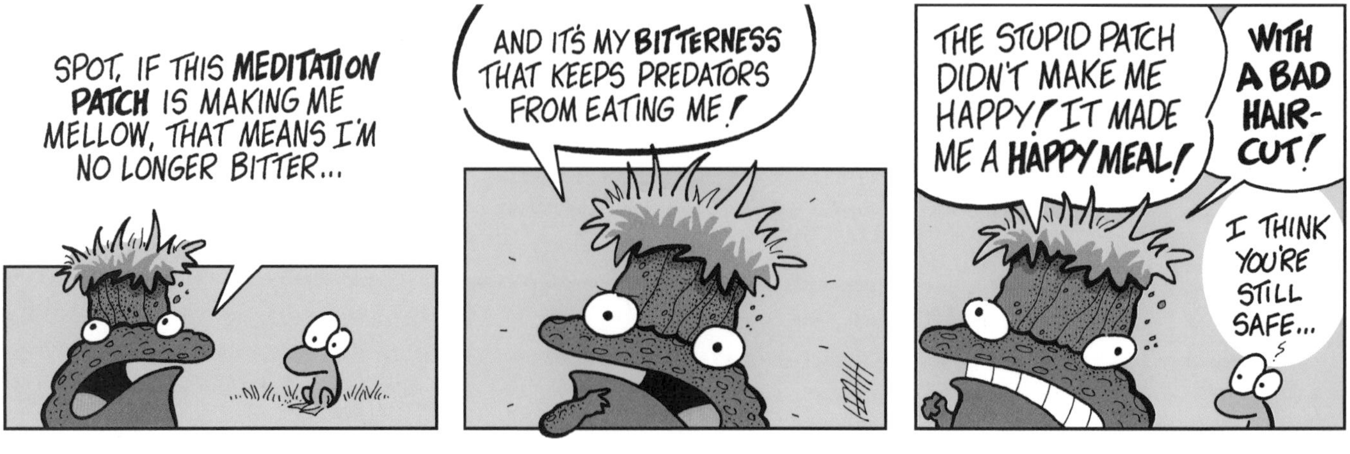
SPOT, IF THIS **MEDITATION PATCH** IS MAKING ME MELLOW, THAT MEANS I'M NO LONGER BITTER...
AND IT'S MY **BITTERNESS** THAT KEEPS PREDATORS FROM EATING ME!
THE STUPID PATCH DIDN'T MAKE ME HAPPY! IT MADE ME A **HAPPY MEAL**!
WITH A BAD HAIR-CUT!
I THINK YOU'RE STILL SAFE...

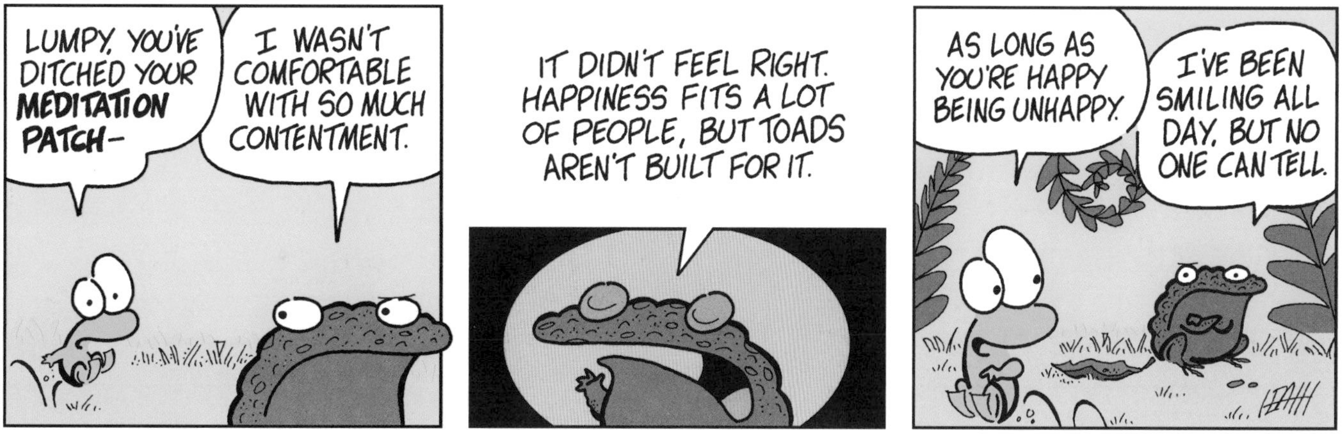
LUMPY, YOU'VE DITCHED YOUR **MEDITATION PATCH**–
I WASN'T COMFORTABLE WITH SO MUCH CONTENTMENT.
IT DIDN'T FEEL RIGHT. HAPPINESS FITS A LOT OF PEOPLE, BUT TOADS AREN'T BUILT FOR IT.
AS LONG AS YOU'RE HAPPY BEING UNHAPPY.
I'VE BEEN SMILING ALL DAY, BUT NO ONE CAN TELL.

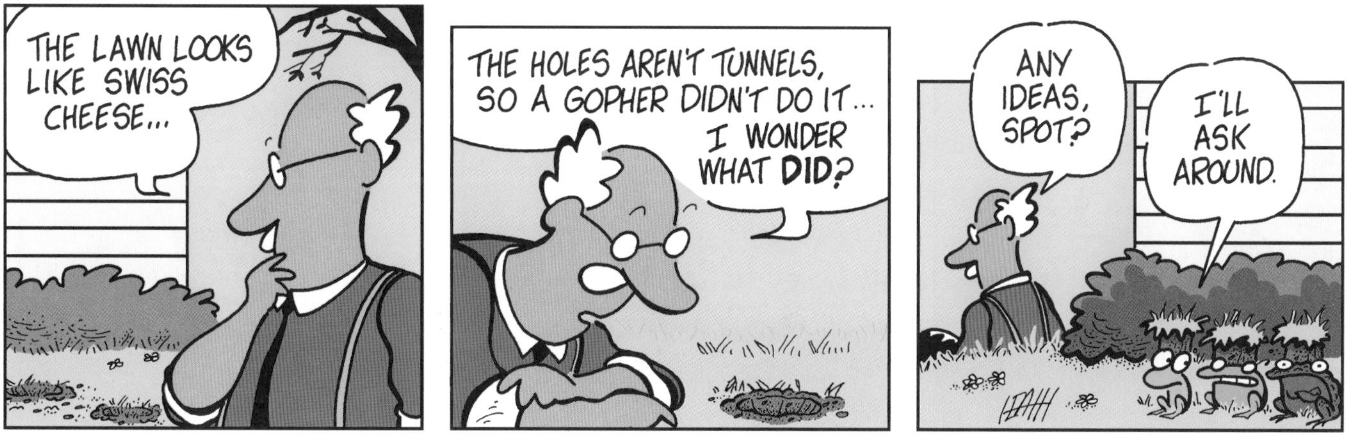
THE LAWN LOOKS LIKE SWISS CHEESE...
THE HOLES AREN'T TUNNELS, SO A GOPHER DIDN'T DO IT... I WONDER WHAT **DID**?
ANY IDEAS, SPOT?
I'LL ASK AROUND.

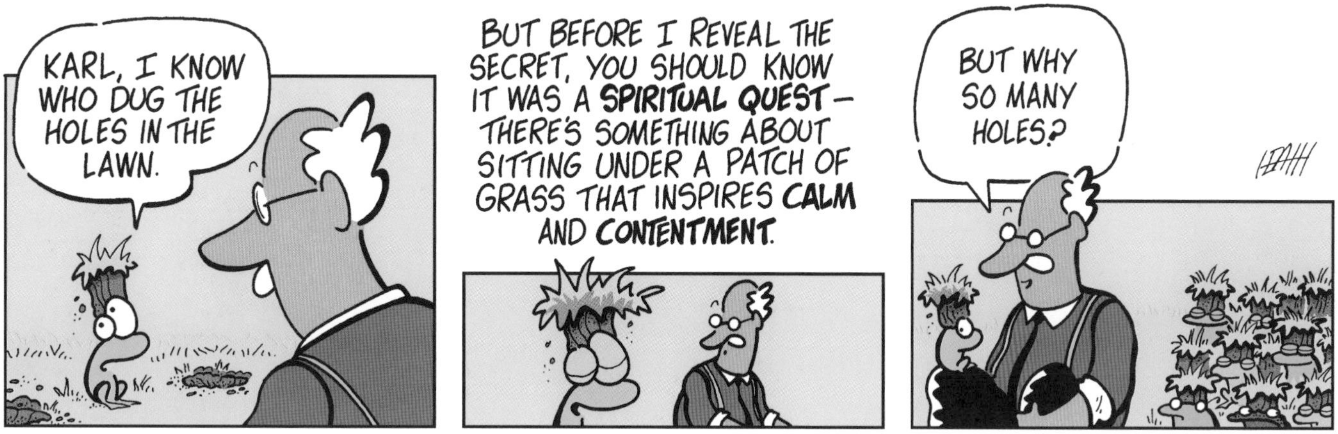
KARL, I KNOW WHO DUG THE HOLES IN THE LAWN.
BUT BEFORE I REVEAL THE SECRET, YOU SHOULD KNOW IT WAS A **SPIRITUAL QUEST**– THERE'S SOMETHING ABOUT SITTING UNDER A PATCH OF GRASS THAT INSPIRES **CALM** AND **CONTENTMENT**.
BUT WHY SO MANY HOLES?

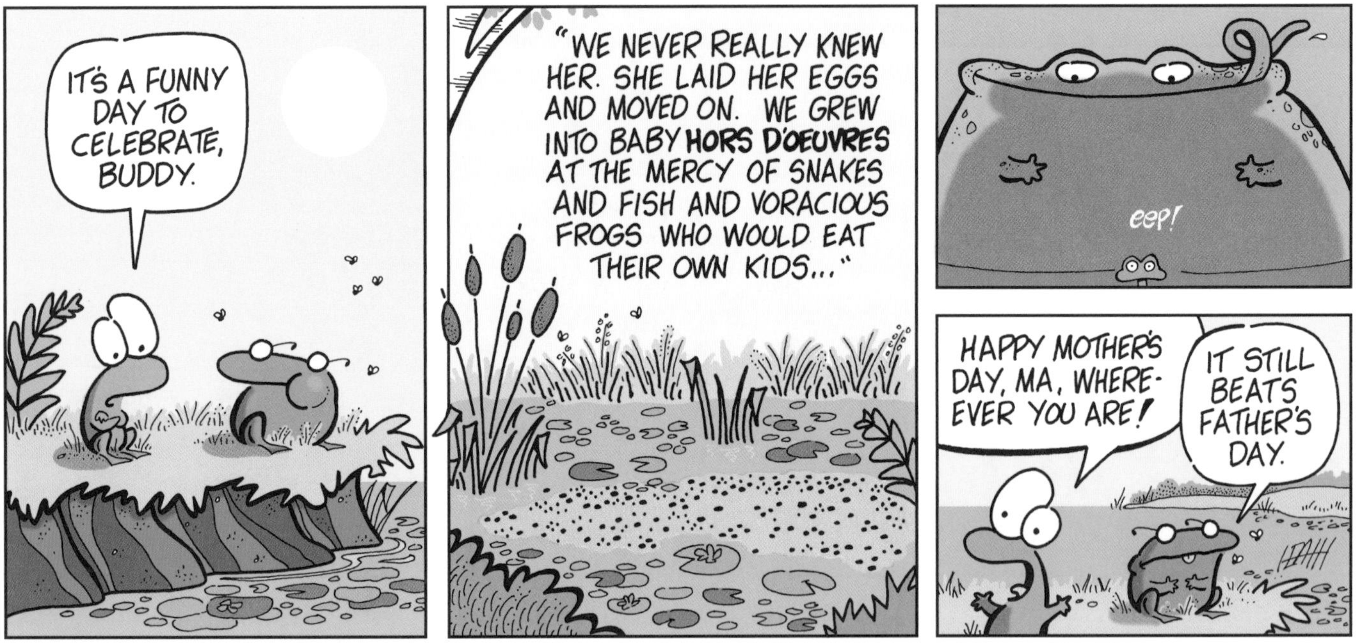
IT'S A FUNNY DAY TO CELEBRATE, BUDDY.
"WE NEVER REALLY KNEW HER. SHE LAID HER EGGS AND MOVED ON. WE GREW INTO BABY **HORS D'OEUVRES** AT THE MERCY OF SNAKES AND FISH AND VORACIOUS FROGS WHO WOULD EAT THEIR OWN KIDS..."
eep!
HAPPY MOTHER'S DAY, MA, WHERE-EVER YOU ARE!
IT STILL BEATS FATHER'S DAY.

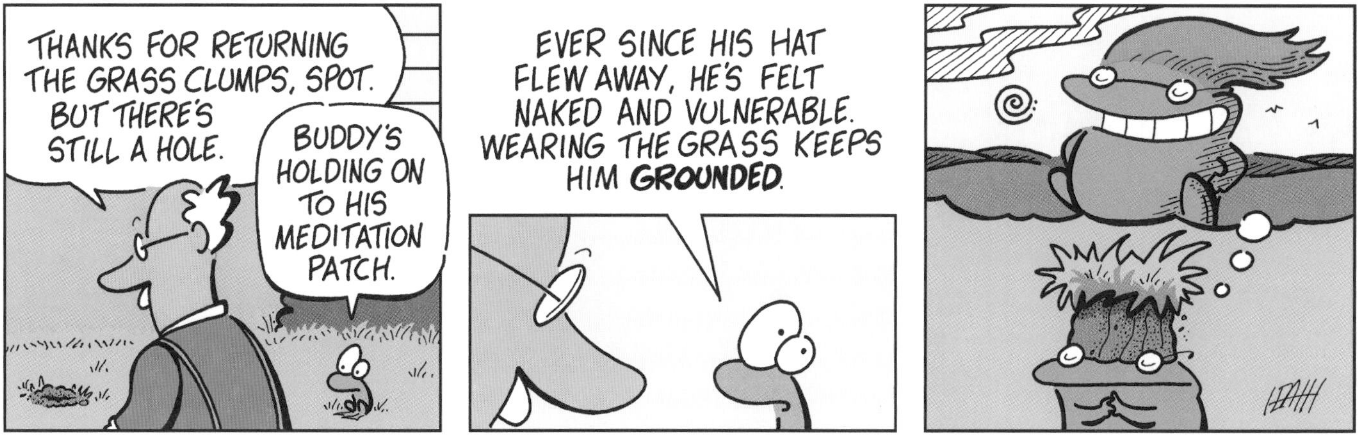
THANKS FOR RETURNING THE GRASS CLUMPS, SPOT. BUT THERE'S STILL A HOLE.
BUDDY'S HOLDING ON TO HIS MEDITATION PATCH.
EVER SINCE HIS HAT FLEW AWAY, HE'S FELT NAKED AND VULNERABLE. WEARING THE GRASS KEEPS HIM **GROUNDED**.

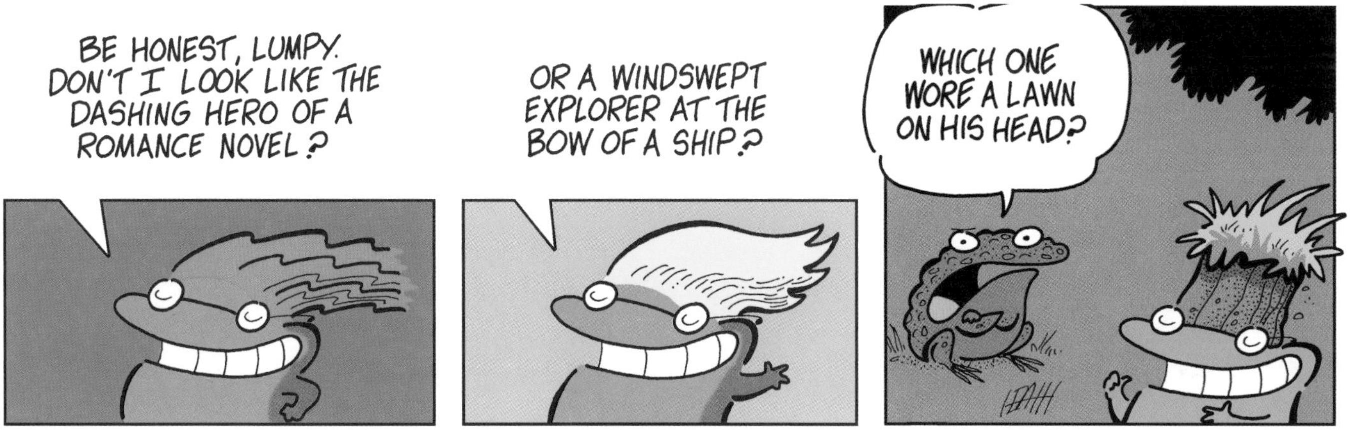
BE HONEST, LUMPY. DON'T I LOOK LIKE THE DASHING HERO OF A ROMANCE NOVEL?
OR A WINDSWEPT EXPLORER AT THE BOW OF A SHIP?
WHICH ONE WORE A LAWN ON HIS HEAD?

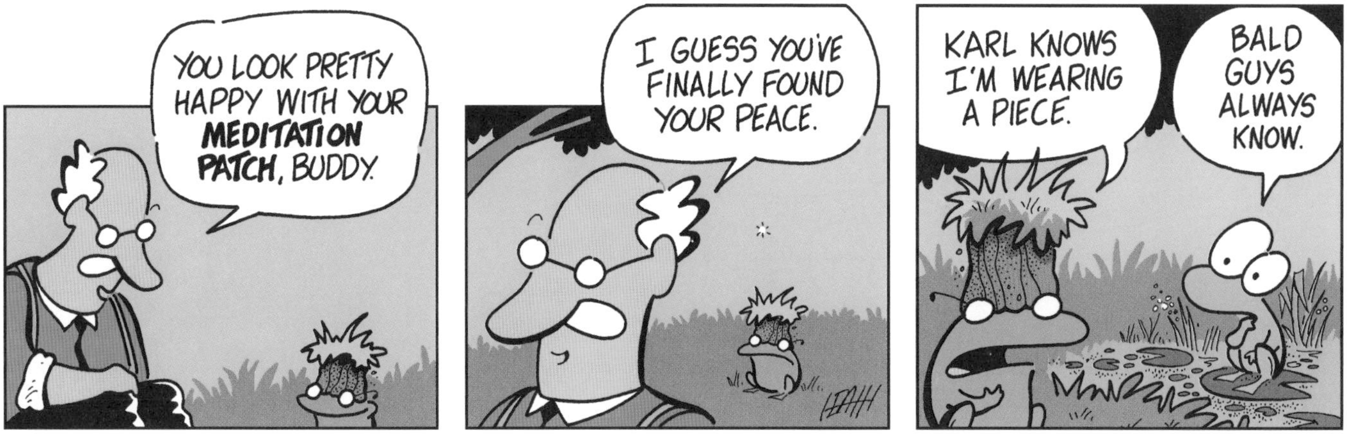
YOU LOOK PRETTY HAPPY WITH YOUR **MEDITATION PATCH**, BUDDY.
I GUESS YOU'VE FINALLY FOUND YOUR PEACE.
KARL KNOWS I'M WEARING A PIECE.
BALD GUYS ALWAYS KNOW.

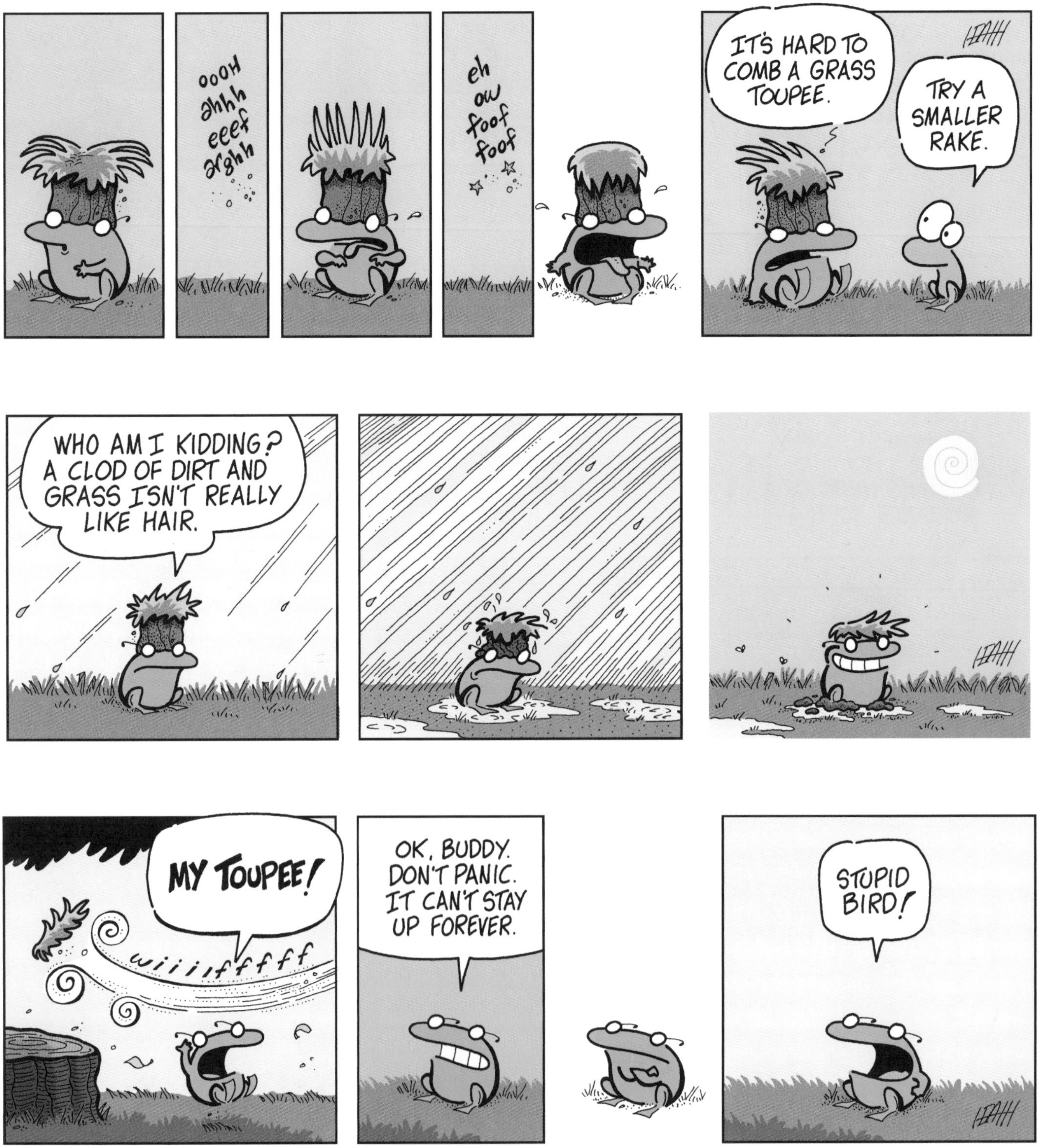
eh
ow
foof
foof
IT'S HARD TO COMB A GRASS TOUPEE.
TRY A SMALLER RAKE.
WHO AM I KIDDING? A CLOD OF DIRT AND GRASS ISN'T REALLY LIKE HAIR.
MY TOUPEE!
wiiiiffffff
OK, BUDDY. DON'T PANIC. IT CAN'T STAY UP FOREVER.
STUPID BIRD!

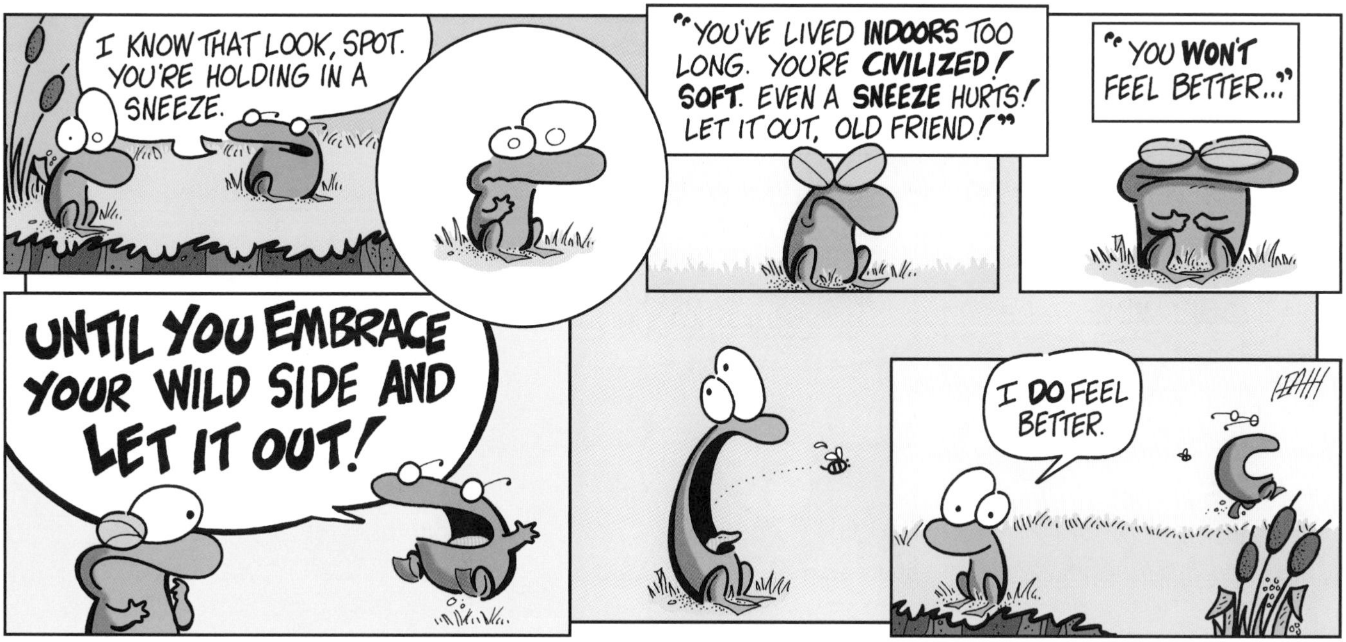
I KNOW THAT LOOK, SPOT. YOU'RE HOLDING IN A SNEEZE.
"YOU'VE LIVED INDOORS TOO LONG. YOU'RE CIVILIZED! SOFT. EVEN A SNEEZE HURTS! LET IT OUT, OLD FRIEND!"
"YOU WON'T FEEL BETTER..."
UNTIL YOU EMBRACE YOUR WILD SIDE AND LET IT OUT!
I DO FEEL BETTER.

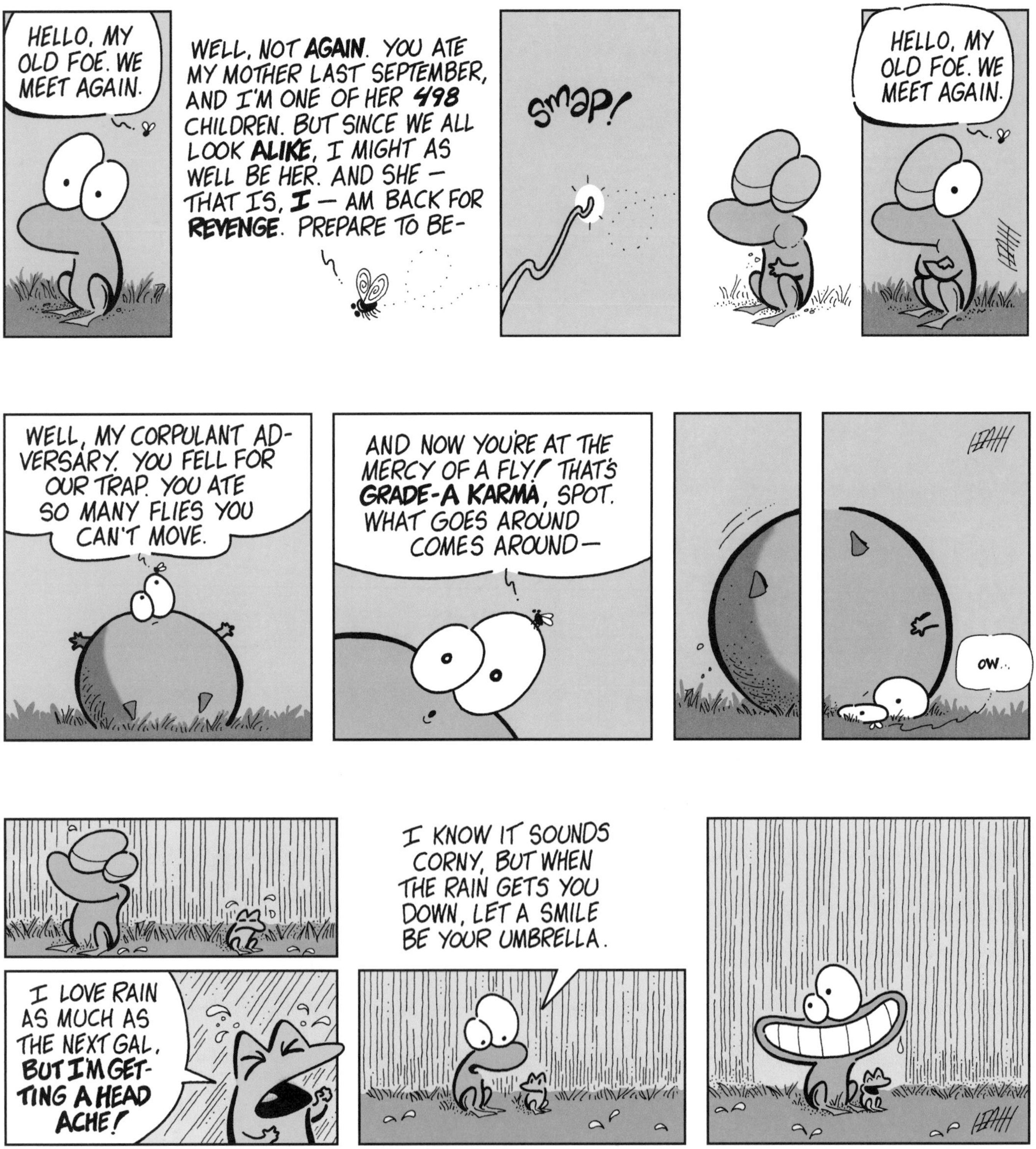

HELLO, MY OLD FOE. WE MEET AGAIN.
WELL, NOT AGAIN. YOU ATE MY MOTHER LAST SEPTEMBER, AND I'M ONE OF HER 498 CHILDREN. BUT SINCE WE ALL LOOK ALIKE, I MIGHT AS WELL BE HER. AND SHE — THAT IS, I — AM BACK FOR REVENGE. PREPARE TO BE-
SMAP!
HELLO, MY OLD FOE. WE MEET AGAIN.
WELL, MY CORPULANT ADVERSARY. YOU FELL FOR OUR TRAP. YOU ATE SO MANY FLIES YOU CAN'T MOVE.
AND NOW YOU'RE AT THE MERCY OF A FLY! THAT'S GRADE-A KARMA, SPOT. WHAT GOES AROUND COMES AROUND—
OW...
I LOVE RAIN AS MUCH AS THE NEXT GAL, BUT I'M GETTING A HEAD ACHE!
I KNOW IT SOUNDS CORNY, BUT WHEN THE RAIN GETS YOU DOWN, LET A SMILE BE YOUR UMBRELLA.

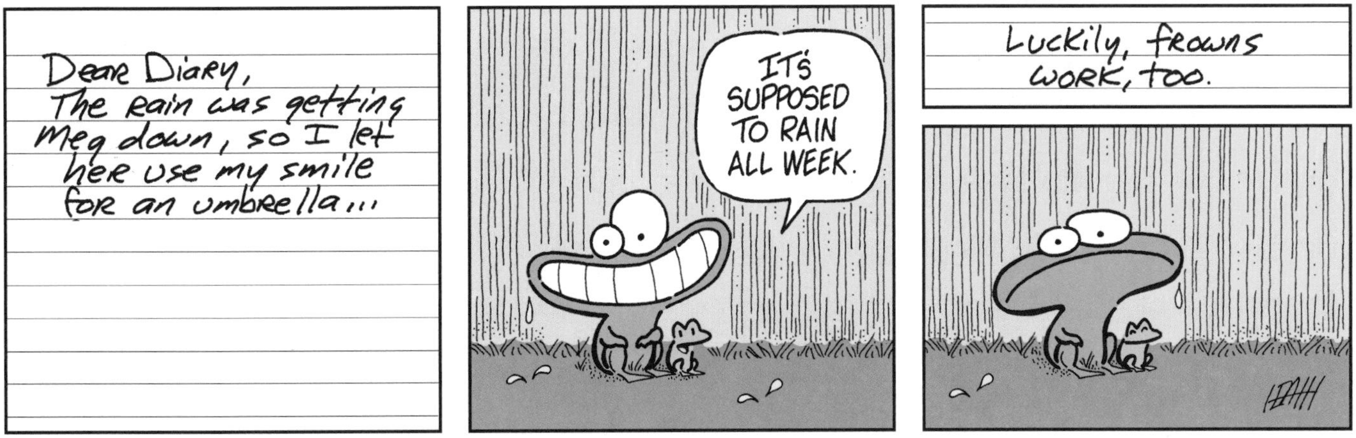
Dear Diary,
The rain was getting Meg down, so I let her use my smile for an umbrella...
IT'S SUPPOSED TO RAIN ALL WEEK.
Luckily, frowns work, too.

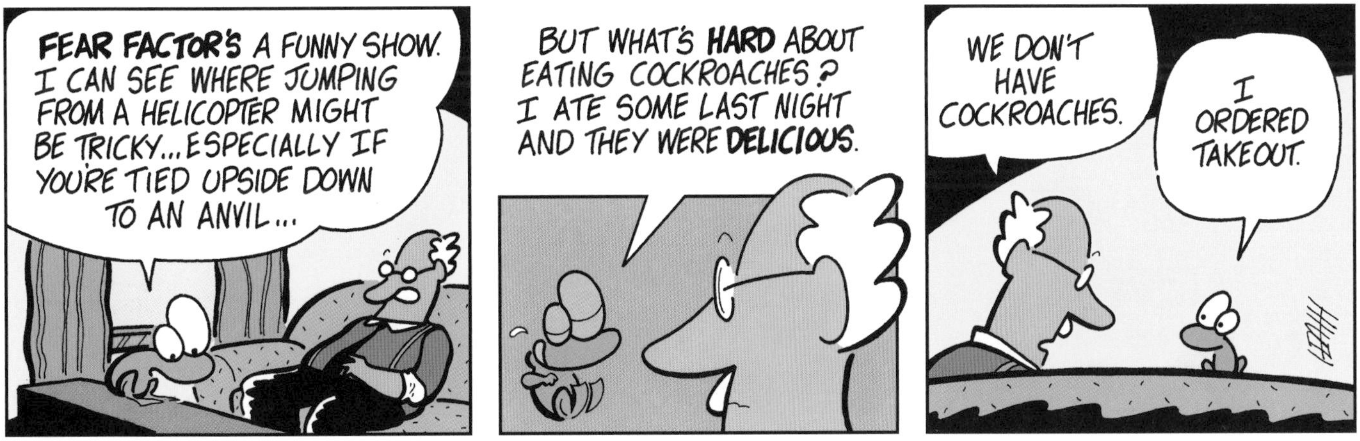
FEAR FACTOR'S A FUNNY SHOW. I CAN SEE WHERE JUMPING FROM A HELICOPTER MIGHT BE TRICKY...ESPECIALLY IF YOU'RE TIED UPSIDE DOWN TO AN ANVIL...
BUT WHAT'S HARD ABOUT EATING COCKROACHES? I ATE SOME LAST NIGHT AND THEY WERE DELICIOUS.
WE DON'T HAVE COCKROACHES.
I ORDERED TAKEOUT.

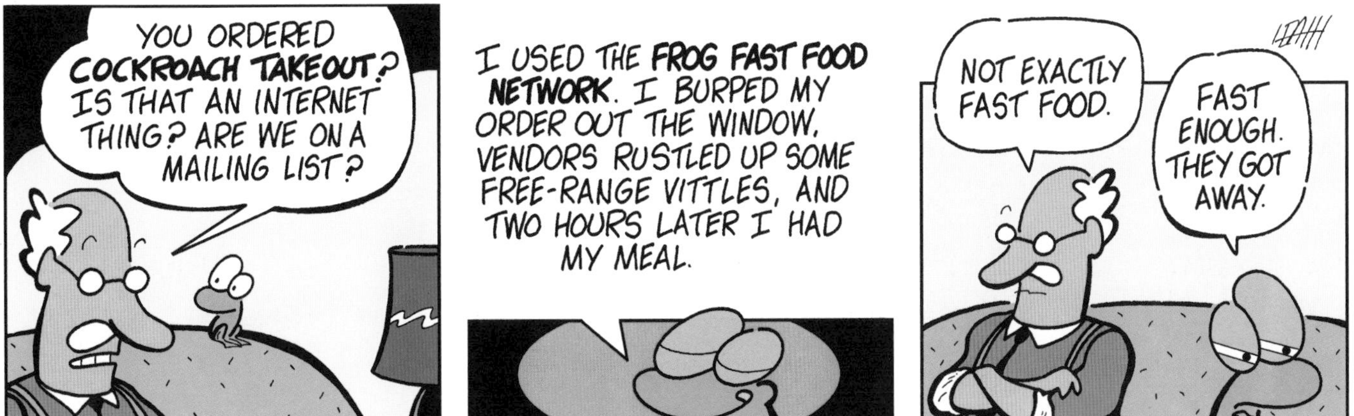
YOU ORDERED COCKROACH TAKEOUT? IS THAT AN INTERNET THING? ARE WE ON A MAILING LIST?
I USED THE FROG FAST FOOD NETWORK. I BURPED MY ORDER OUT THE WINDOW, VENDORS RUSTLED UP SOME FREE-RANGE VITTLES, AND TWO HOURS LATER I HAD MY MEAL.
NOT EXACTLY FAST FOOD.
FAST ENOUGH. THEY GOT AWAY.

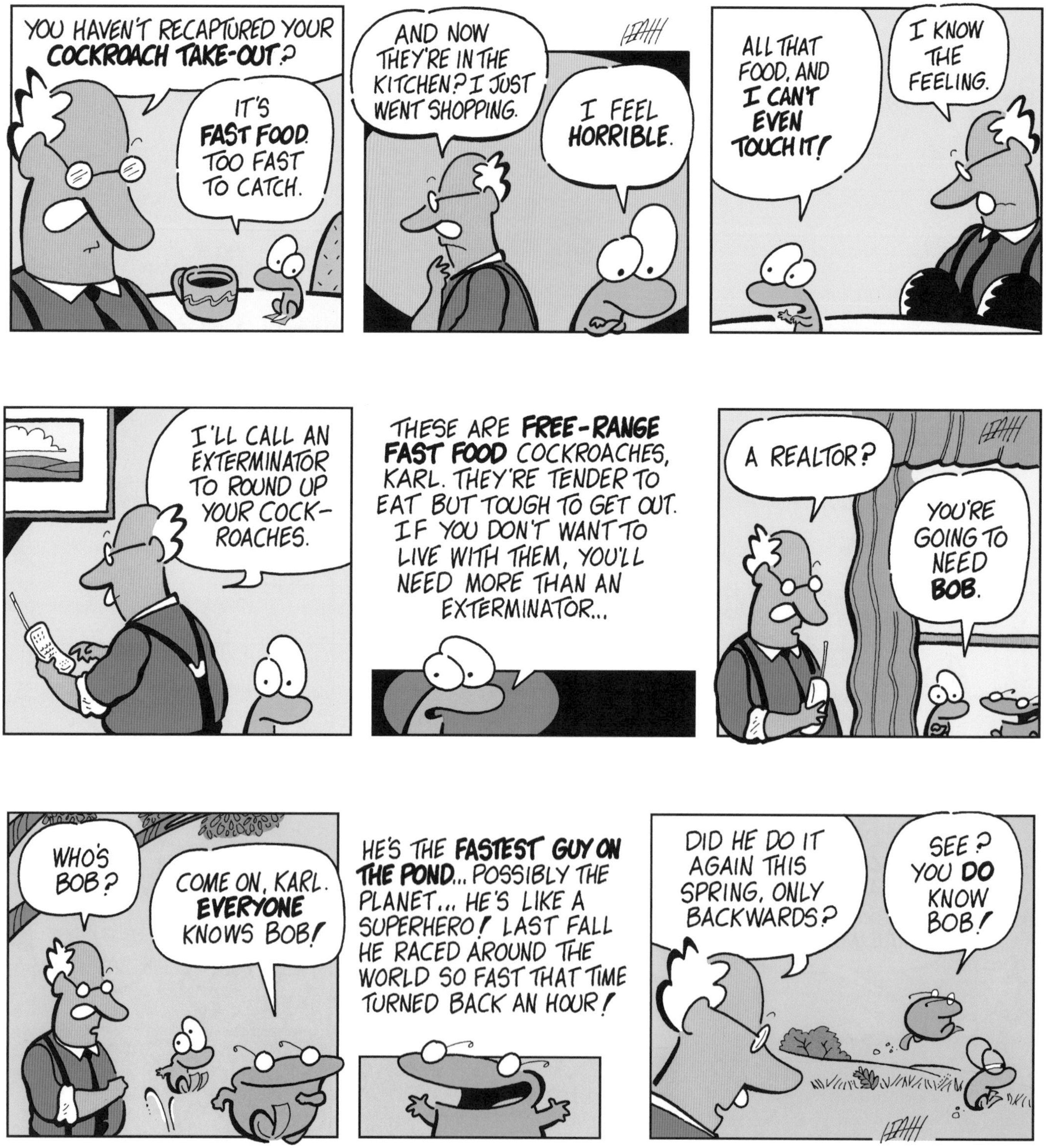
YOU HAVEN'T RECAPTURED YOUR **COCKROACH TAKE-OUT**?
IT'S **FAST FOOD**. TOO FAST TO CATCH.
AND NOW THEY'RE IN THE KITCHEN? I JUST WENT SHOPPING.
I FEEL **HORRIBLE**.
ALL THAT FOOD, AND **I CAN'T EVEN TOUCH IT!**
I KNOW THE FEELING.
I'LL CALL AN EXTERMINATOR TO ROUND UP YOUR COCK-ROACHES.
THESE ARE **FREE-RANGE FAST FOOD** COCKROACHES, KARL. THEY'RE TENDER TO EAT BUT TOUGH TO GET OUT. IF YOU DON'T WANT TO LIVE WITH THEM, YOU'LL NEED MORE THAN AN EXTERMINATOR...
A REALTOR?
YOU'RE GOING TO NEED **BOB**.
WHO'S BOB?
COME ON, KARL. **EVERYONE** KNOWS BOB!
HE'S THE **FASTEST GUY ON THE POND**... POSSIBLY THE PLANET... HE'S LIKE A SUPERHERO! LAST FALL HE RACED AROUND THE WORLD SO FAST THAT TIME TURNED BACK AN HOUR!
DID HE DO IT AGAIN THIS SPRING, ONLY BACKWARDS?
SEE? YOU **DO** KNOW BOB!

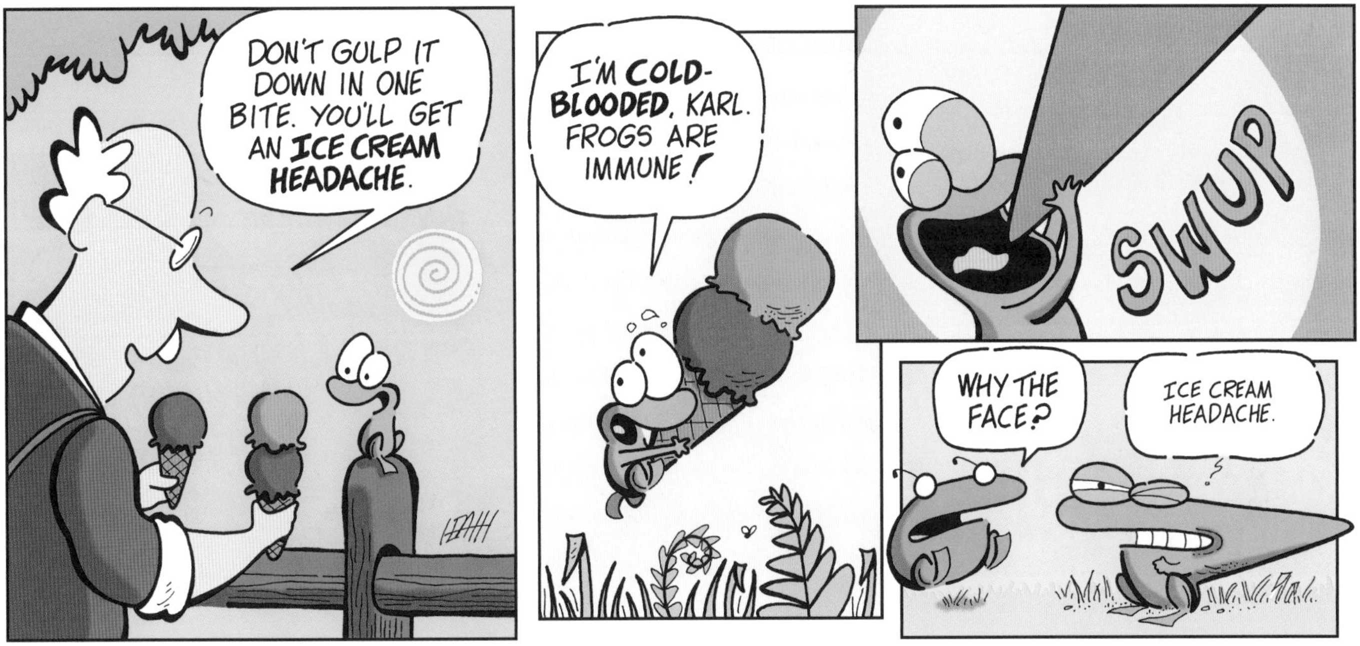
DON'T GULP IT DOWN IN ONE BITE. YOU'LL GET AN ICE CREAM HEADACHE.
I'M COLD-BLOODED, KARL. FROGS ARE IMMUNE!
SWUP
WHY THE FACE?
ICE CREAM HEADACHE.

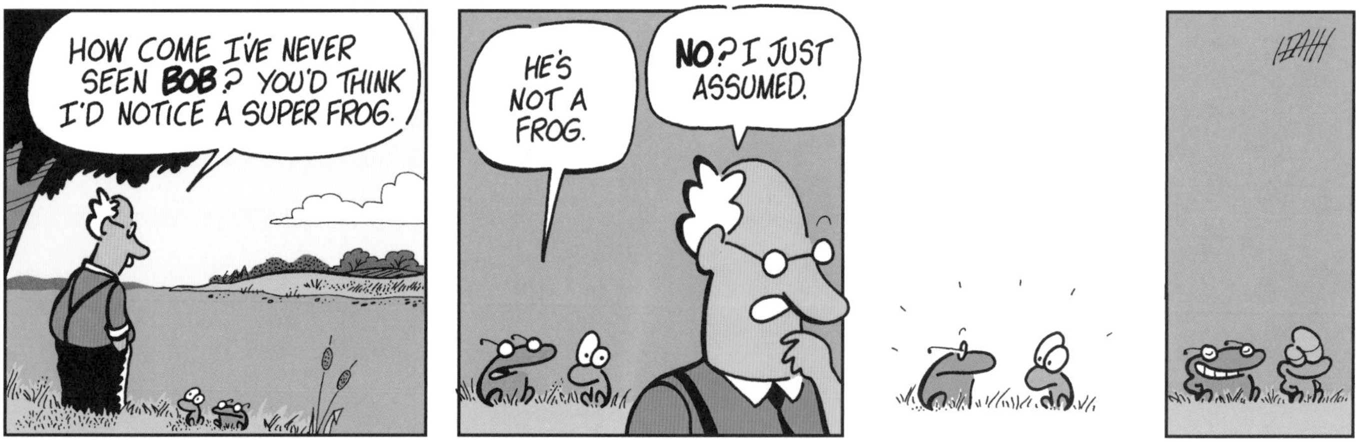
HOW COME I'VE NEVER SEEN BOB? YOU'D THINK I'D NOTICE A SUPER FROG.
HE'S NOT A FROG.
NO? I JUST ASSUMED.

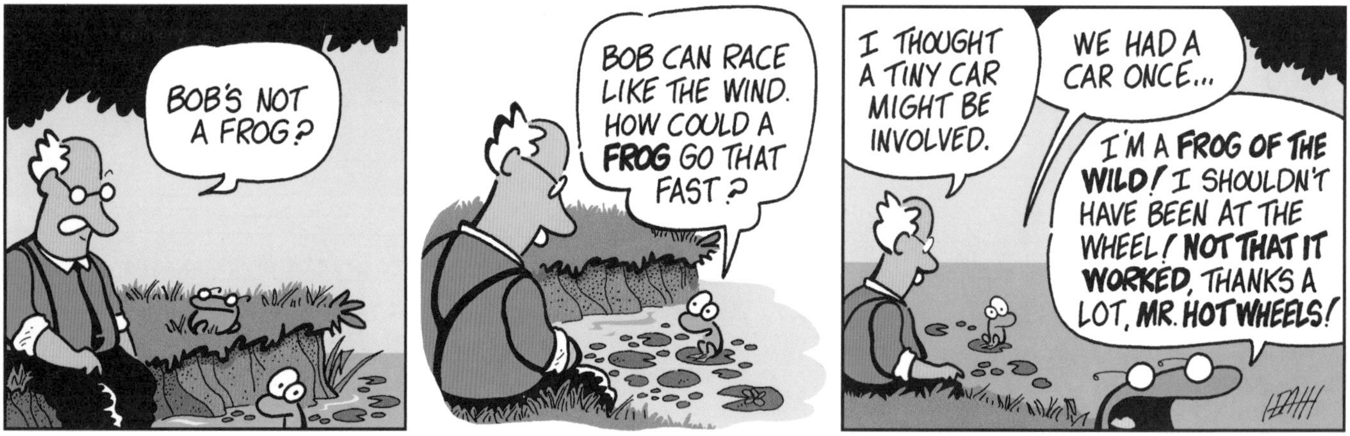
BOB'S NOT A FROG?
BOB CAN RACE LIKE THE WIND. HOW COULD A FROG GO THAT FAST?
I THOUGHT A TINY CAR MIGHT BE INVOLVED.
WE HAD A CAR ONCE...
I'M A FROG OF THE WILD! I SHOULDN'T HAVE BEEN AT THE WHEEL! NOT THAT IT WORKED, THANKS A LOT, MR. HOT WHEELS!

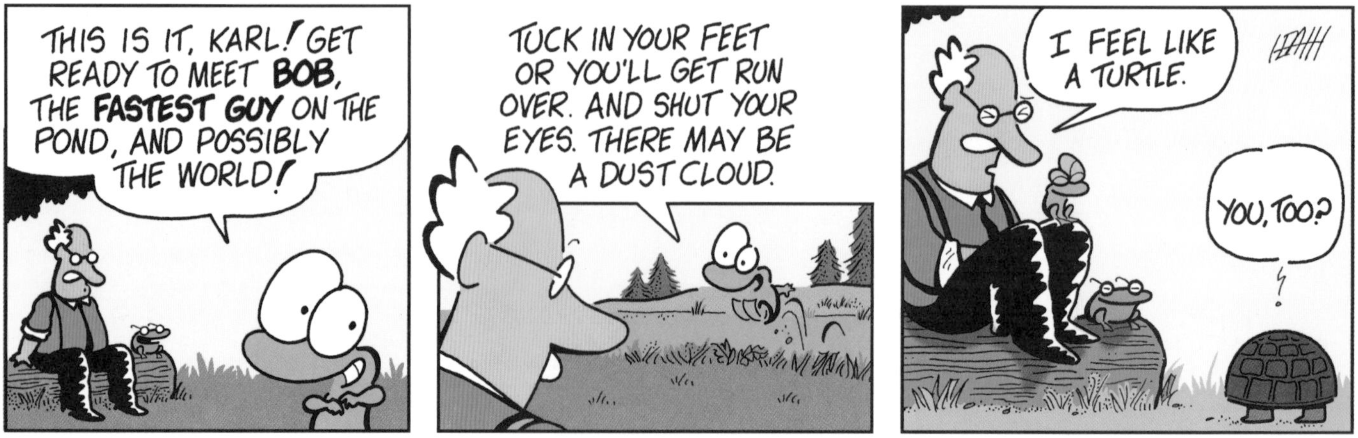
THIS IS IT, KARL! GET READY TO MEET BOB, THE FASTEST GUY ON THE POND, AND POSSIBLY THE WORLD!
TUCK IN YOUR FEET OR YOU'LL GET RUN OVER. AND SHUT YOUR EYES. THERE MAY BE A DUST CLOUD.
I FEEL LIKE A TURTLE.
YOU, TOO?

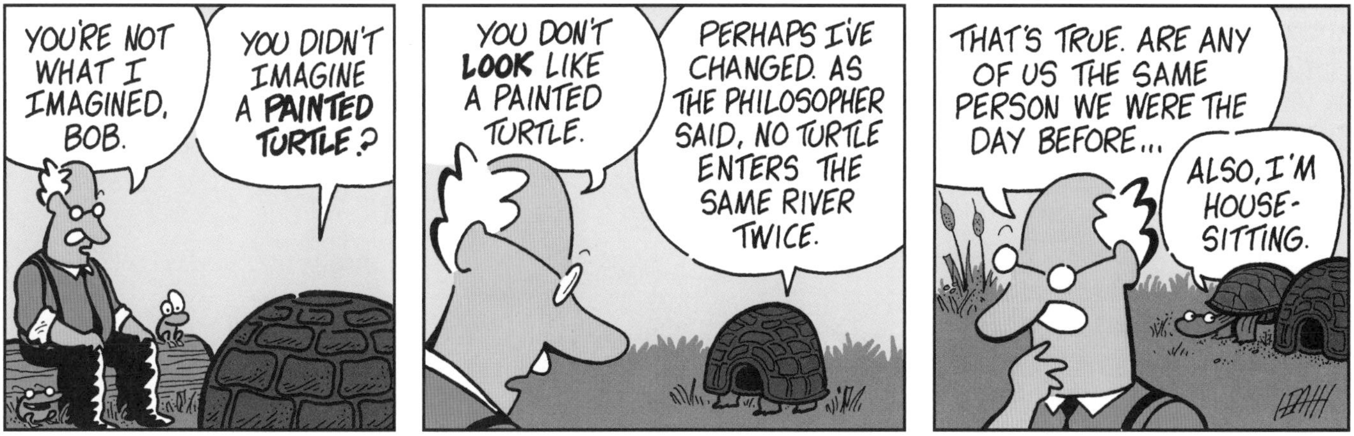
YOU'RE NOT WHAT I IMAGINED, BOB.
YOU DIDN'T IMAGINE A **PAINTED TURTLE**?
YOU DON'T **LOOK** LIKE A PAINTED TURTLE.
PERHAPS I'VE CHANGED. AS THE PHILOSOPHER SAID, NO TURTLE ENTERS THE SAME RIVER TWICE.
THAT'S TRUE. ARE ANY OF US THE SAME PERSON WE WERE THE DAY BEFORE...
ALSO, I'M HOUSE-SITTING.

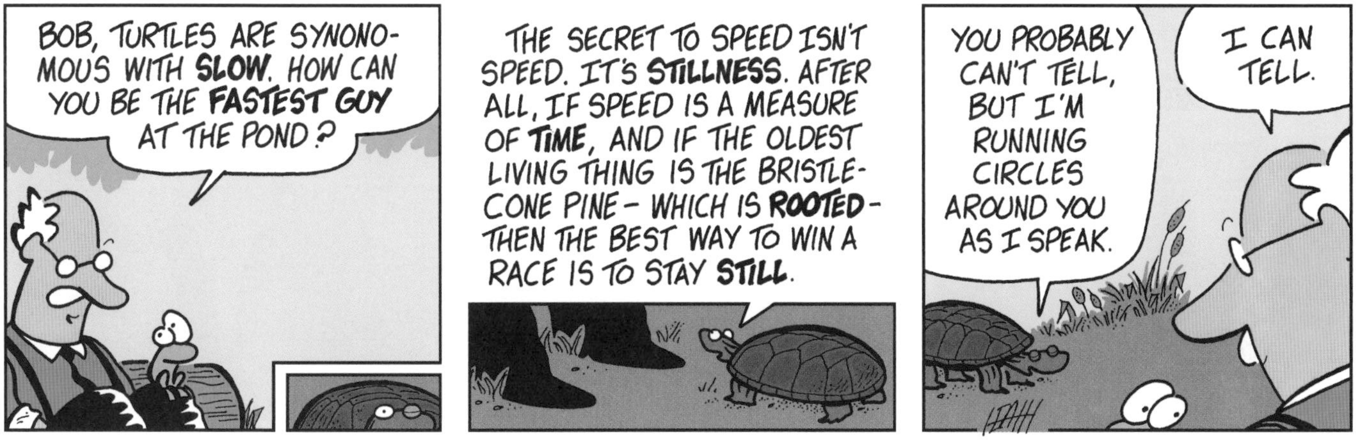
BOB, TURTLES ARE SYNONOMOUS WITH **SLOW**. HOW CAN YOU BE THE **FASTEST GUY** AT THE POND?
THE SECRET TO SPEED ISN'T SPEED. IT'S **STILLNESS**. AFTER ALL, IF SPEED IS A MEASURE OF **TIME**, AND IF THE OLDEST LIVING THING IS THE BRISTLECONE PINE – WHICH IS **ROOTED** – THEN THE BEST WAY TO WIN A RACE IS TO STAY **STILL**.
YOU PROBABLY CAN'T TELL, BUT I'M RUNNING CIRCLES AROUND YOU AS I SPEAK.
I CAN TELL.

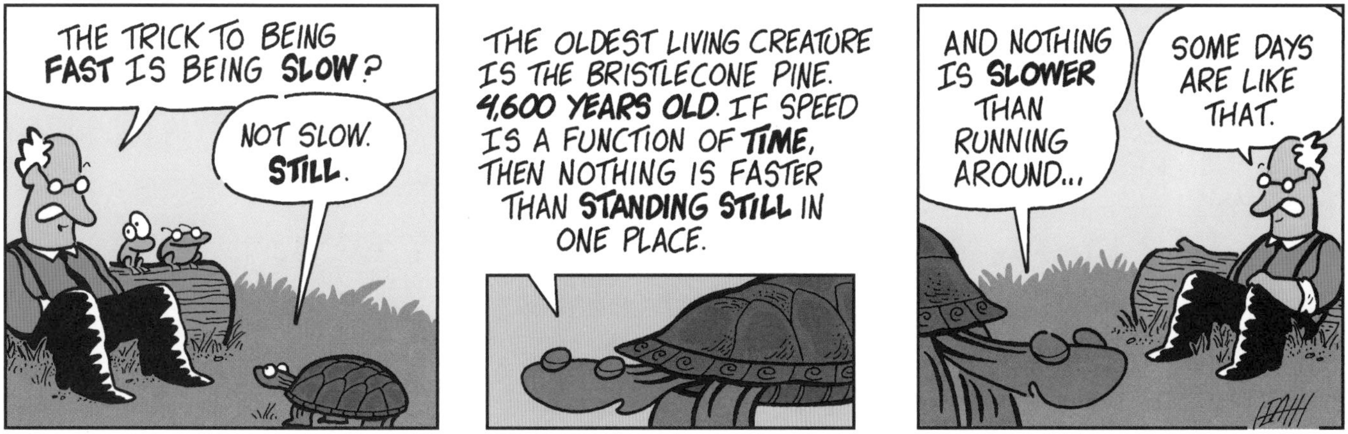
THE TRICK TO BEING **FAST** IS BEING **SLOW**?
NOT SLOW. **STILL**.
THE OLDEST LIVING CREATURE IS THE BRISTLECONE PINE. **4,600 YEARS OLD**. IF SPEED IS A FUNCTION OF **TIME**, THEN NOTHING IS FASTER THAN **STANDING STILL** IN ONE PLACE.
AND NOTHING IS **SLOWER** THAN RUNNING AROUND...
SOME DAYS ARE LIKE THAT.

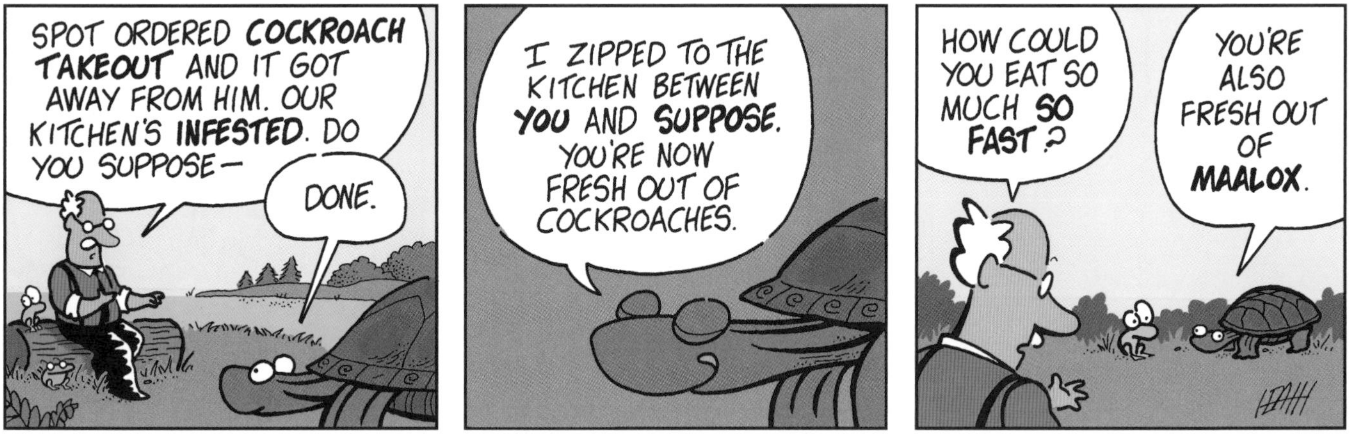
SPOT ORDERED **COCKROACH TAKEOUT** AND IT GOT AWAY FROM HIM. OUR KITCHEN'S **INFESTED**. DO YOU SUPPOSE—
DONE.
I ZIPPED TO THE KITCHEN BETWEEN **YOU** AND **SUPPOSE**. YOU'RE NOW FRESH OUT OF COCKROACHES.
HOW COULD YOU EAT SO MUCH **SO FAST**?
YOU'RE ALSO FRESH OUT OF **MAALOX**.

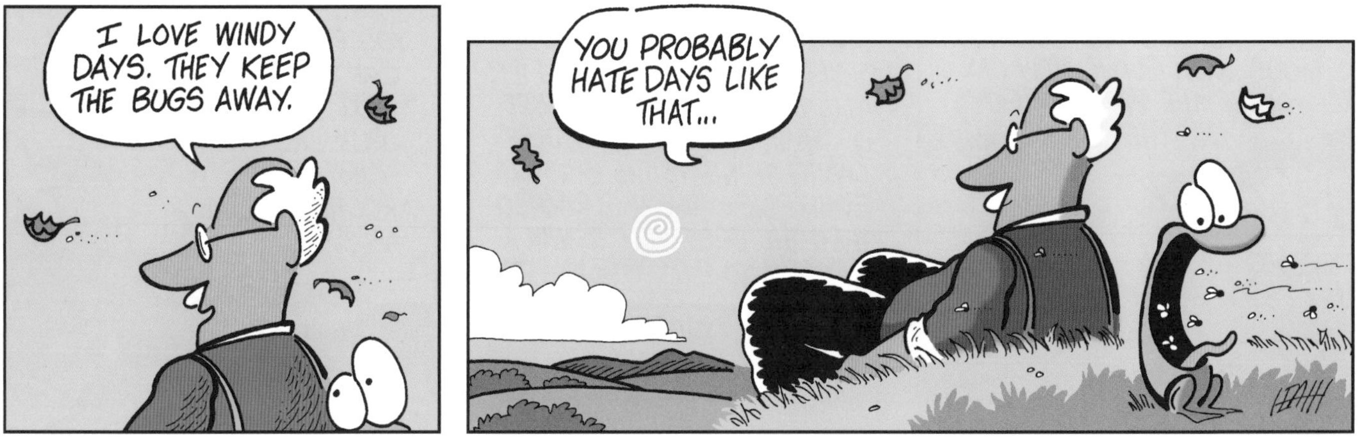
I LOVE WINDY DAYS. THEY KEEP THE BUGS AWAY.
YOU PROBABLY HATE DAYS LIKE THAT...

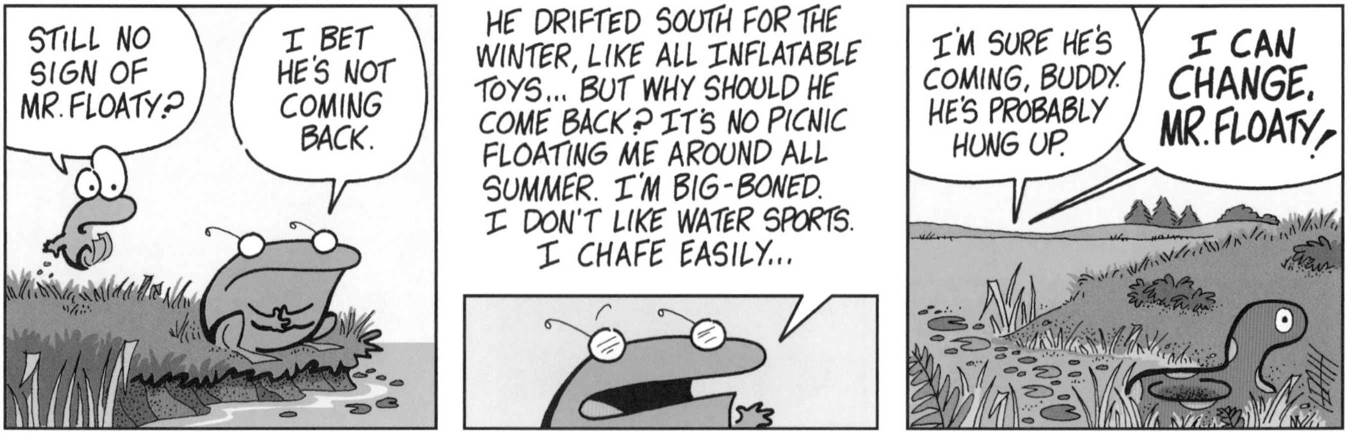
STILL NO SIGN OF MR. FLOATY?
I BET HE'S NOT COMING BACK.
HE DRIFTED SOUTH FOR THE WINTER, LIKE ALL INFLATABLE TOYS... BUT WHY SHOULD HE COME BACK? IT'S NO PICNIC FLOATING ME AROUND ALL SUMMER. I'M BIG-BONED. I DON'T LIKE WATER SPORTS. I CHAFE EASILY...
I'M SURE HE'S COMING, BUDDY. HE'S PROBABLY HUNG UP.
I CAN CHANGE, MR. FLOATY!

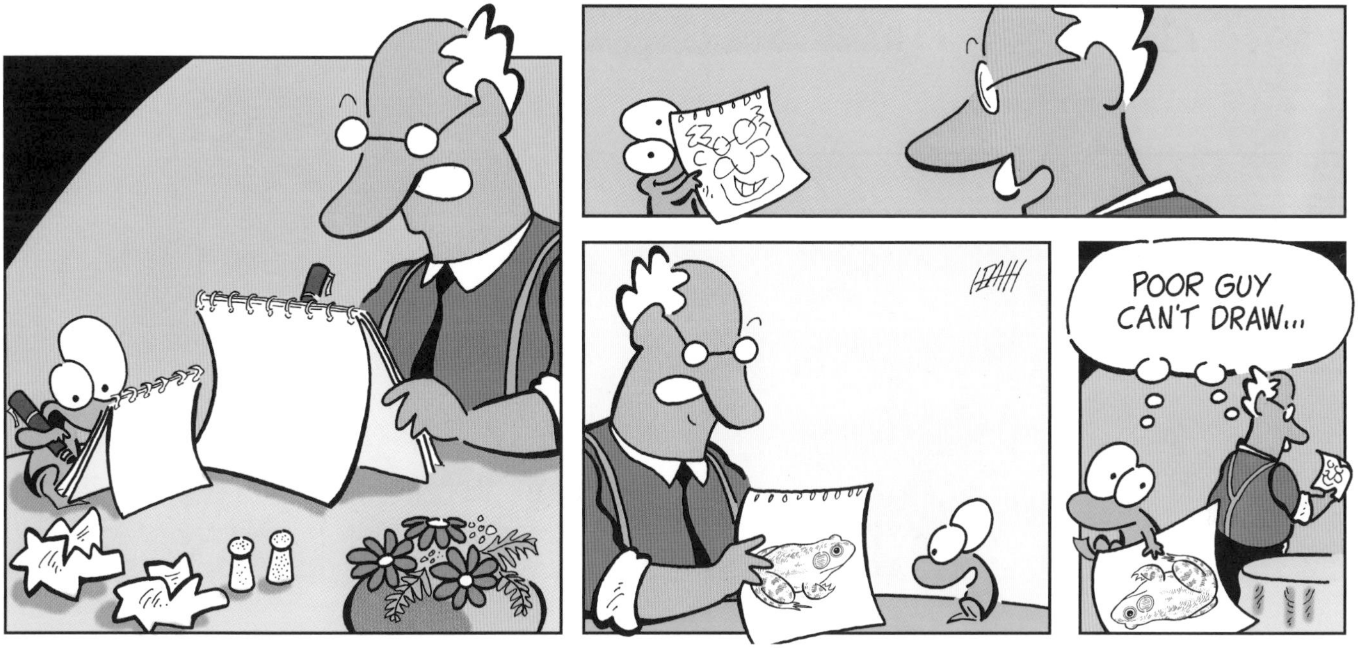
POOR GUY
CAN'T DRAW...

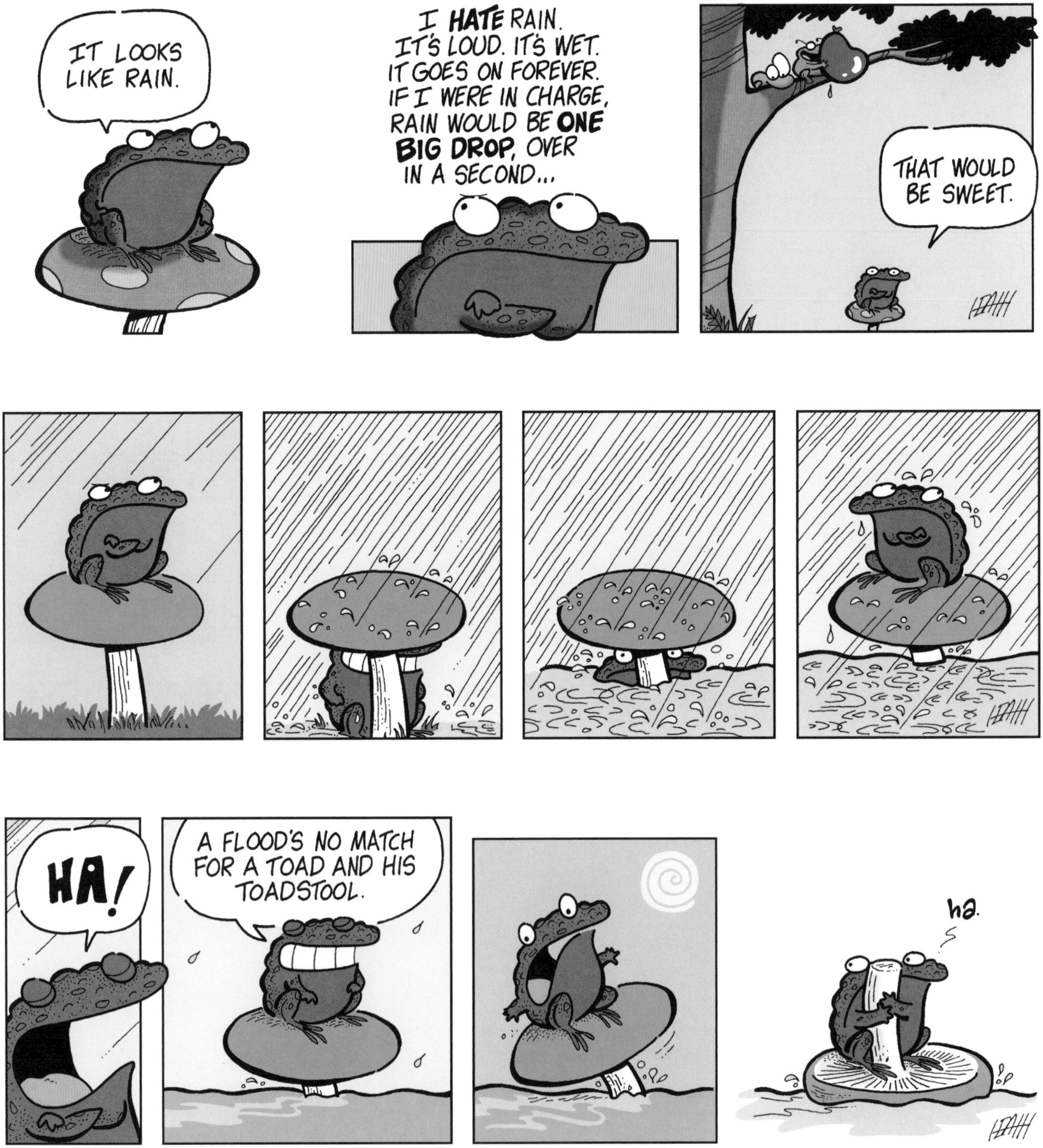
IT LOOKS LIKE RAIN.
I HATE RAIN. IT'S LOUD. IT'S WET. IT GOES ON FOREVER. IF I WERE IN CHARGE, RAIN WOULD BE ONE BIG DROP, OVER IN A SECOND...
THAT WOULD BE SWEET.
HA!
A FLOOD'S NO MATCH FOR A TOAD AND HIS TOADSTOOL.
ha.

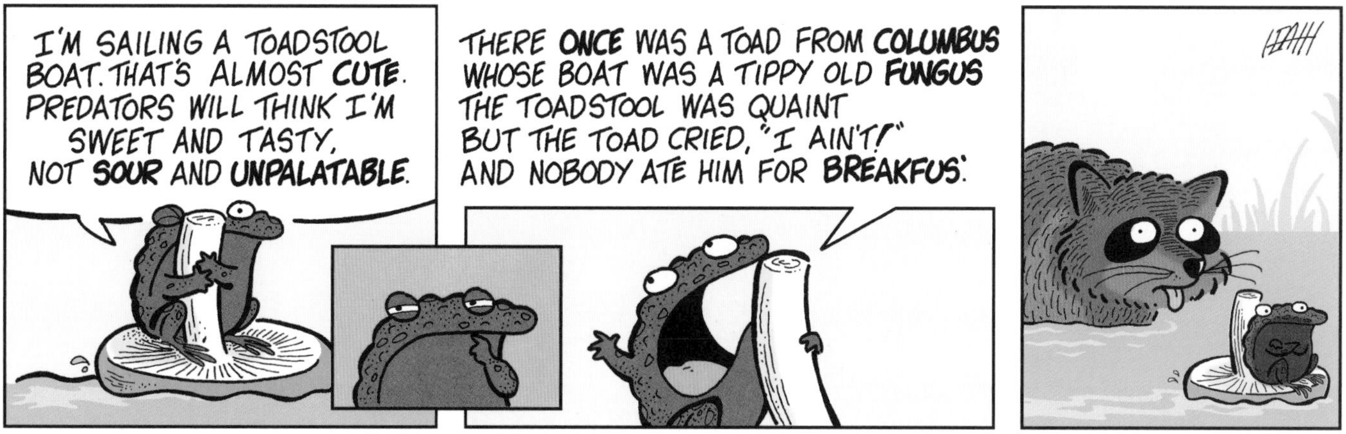
I'M SAILING A TOADSTOOL BOAT. THAT'S ALMOST CUTE. PREDATORS WILL THINK I'M SWEET AND TASTY, NOT SOUR AND UNPALATABLE.
THERE ONCE WAS A TOAD FROM COLUMBUS
WHOSE BOAT WAS A TIPPY OLD FUNGUS
THE TOADSTOOL WAS QUAINT
BUT THE TOAD CRIED, "I AIN'T!"
AND NOBODY ATE HIM FOR BREAKFUS.

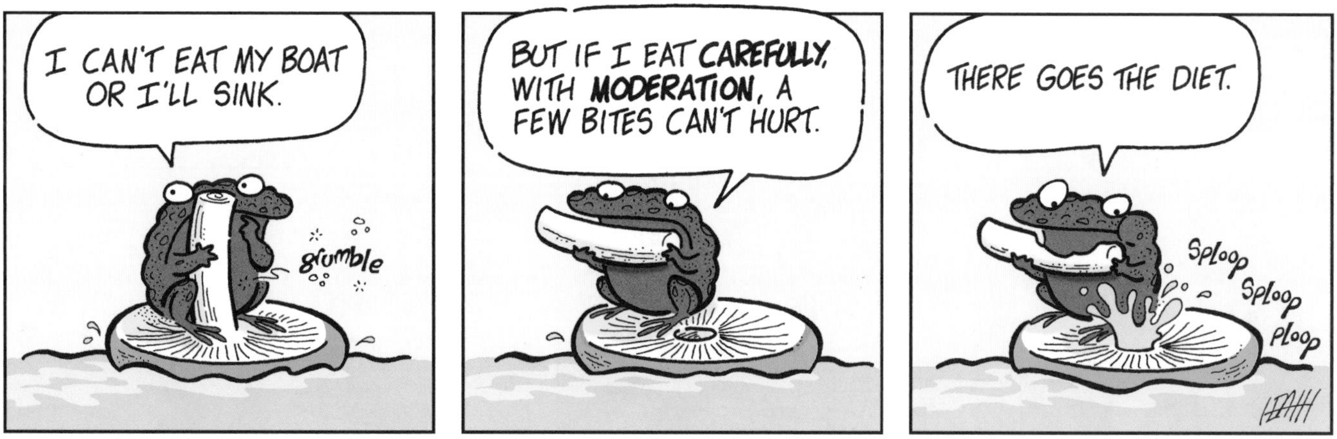
I CAN'T EAT MY BOAT OR I'LL SINK.
grumble
BUT IF I EAT CAREFULLY, WITH MODERATION, A FEW BITES CAN'T HURT.
THERE GOES THE DIET.
Sploop
Sploop
Ploop

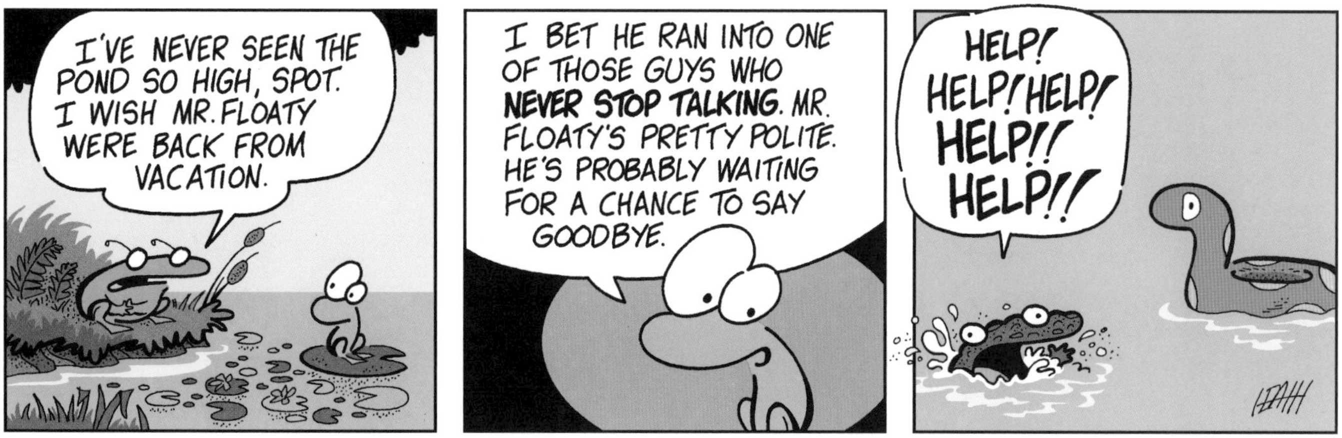
I'VE NEVER SEEN THE POND SO HIGH, SPOT. I WISH MR. FLOATY WERE BACK FROM VACATION.
I BET HE RAN INTO ONE OF THOSE GUYS WHO NEVER STOP TALKING. MR. FLOATY'S PRETTY POLITE. HE'S PROBABLY WAITING FOR A CHANCE TO SAY GOODBYE.
HELP! HELP! HELP! HELP!! HELP!!

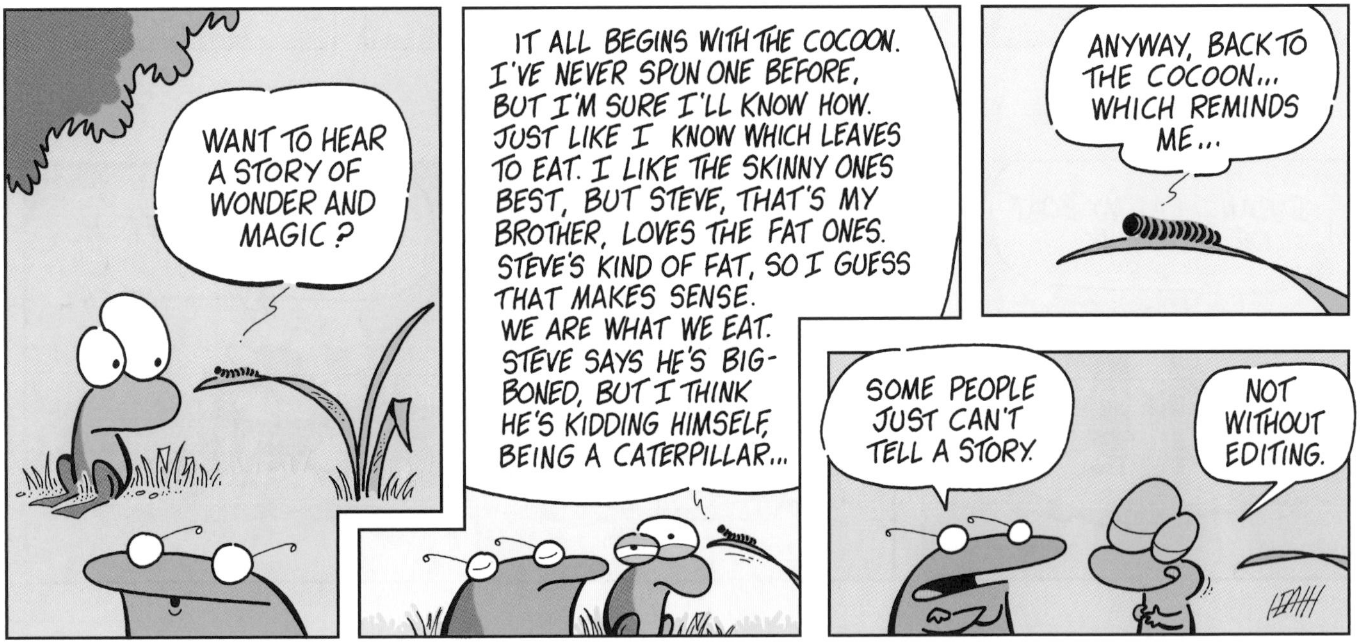
WANT TO HEAR A STORY OF WONDER AND MAGIC?
IT ALL BEGINS WITH THE COCOON. I'VE NEVER SPUN ONE BEFORE, BUT I'M SURE I'LL KNOW HOW. JUST LIKE I KNOW WHICH LEAVES TO EAT. I LIKE THE SKINNY ONES BEST, BUT STEVE, THAT'S MY BROTHER, LOVES THE FAT ONES. STEVE'S KIND OF FAT, SO I GUESS THAT MAKES SENSE. WE ARE WHAT WE EAT. STEVE SAYS HE'S BIG-BONED, BUT I THINK HE'S KIDDING HIMSELF, BEING A CATERPILLAR...
ANYWAY, BACK TO THE COCOON... WHICH REMINDS ME...
SOME PEOPLE JUST CAN'T TELL A STORY.
NOT WITHOUT EDITING.

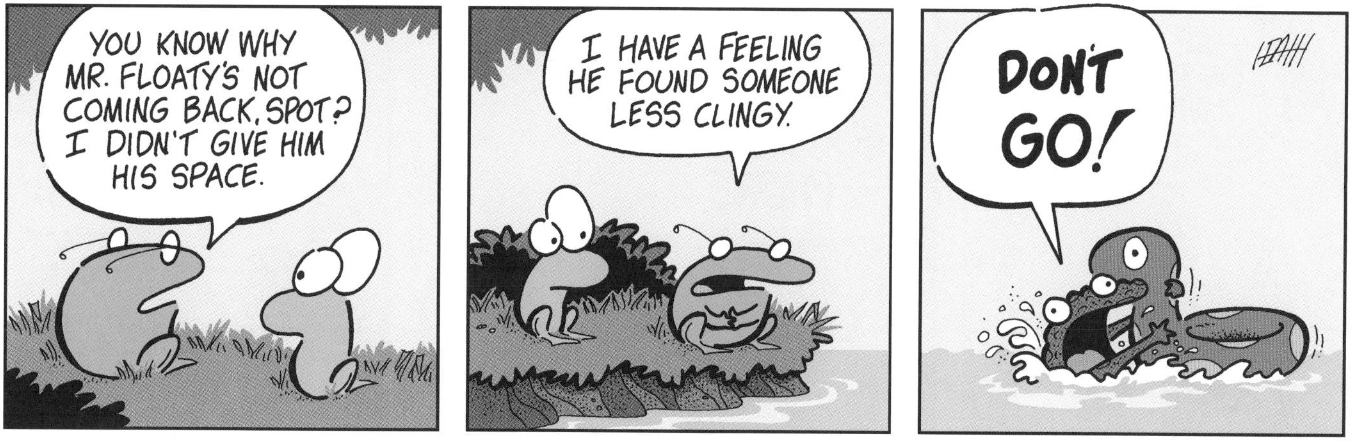
YOU KNOW WHY MR. FLOATY'S NOT COMING BACK, SPOT? I DIDN'T GIVE HIM HIS SPACE.
I HAVE A FEELING HE FOUND SOMEONE LESS CLINGY.
DON'T GO!

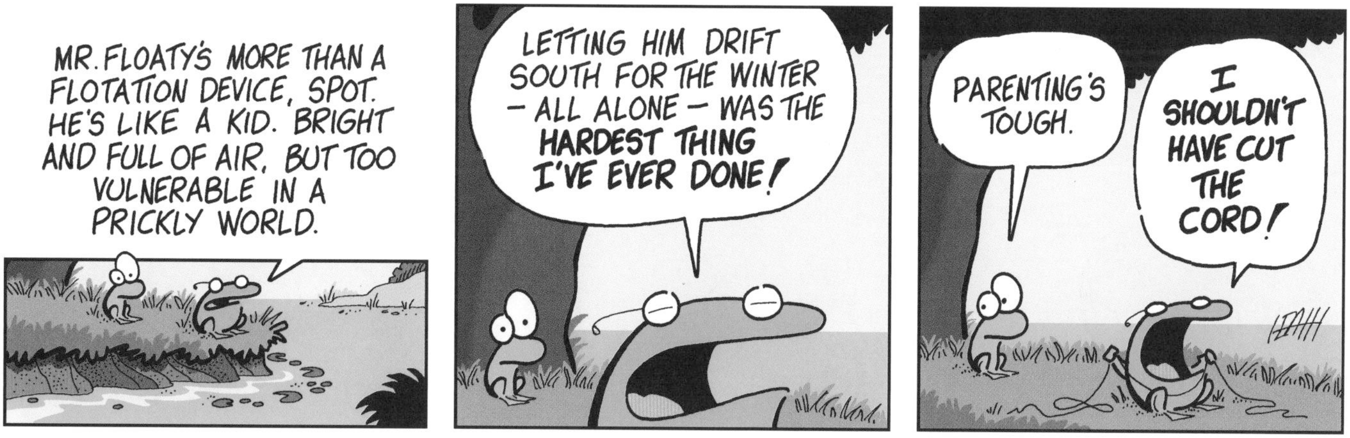
MR. FLOATY'S MORE THAN A FLOTATION DEVICE, SPOT. HE'S LIKE A KID. BRIGHT AND FULL OF AIR, BUT TOO VULNERABLE IN A PRICKLY WORLD.
LETTING HIM DRIFT SOUTH FOR THE WINTER – ALL ALONE – WAS THE HARDEST THING I'VE EVER DONE!
PARENTING'S TOUGH.
I SHOULDN'T HAVE CUT THE CORD!

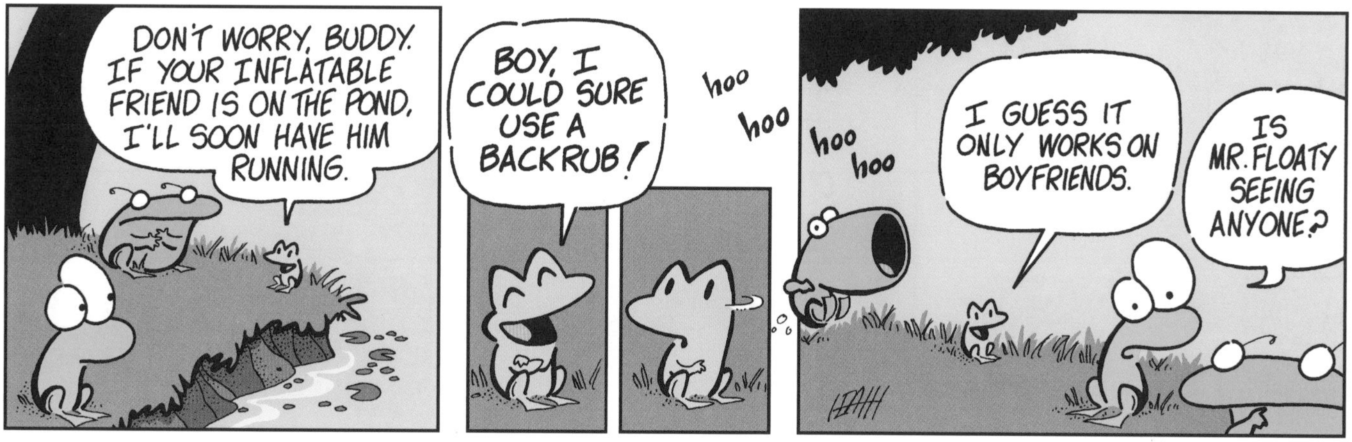
DON'T WORRY, BUDDY. IF YOUR INFLATABLE FRIEND IS ON THE POND, I'LL SOON HAVE HIM RUNNING.
BOY, I COULD SURE USE A BACKRUB!
hoo
hoo
hoo
hoo
I GUESS IT ONLY WORKS ON BOYFRIENDS.
IS MR. FLOATY SEEING ANYONE?

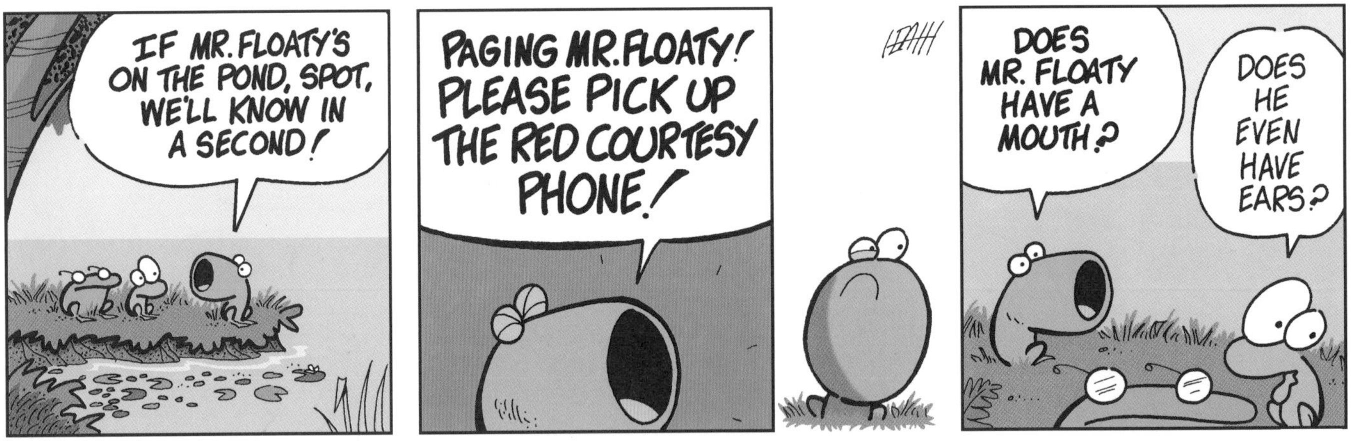
IF MR. FLOATY'S ON THE POND, SPOT, WE'LL KNOW IN A SECOND!
PAGING MR. FLOATY! PLEASE PICK UP THE RED COURTESY PHONE!
DOES MR. FLOATY HAVE A MOUTH?
DOES HE EVEN HAVE EARS?

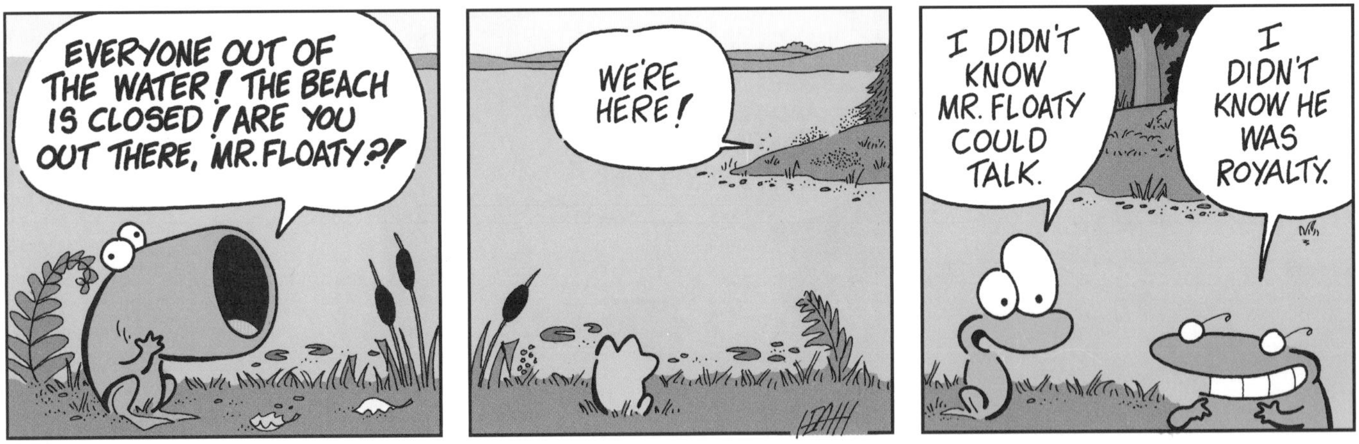
EVERYONE OUT OF THE WATER! THE BEACH IS CLOSED! ARE YOU OUT THERE, MR. FLOATY?!
WE'RE HERE!
I DIDN'T KNOW MR. FLOATY COULD TALK.
I DIDN'T KNOW HE WAS ROYALTY.

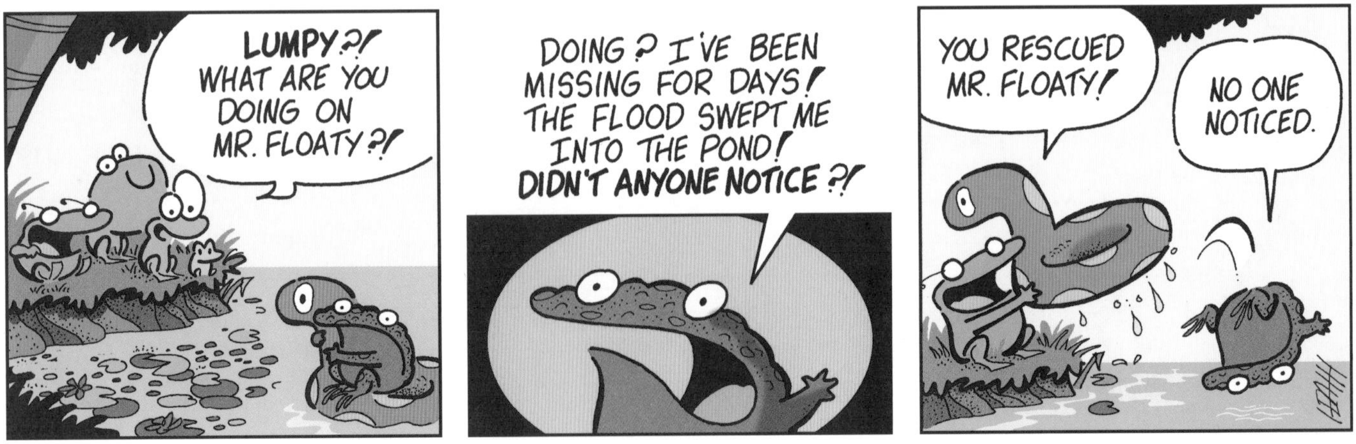
LUMPY?! WHAT ARE YOU DOING ON MR. FLOATY?!
DOING? I'VE BEEN MISSING FOR DAYS! THE FLOOD SWEPT ME INTO THE POND! DIDN'T ANYONE NOTICE?!
YOU RESCUED MR. FLOATY!
NO ONE NOTICED.

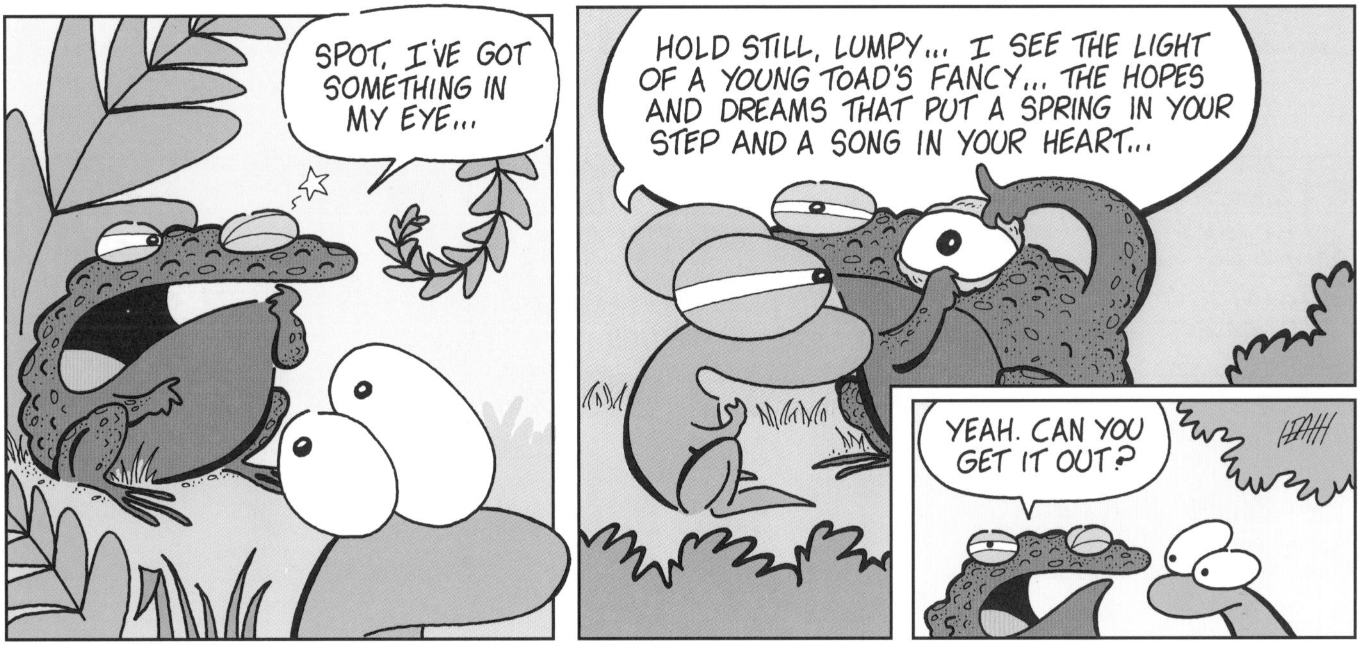
SPOT, I'VE GOT SOMETHING IN MY EYE...
HOLD STILL, LUMPY... I SEE THE LIGHT OF A YOUNG TOAD'S FANCY... THE HOPES AND DREAMS THAT PUT A SPRING IN YOUR STEP AND A SONG IN YOUR HEART...
YEAH. CAN YOU GET IT OUT?

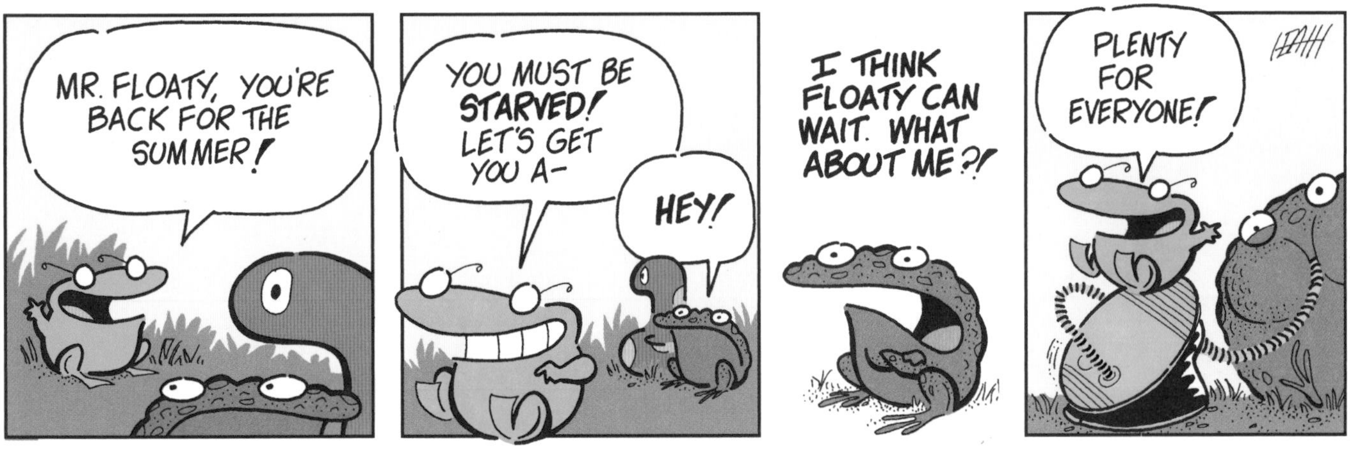
MR. FLOATY, YOU'RE BACK FOR THE SUMMER!
YOU MUST BE STARVED! LET'S GET YOU A-
HEY!
I THINK FLOATY CAN WAIT. WHAT ABOUT ME?!
PLENTY FOR EVERYONE!

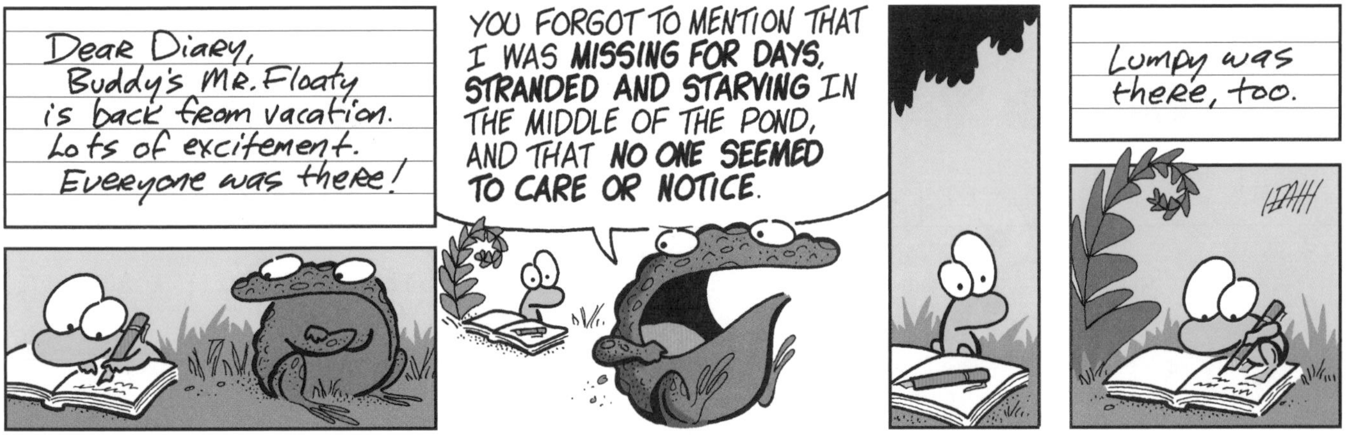
Dear Diary,
Buddy's Mr. Floaty is back from vacation. Lots of excitement. Everyone was there!
YOU FORGOT TO MENTION THAT I WAS MISSING FOR DAYS, STRANDED AND STARVING IN THE MIDDLE OF THE POND, AND THAT NO ONE SEEMED TO CARE OR NOTICE.
Lumpy was there, too.

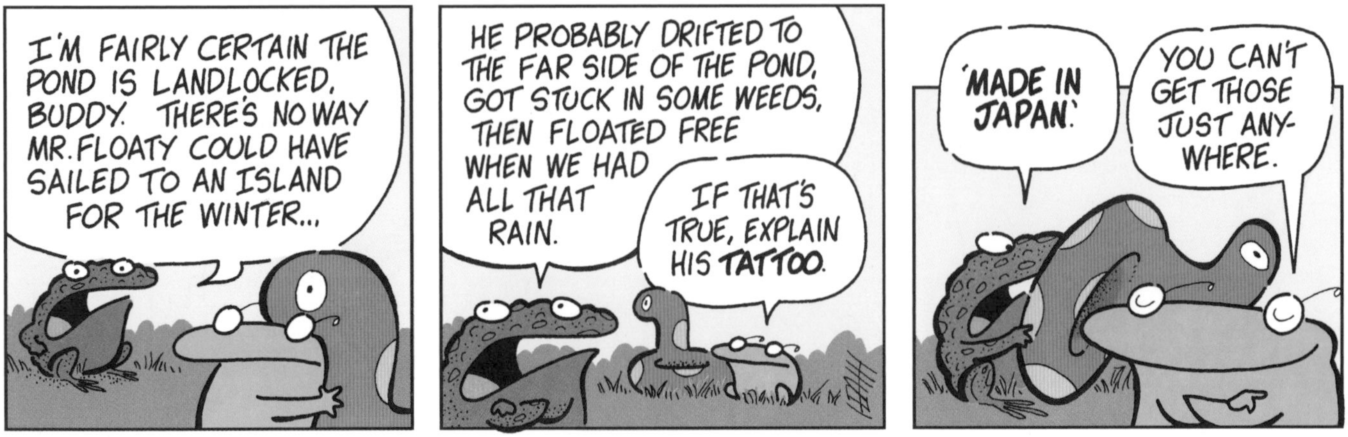
I'M FAIRLY CERTAIN THE POND IS LANDLOCKED, BUDDY. THERE'S NO WAY MR. FLOATY COULD HAVE SAILED TO AN ISLAND FOR THE WINTER...
HE PROBABLY DRIFTED TO THE FAR SIDE OF THE POND, GOT STUCK IN SOME WEEDS, THEN FLOATED FREE WHEN WE HAD ALL THAT RAIN.
IF THAT'S TRUE, EXPLAIN HIS TATTOO.
'MADE IN JAPAN.'
YOU CAN'T GET THOSE JUST ANYWHERE.

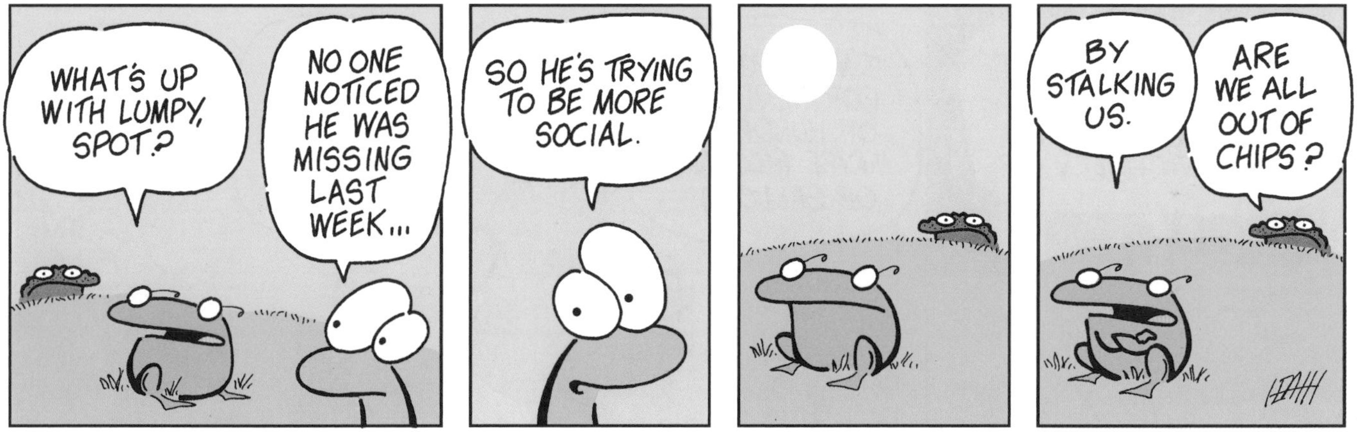
WHAT'S UP WITH LUMPY, SPOT?
NO ONE NOTICED HE WAS MISSING LAST WEEK...
SO HE'S TRYING TO BE MORE SOCIAL.
BY STALKING US.
ARE WE ALL OUT OF CHIPS?

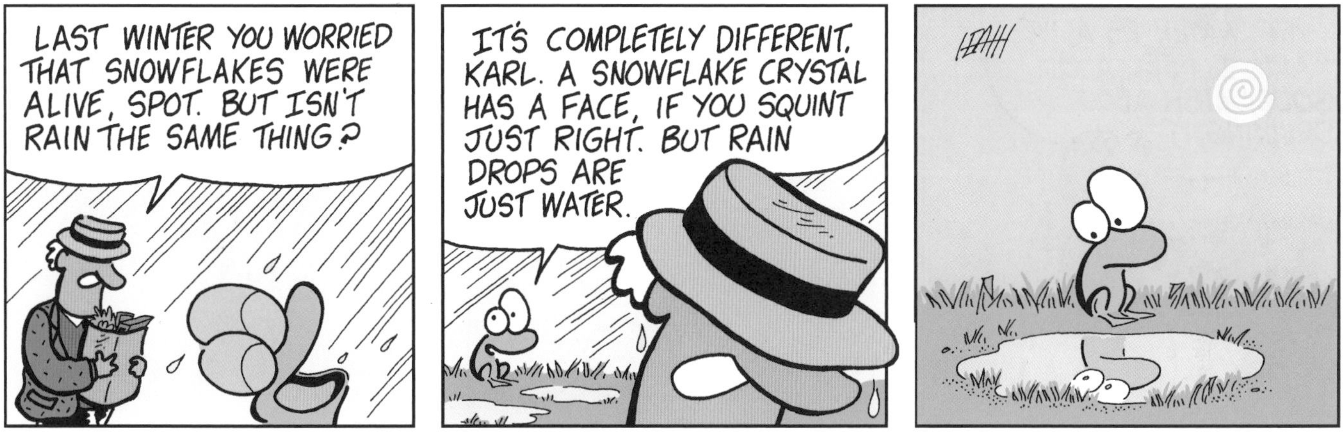
LAST WINTER YOU WORRIED THAT SNOWFLAKES WERE ALIVE, SPOT. BUT ISN'T RAIN THE SAME THING?
IT'S COMPLETELY DIFFERENT, KARL. A SNOWFLAKE CRYSTAL HAS A FACE, IF YOU SQUINT JUST RIGHT. BUT RAIN DROPS ARE JUST WATER.

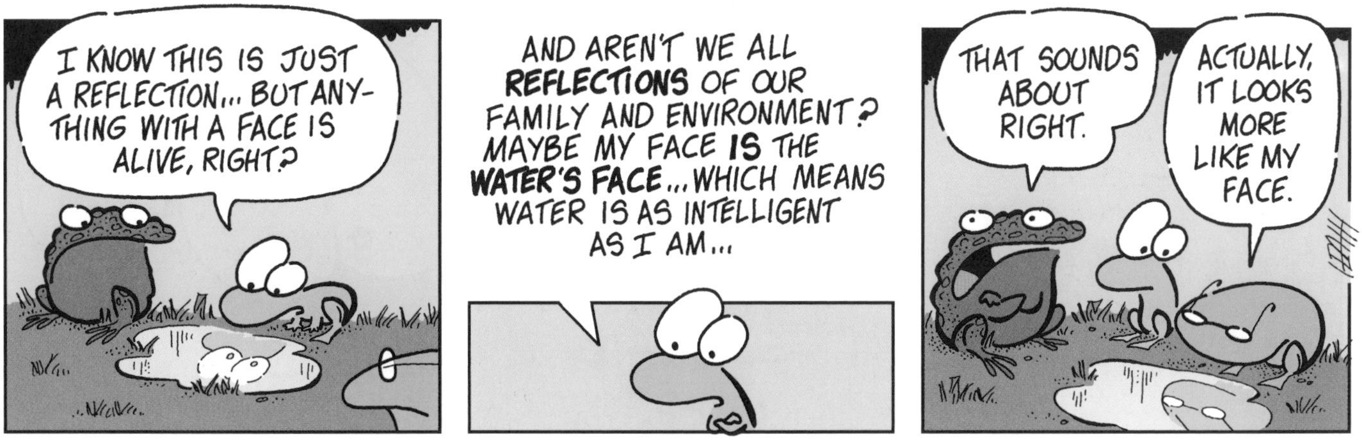
I KNOW THIS IS JUST A REFLECTION... BUT ANYTHING WITH A FACE IS ALIVE, RIGHT?
AND AREN'T WE ALL **REFLECTIONS** OF OUR FAMILY AND ENVIRONMENT? MAYBE MY FACE **IS** THE **WATER'S FACE**... WHICH MEANS WATER IS AS INTELLIGENT AS I AM...
THAT SOUNDS ABOUT RIGHT.
ACTUALLY, IT LOOKS MORE LIKE MY FACE.

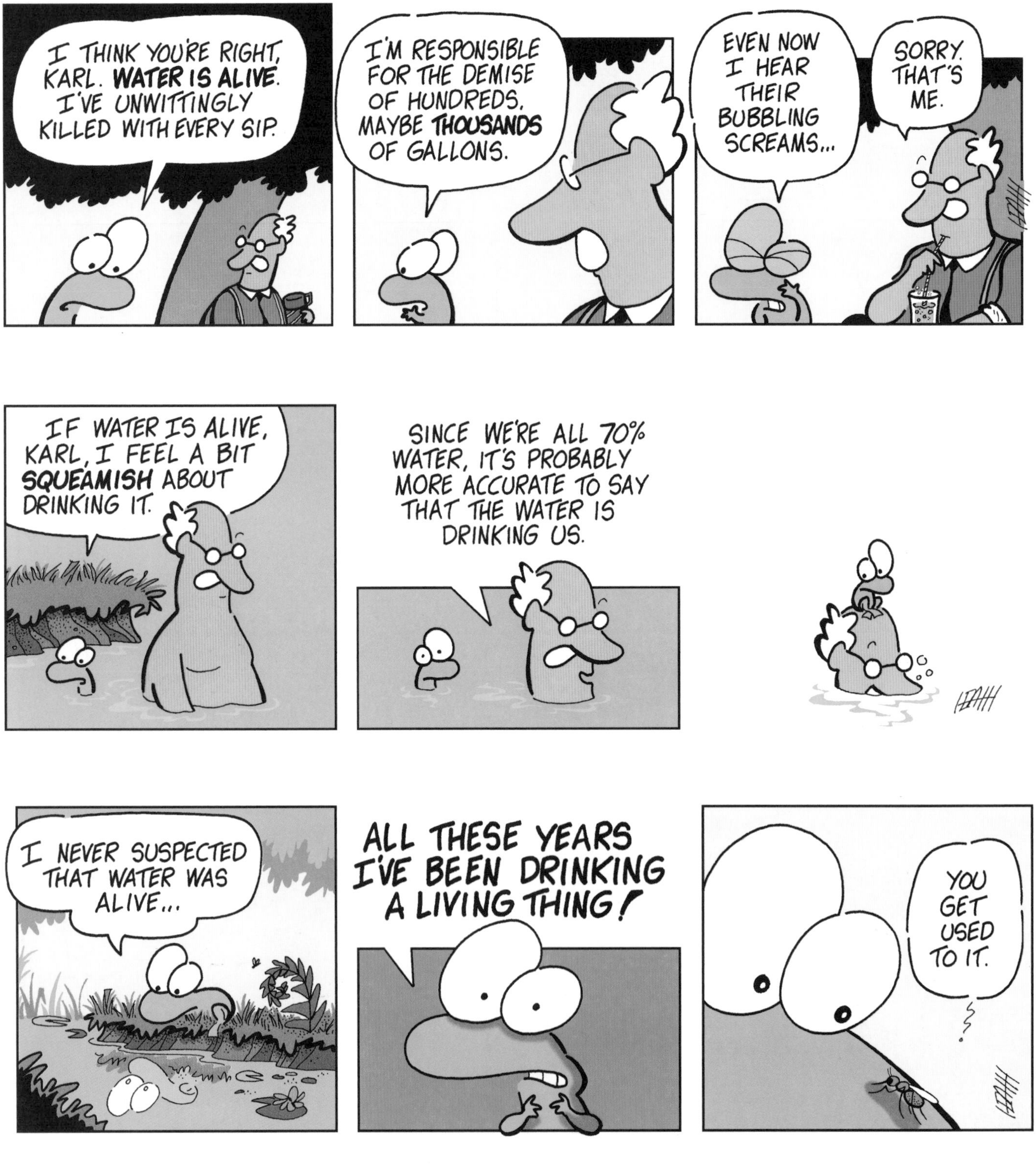
I THINK YOU'RE RIGHT, KARL. **WATER IS ALIVE**. I'VE UNWITTINGLY KILLED WITH EVERY SIP.
I'M RESPONSIBLE FOR THE DEMISE OF HUNDREDS, MAYBE **THOUSANDS** OF GALLONS.
EVEN NOW I HEAR THEIR BUBBLING SCREAMS...
SORRY. THAT'S ME.
IF WATER IS ALIVE, KARL, I FEEL A BIT **SQUEAMISH** ABOUT DRINKING IT.
SINCE WE'RE ALL 70% WATER, IT'S PROBABLY MORE ACCURATE TO SAY THAT THE WATER IS DRINKING US.
I NEVER SUSPECTED THAT WATER WAS ALIVE...
ALL THESE YEARS I'VE BEEN DRINKING A LIVING THING!
YOU GET USED TO IT.

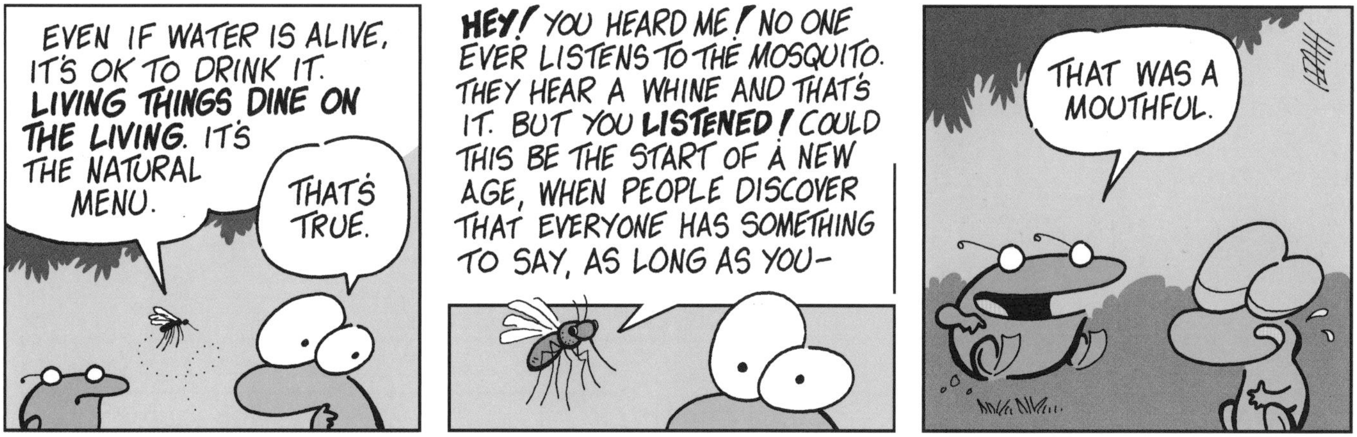
EVEN IF WATER IS ALIVE, IT'S OK TO DRINK IT. **LIVING THINGS DINE ON THE LIVING**. IT'S THE NATURAL MENU.
THAT'S TRUE.
HEY! YOU HEARD ME! NO ONE EVER LISTENS TO THE MOSQUITO. THEY HEAR A WHINE AND THAT'S IT. BUT YOU **LISTENED!** COULD THIS BE THE START OF A NEW AGE, WHEN PEOPLE DISCOVER THAT EVERYONE HAS SOMETHING TO SAY, AS LONG AS YOU-
THAT WAS A MOUTHFUL.

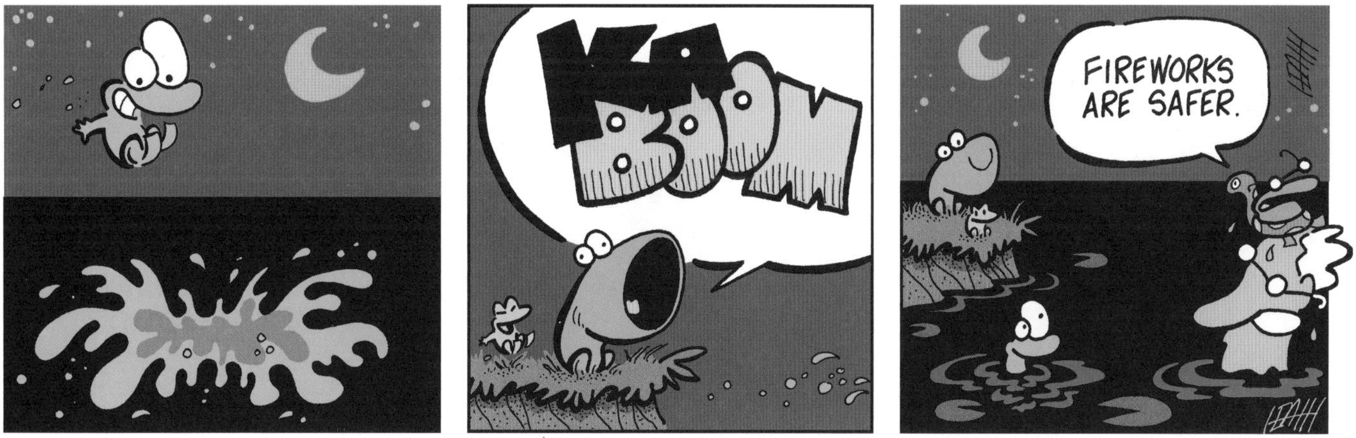
KA BOOM
FIREWORKS ARE SAFER.

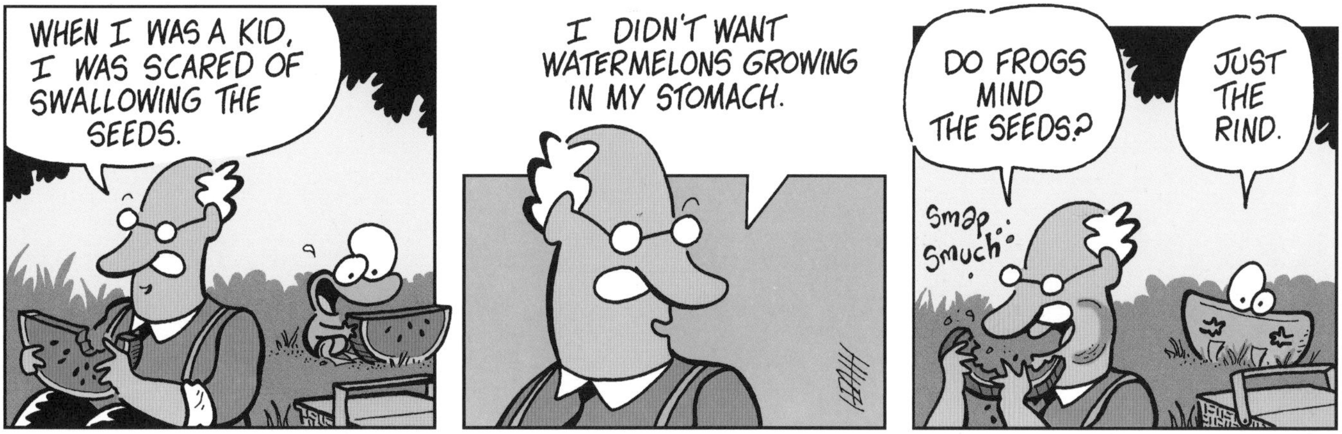
WHEN I WAS A KID, I WAS SCARED OF SWALLOWING THE SEEDS.
I DIDN'T WANT WATERMELONS GROWING IN MY STOMACH.
DO FROGS MIND THE SEEDS?
JUST THE RIND.
Smap Smuch

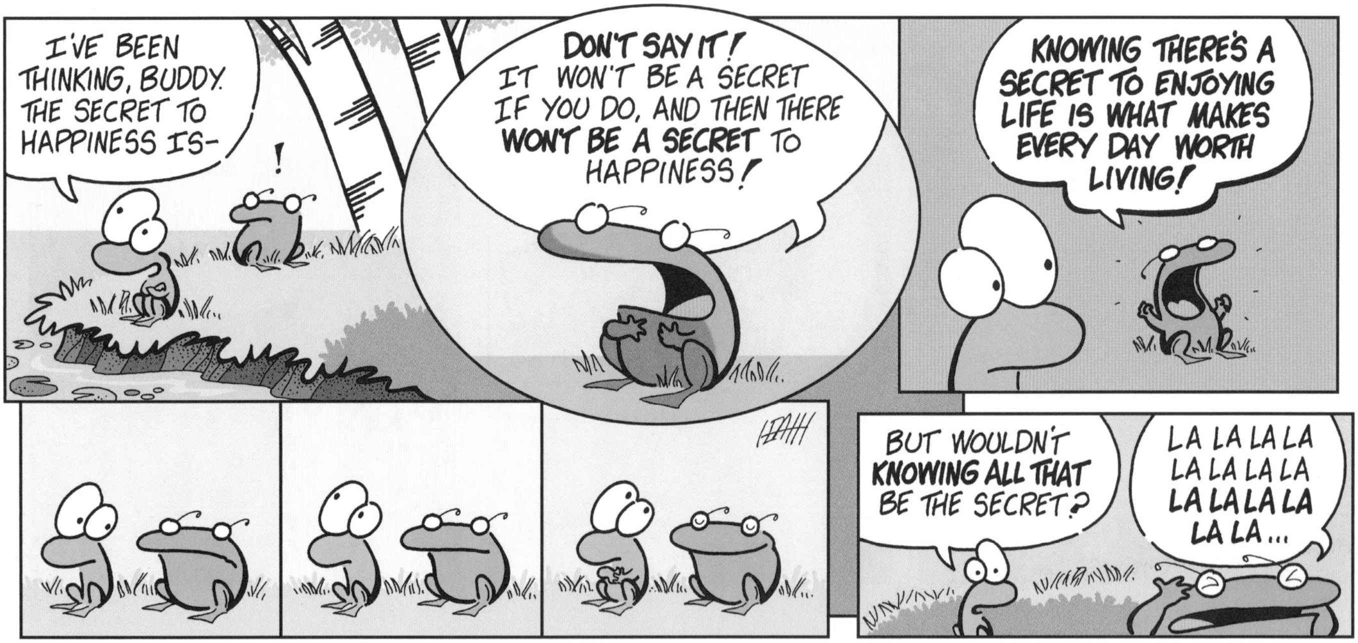
I'VE BEEN THINKING, BUDDY. THE SECRET TO HAPPINESS IS-
!
DON'T SAY IT! IT WON'T BE A SECRET IF YOU DO, AND THEN THERE WON'T BE A SECRET TO HAPPINESS!
KNOWING THERE'S A SECRET TO ENJOYING LIFE IS WHAT MAKES EVERY DAY WORTH LIVING!
BUT WOULDN'T KNOWING ALL THAT BE THE SECRET?
LA LA LA LA LA LA LA LA LA LA LA LA LA LA...

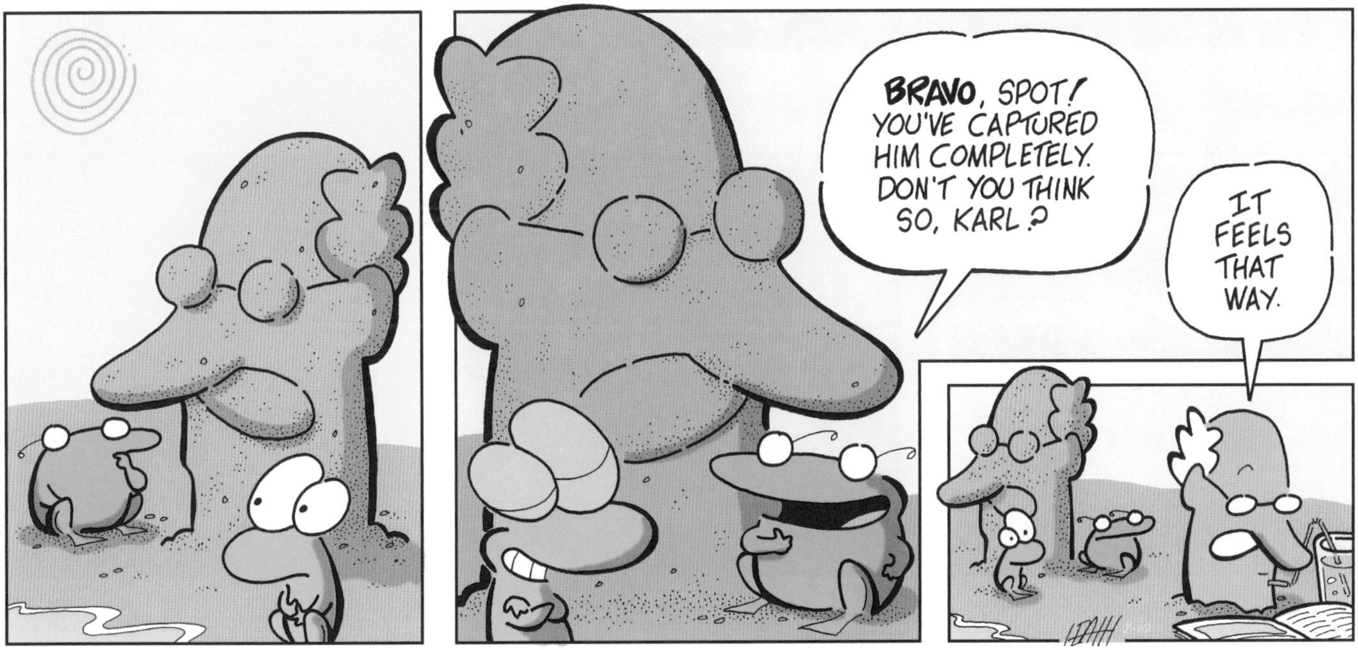
BRAVO, SPOT! YOU'VE CAPTURED HIM COMPLETELY. DON'T YOU THINK SO, KARL?
IT FEELS THAT WAY.

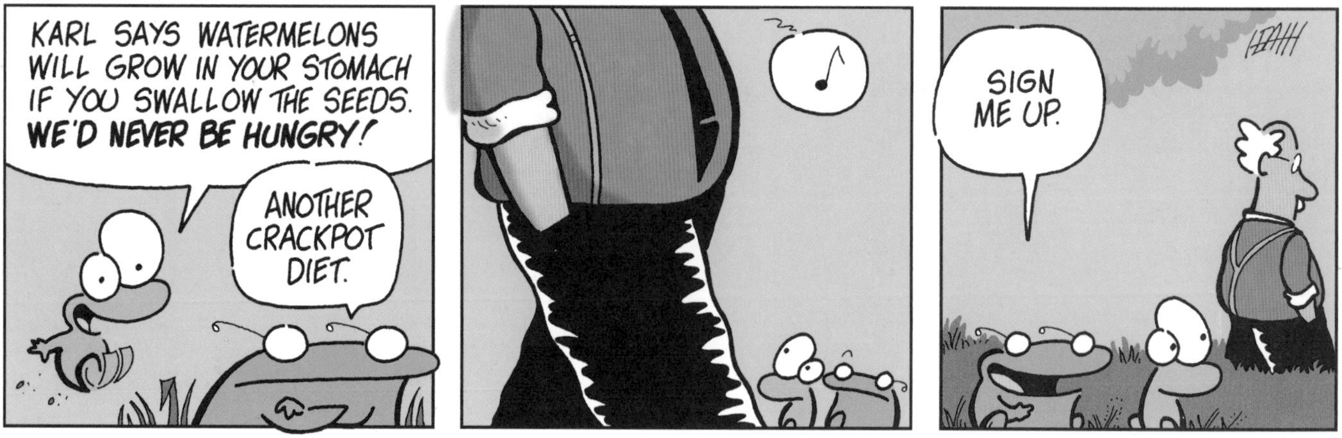
KARL SAYS WATERMELONS WILL GROW IN YOUR STOMACH IF YOU SWALLOW THE SEEDS. **WE'D NEVER BE HUNGRY!**
ANOTHER CRACKPOT DIET.
SIGN ME UP.

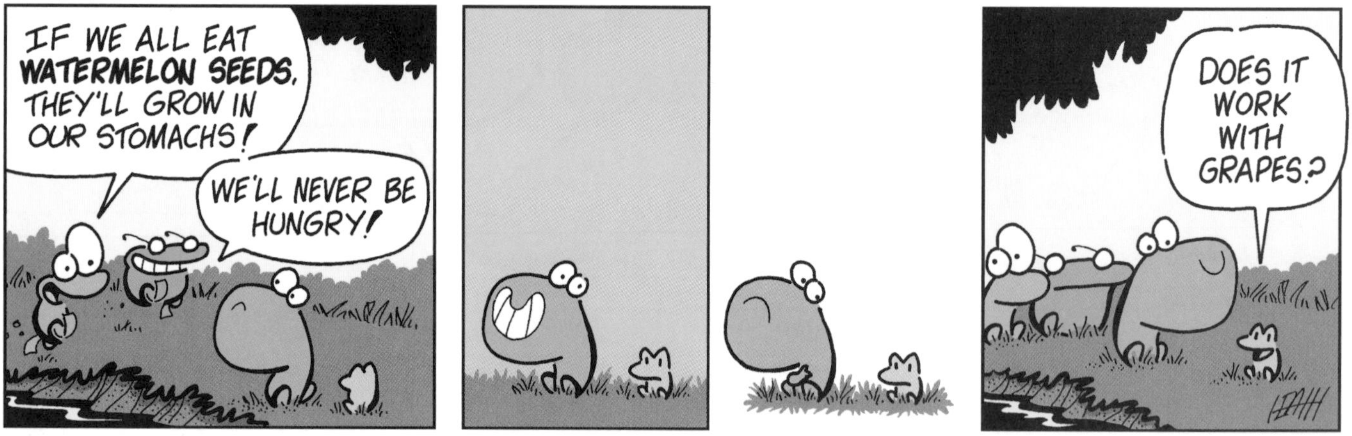
IF WE ALL EAT **WATERMELON SEEDS**, THEY'LL GROW IN OUR STOMACHS!
WE'LL NEVER BE HUNGRY!
DOES IT WORK WITH GRAPES?

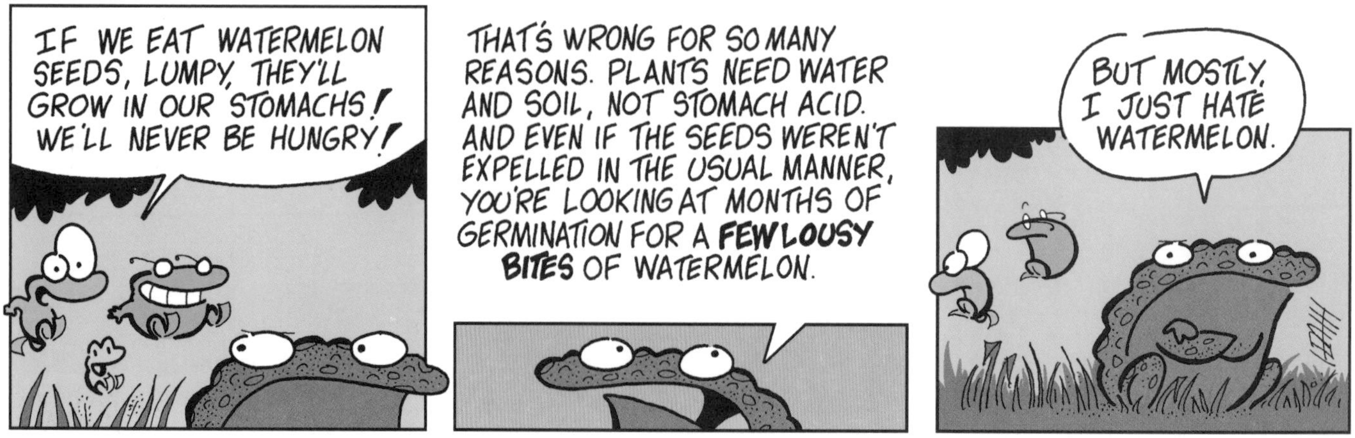
IF WE EAT WATERMELON SEEDS, LUMPY, THEY'LL GROW IN OUR STOMACHS! WE'LL NEVER BE HUNGRY!
THAT'S WRONG FOR SO MANY REASONS. PLANTS NEED WATER AND SOIL, NOT STOMACH ACID. AND EVEN IF THE SEEDS WEREN'T EXPELLED IN THE USUAL MANNER, YOU'RE LOOKING AT MONTHS OF GERMINATION FOR A **FEW LOUSY BITES** OF WATERMELON.
BUT MOSTLY, I JUST HATE WATERMELON.

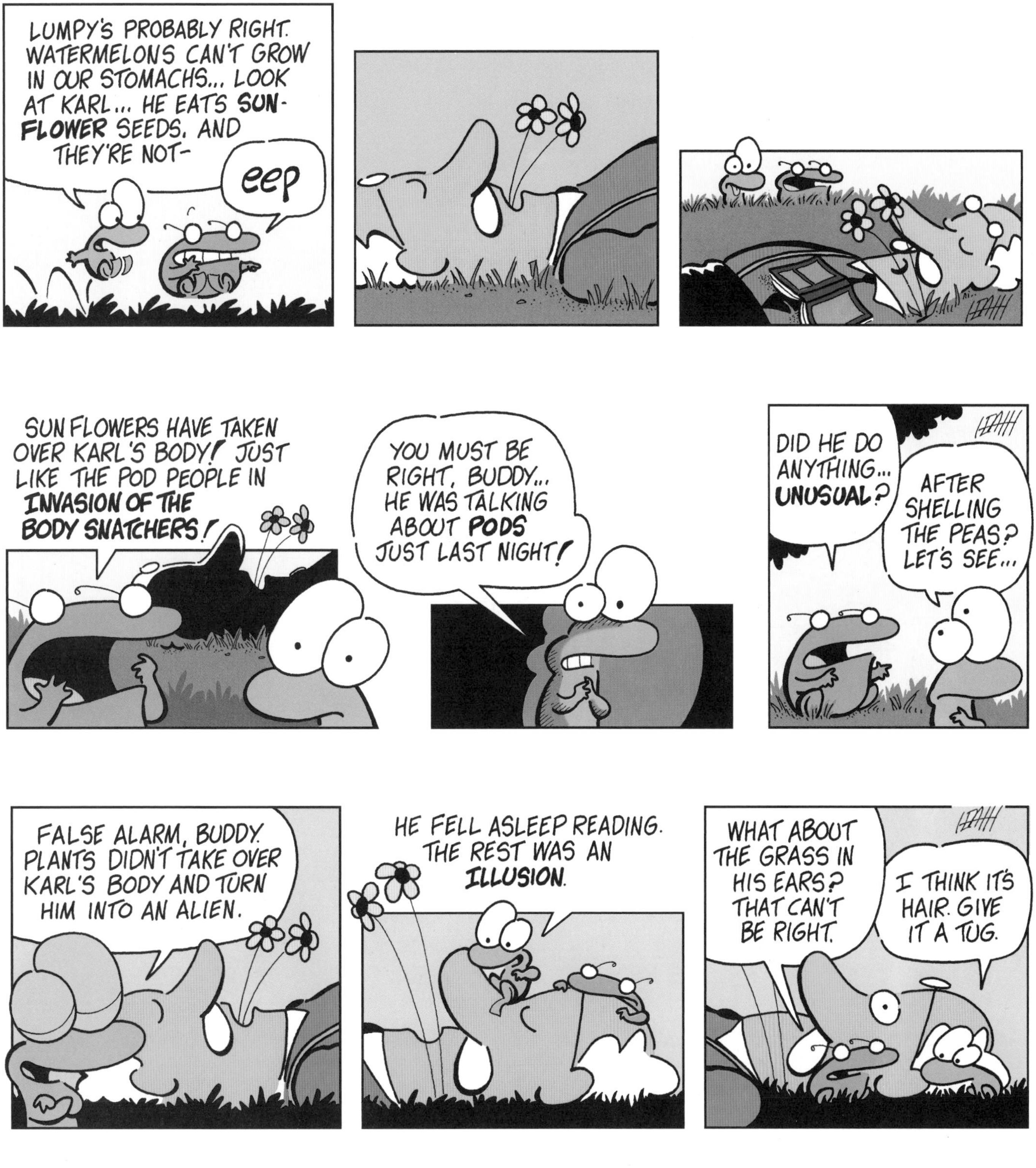
LUMPY'S PROBABLY RIGHT. WATERMELONS CAN'T GROW IN OUR STOMACHS... LOOK AT KARL... HE EATS **SUN-FLOWER** SEEDS, AND THEY'RE NOT-
eep
SUN FLOWERS HAVE TAKEN OVER KARL'S BODY! JUST LIKE THE POD PEOPLE IN **INVASION OF THE BODY SNATCHERS**!
YOU MUST BE RIGHT, BUDDY... HE WAS TALKING ABOUT **PODS** JUST LAST NIGHT!
DID HE DO ANYTHING... **UNUSUAL**?
AFTER SHELLING THE PEAS? LET'S SEE...
FALSE ALARM, BUDDY. PLANTS DIDN'T TAKE OVER KARL'S BODY AND TURN HIM INTO AN ALIEN.
HE FELL ASLEEP READING. THE REST WAS AN **ILLUSION**.
WHAT ABOUT THE GRASS IN HIS EARS? THAT CAN'T BE RIGHT.
I THINK IT'S HAIR. GIVE IT A TUG.

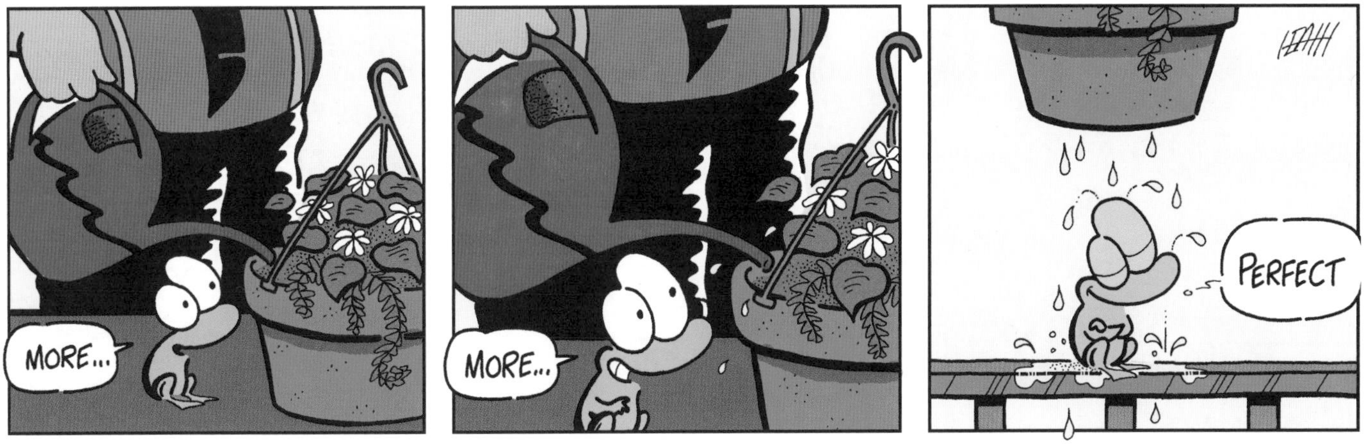
MORE...
MORE...
PERFECT

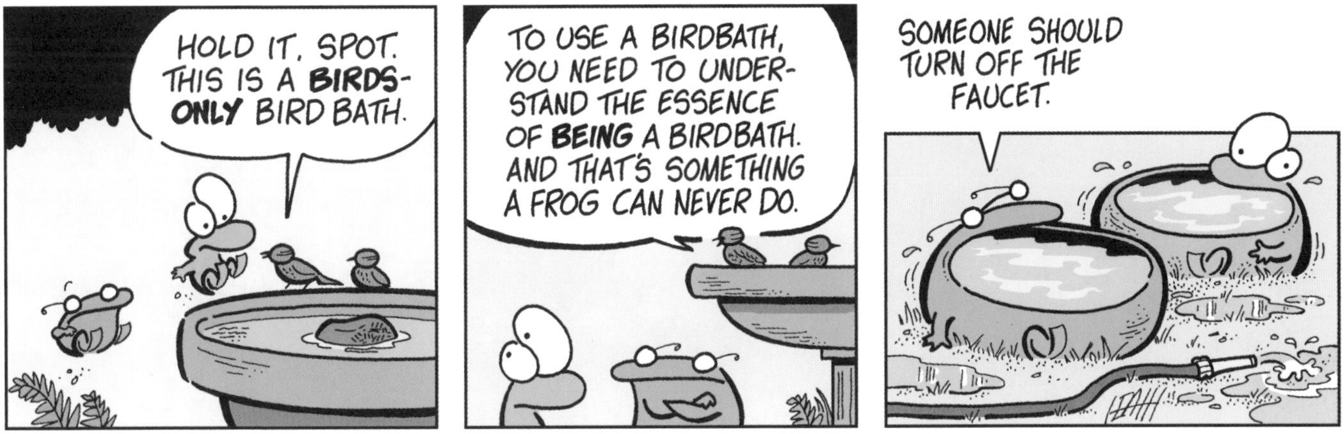
HOLD IT, SPOT. THIS IS A BIRDS-ONLY BIRD BATH.
TO USE A BIRDBATH, YOU NEED TO UNDERSTAND THE ESSENCE OF BEING A BIRDBATH. AND THAT'S SOMETHING A FROG CAN NEVER DO.
SOMEONE SHOULD TURN OFF THE FAUCET.

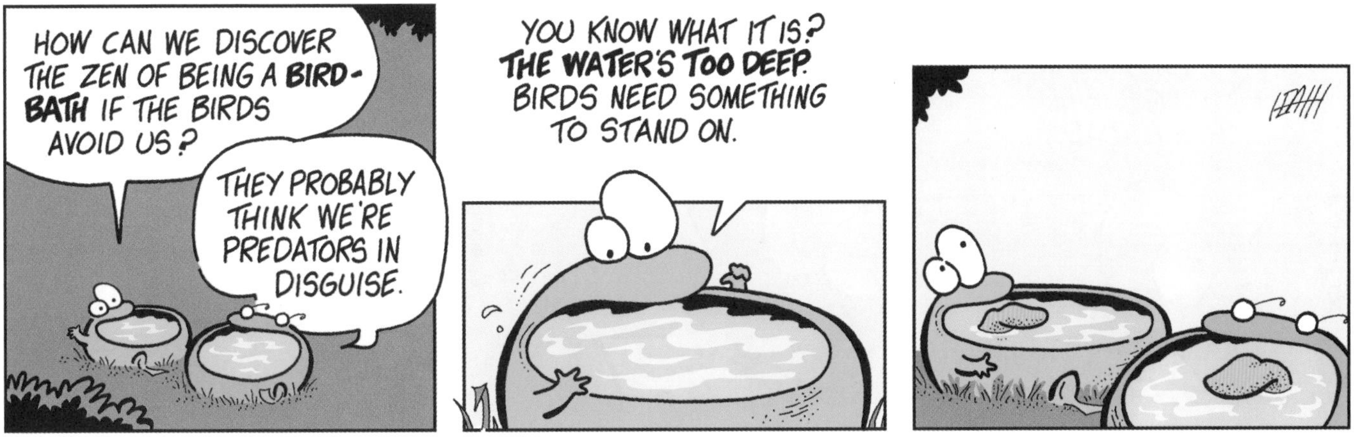
HOW CAN WE DISCOVER THE ZEN OF BEING A BIRD-BATH IF THE BIRDS AVOID US?
THEY PROBABLY THINK WE'RE PREDATORS IN DISGUISE.
YOU KNOW WHAT IT IS? THE WATER'S TOO DEEP. BIRDS NEED SOMETHING TO STAND ON.

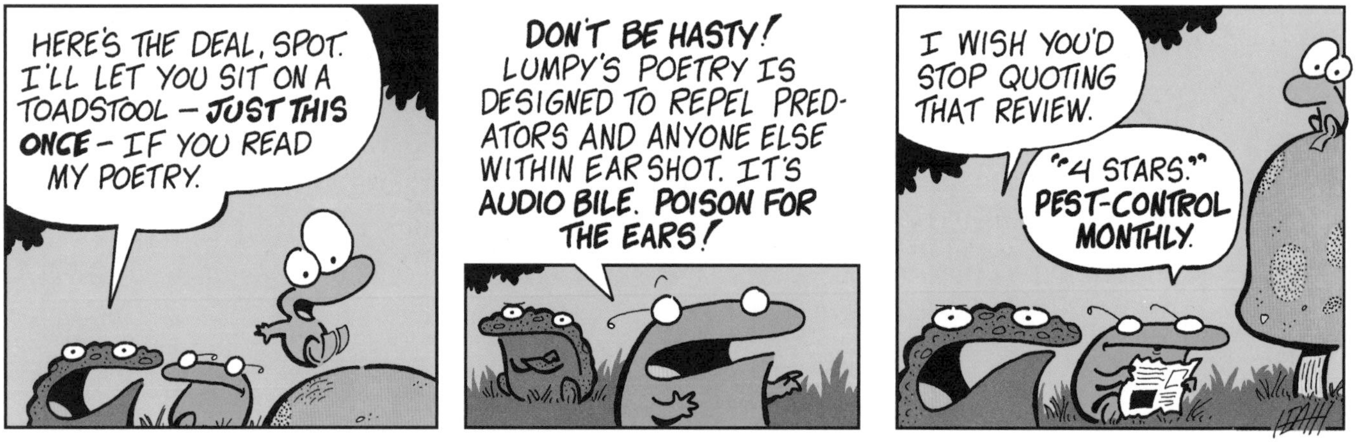
HERE'S THE DEAL, SPOT. I'LL LET YOU SIT ON A TOADSTOOL – JUST THIS ONCE – IF YOU READ MY POETRY.
DON'T BE HASTY! LUMPY'S POETRY IS DESIGNED TO REPEL PREDATORS AND ANYONE ELSE WITHIN EARSHOT. IT'S AUDIO BILE. POISON FOR THE EARS!
I WISH YOU'D STOP QUOTING THAT REVIEW.
"4 STARS." PEST-CONTROL MONTHLY.

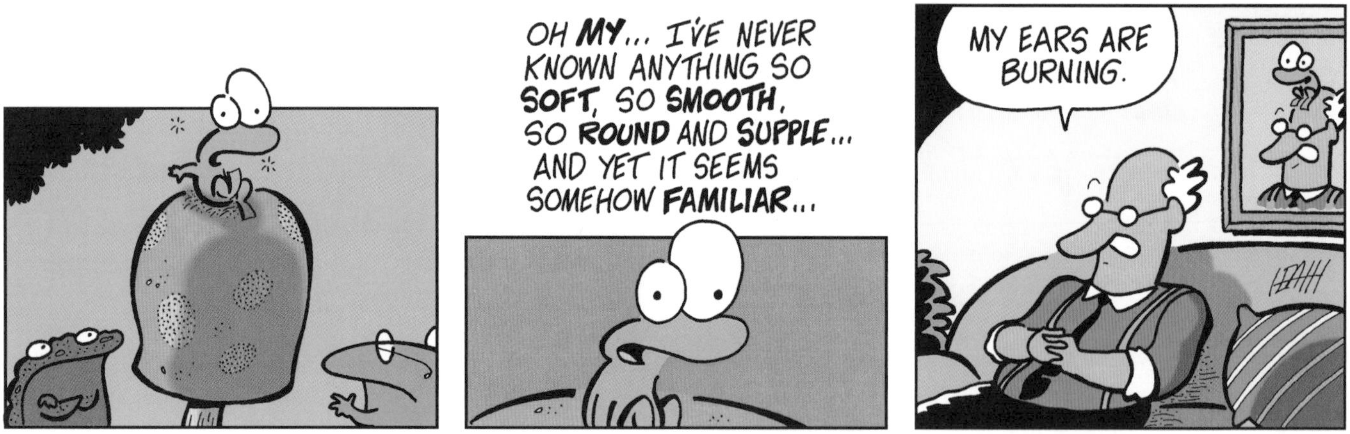
OH MY... I'VE NEVER KNOWN ANYTHING SO SOFT, SO SMOOTH, SO ROUND AND SUPPLE... AND YET IT SEEMS SOMEHOW FAMILIAR...
MY EARS ARE BURNING.

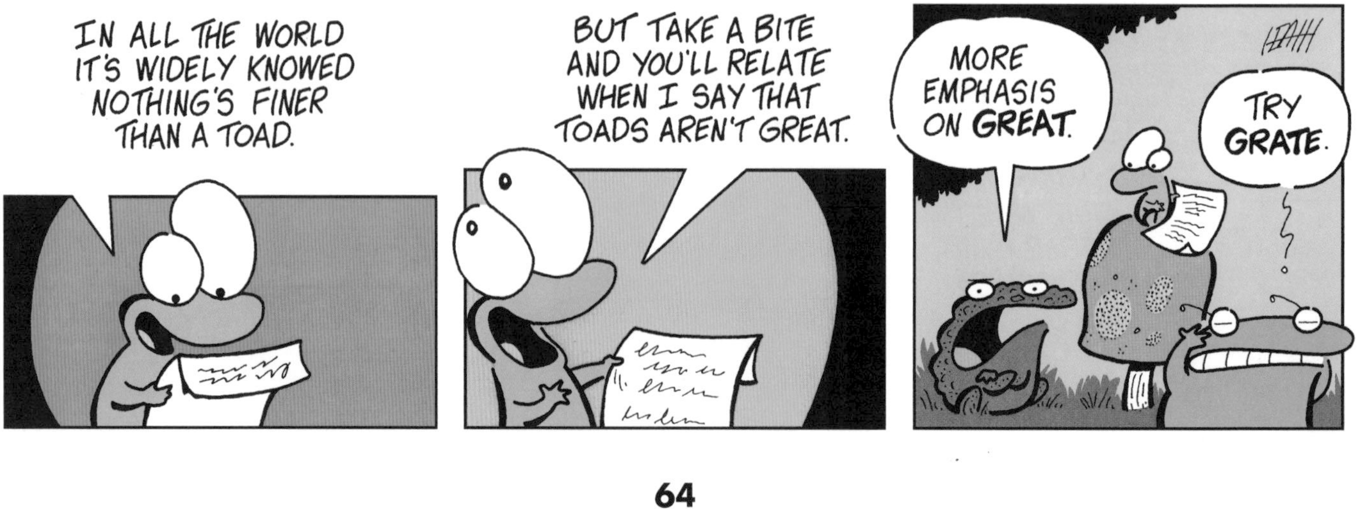
IN ALL THE WORLD IT'S WIDELY KNOWED NOTHING'S FINER THAN A TOAD.
BUT TAKE A BITE AND YOU'LL RELATE WHEN I SAY THAT TOADS AREN'T GREAT.
MORE EMPHASIS ON GREAT.
TRY GRATE.

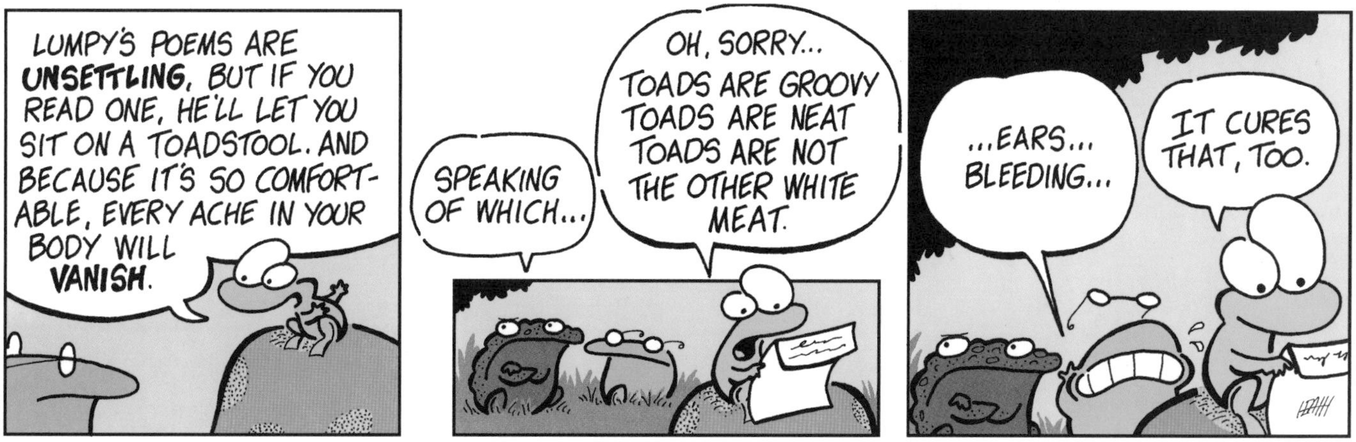
LUMPY'S POEMS ARE **UNSETTLING**, BUT IF YOU READ ONE, HE'LL LET YOU SIT ON A TOADSTOOL. AND BECAUSE IT'S SO COMFORTABLE, EVERY ACHE IN YOUR BODY WILL **VANISH**.
SPEAKING OF WHICH...
OH, SORRY... TOADS ARE GROOVY TOADS ARE NEAT TOADS ARE NOT THE OTHER WHITE MEAT.
...EARS... BLEEDING...
IT CURES THAT, TOO.

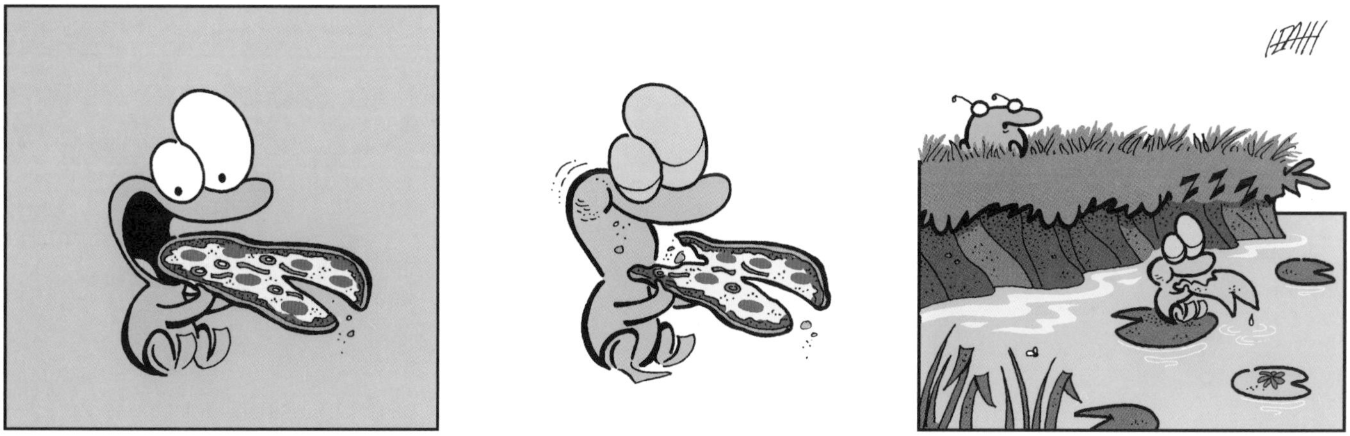

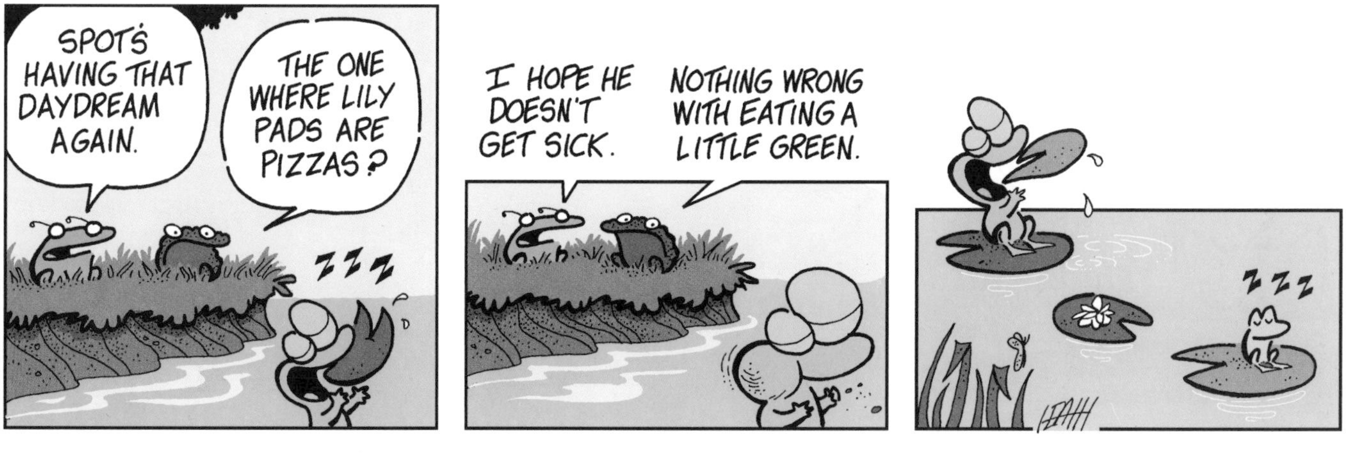
SPOT'S HAVING THAT DAYDREAM AGAIN.
THE ONE WHERE LILY PADS ARE PIZZAS?
I HOPE HE DOESN'T GET SICK.
NOTHING WRONG WITH EATING A LITTLE GREEN.

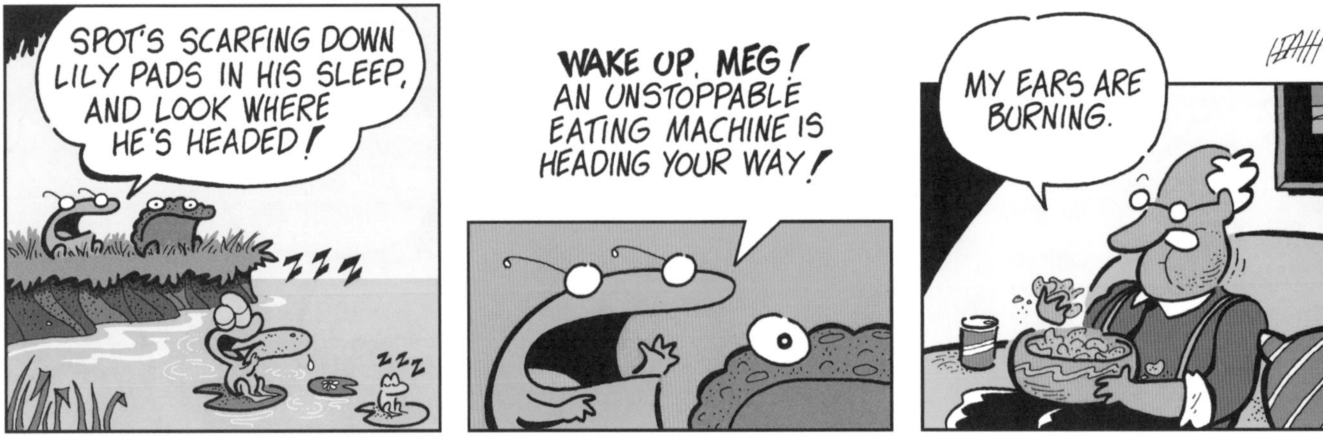
SPOT'S SCARFING DOWN LILY PADS IN HIS SLEEP, AND LOOK WHERE HE'S HEADED!
Z Z Z
Z Z Z
WAKE UP, MEG! AN UNSTOPPABLE EATING MACHINE IS HEADING YOUR WAY!
MY EARS ARE BURNING.

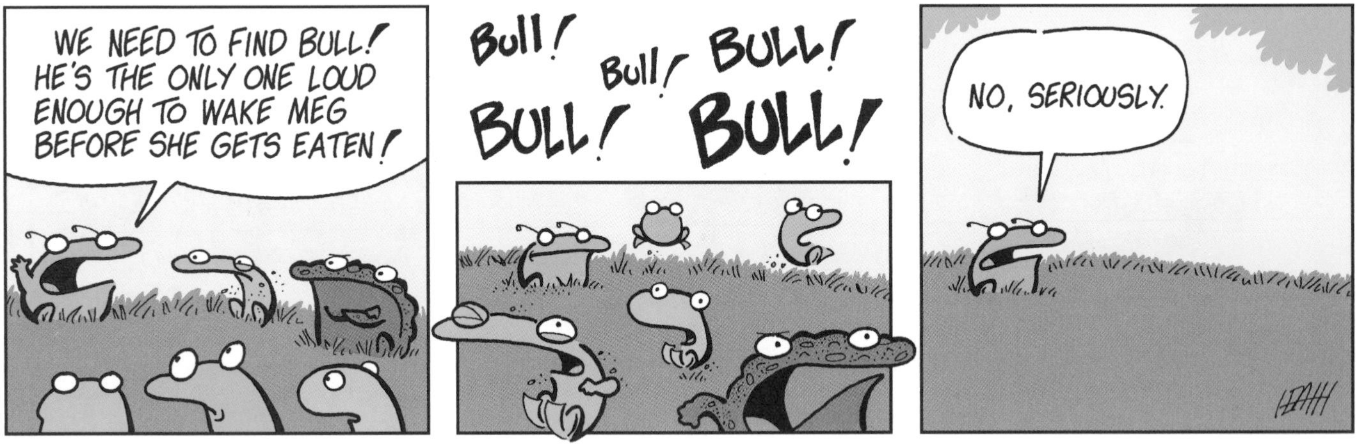
WE NEED TO FIND BULL! HE'S THE ONLY ONE LOUD ENOUGH TO WAKE MEG BEFORE SHE GETS EATEN!
Bull!
Bull!
BULL!
BULL!
BULL!
NO, SERIOUSLY.

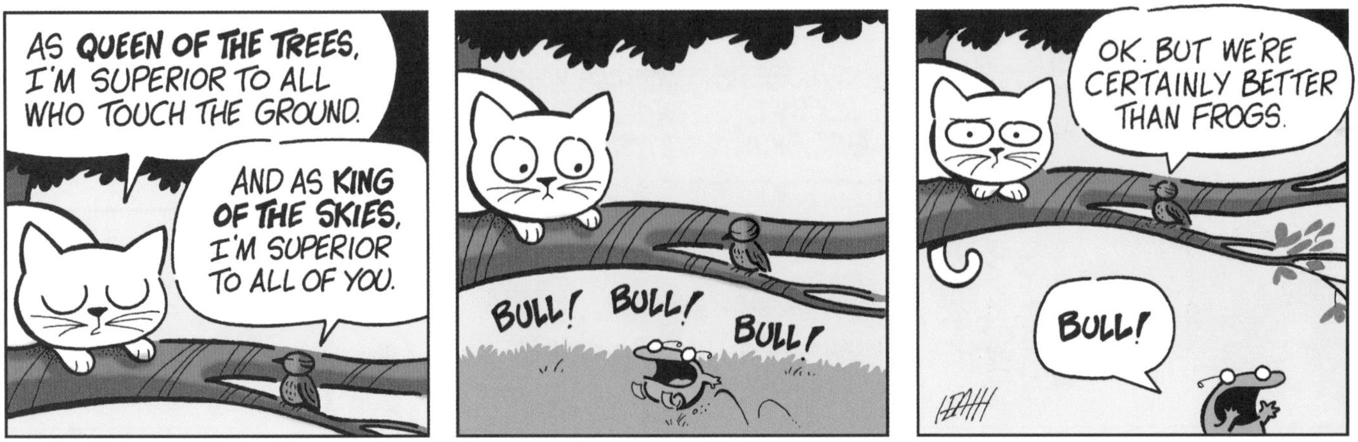
AS **QUEEN OF THE TREES**, I'M SUPERIOR TO ALL WHO TOUCH THE GROUND.
AND AS **KING OF THE SKIES**, I'M SUPERIOR TO ALL OF YOU.
BULL! BULL! BULL!
OK. BUT WE'RE CERTAINLY BETTER THAN FROGS.
BULL!

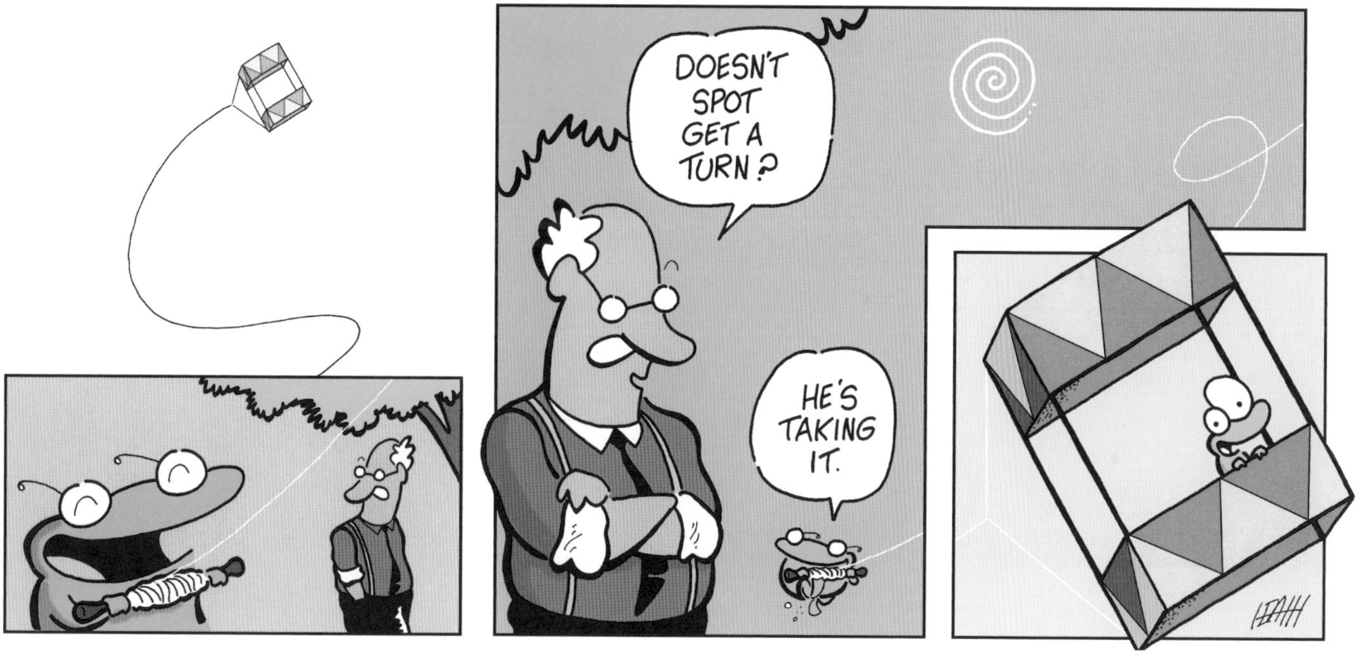
DOESN'T SPOT GET A TURN?
HE'S TAKING IT.

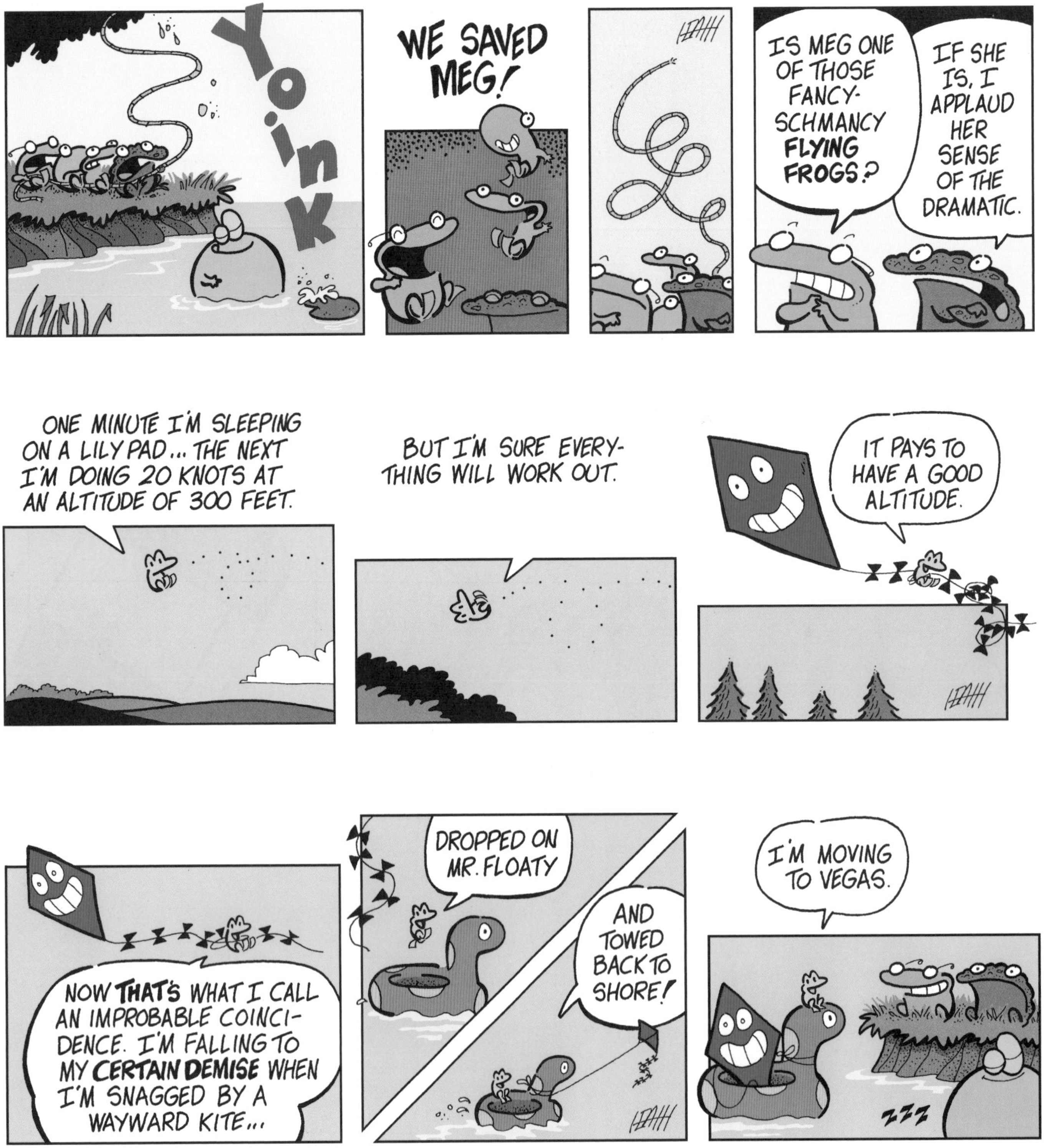

YOINK
WE SAVED MEG!
IS MEG ONE OF THOSE FANCY-SCHMANCY FLYING FROGS?
IF SHE IS, I APPLAUD HER SENSE OF THE DRAMATIC.
ONE MINUTE I'M SLEEPING ON A LILY PAD... THE NEXT I'M DOING 20 KNOTS AT AN ALTITUDE OF 300 FEET.
BUT I'M SURE EVERYTHING WILL WORK OUT.
IT PAYS TO HAVE A GOOD ALTITUDE.
NOW THAT'S WHAT I CALL AN IMPROBABLE COINCIDENCE. I'M FALLING TO MY CERTAIN DEMISE WHEN I'M SNAGGED BY A WAYWARD KITE...
DROPPED ON MR. FLOATY
AND TOWED BACK TO SHORE!
I'M MOVING TO VEGAS.
ZZZ

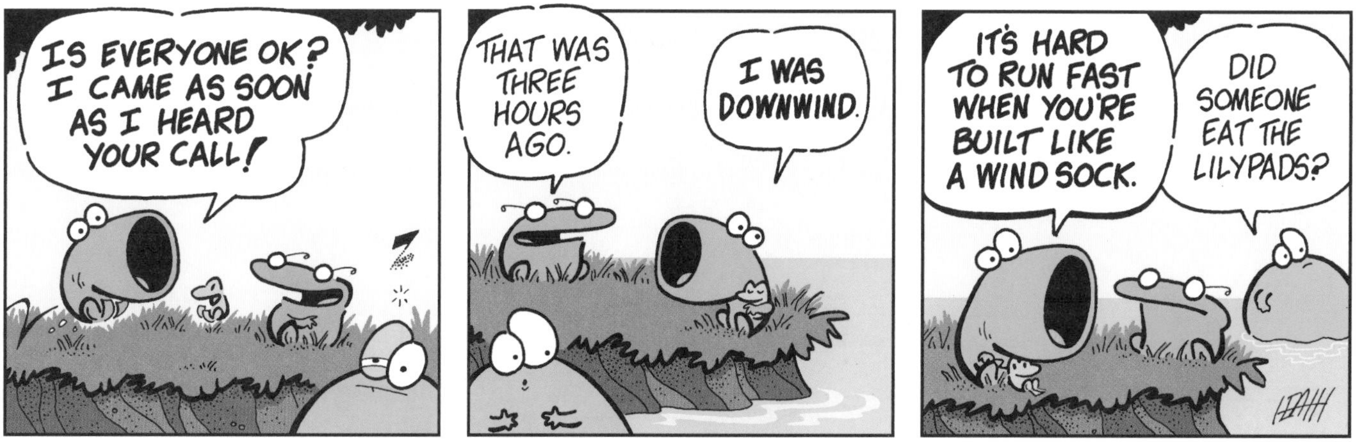
IS EVERYONE OK? I CAME AS SOON AS I HEARD YOUR CALL!
THAT WAS THREE HOURS AGO.
I WAS DOWNWIND.
IT'S HARD TO RUN FAST WHEN YOU'RE BUILT LIKE A WIND SOCK.
DID SOMEONE EAT THE LILYPADS?

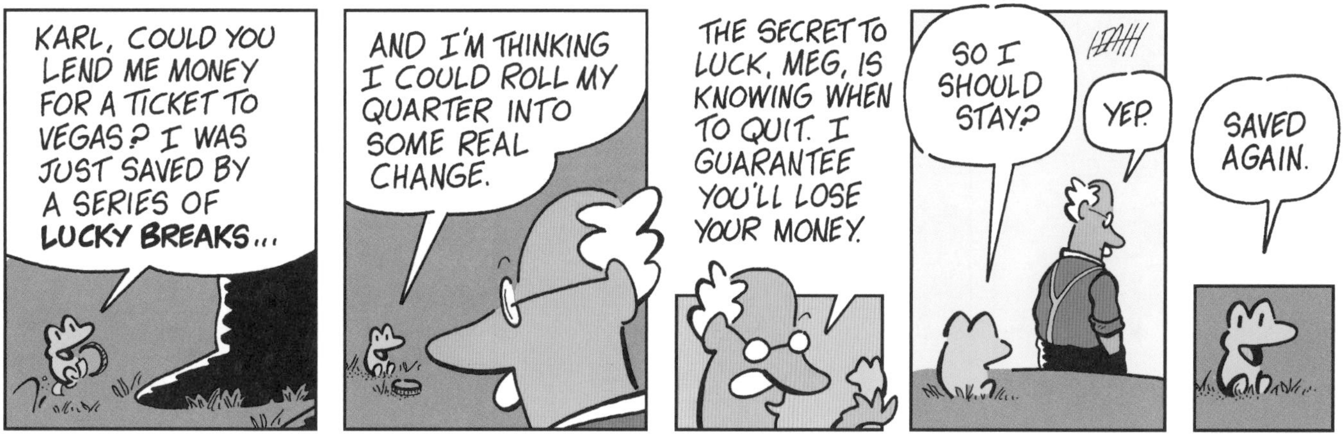
KARL, COULD YOU LEND ME MONEY FOR A TICKET TO VEGAS? I WAS JUST SAVED BY A SERIES OF LUCKY BREAKS...
AND I'M THINKING I COULD ROLL MY QUARTER INTO SOME REAL CHANGE.
THE SECRET TO LUCK, MEG, IS KNOWING WHEN TO QUIT. I GUARANTEE YOU'LL LOSE YOUR MONEY.
SO I SHOULD STAY?
YEP.
SAVED AGAIN.

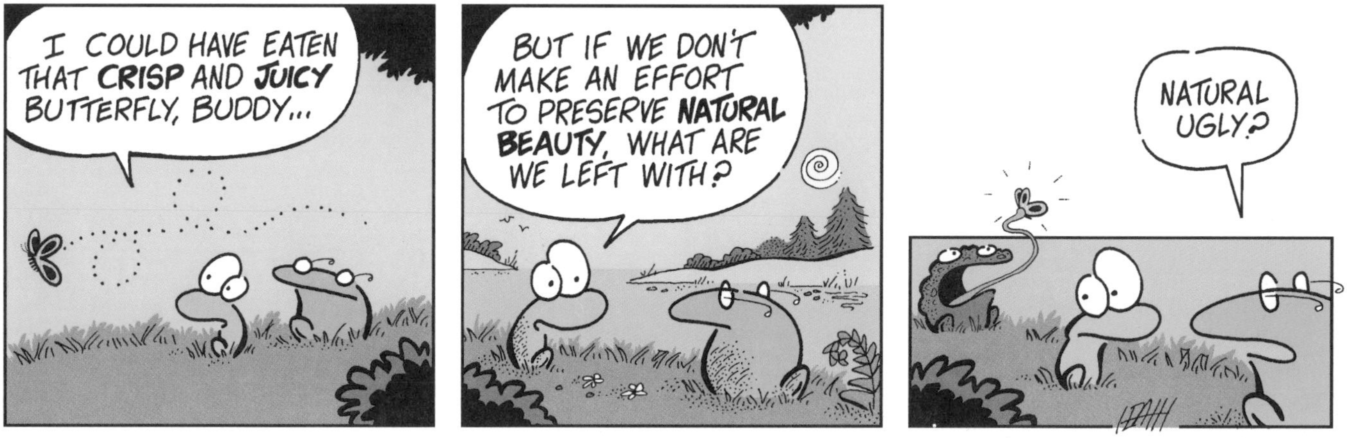
I COULD HAVE EATEN THAT CRISP AND JUICY BUTTERFLY, BUDDY...
BUT IF WE DON'T MAKE AN EFFORT TO PRESERVE NATURAL BEAUTY, WHAT ARE WE LEFT WITH?
NATURAL UGLY?

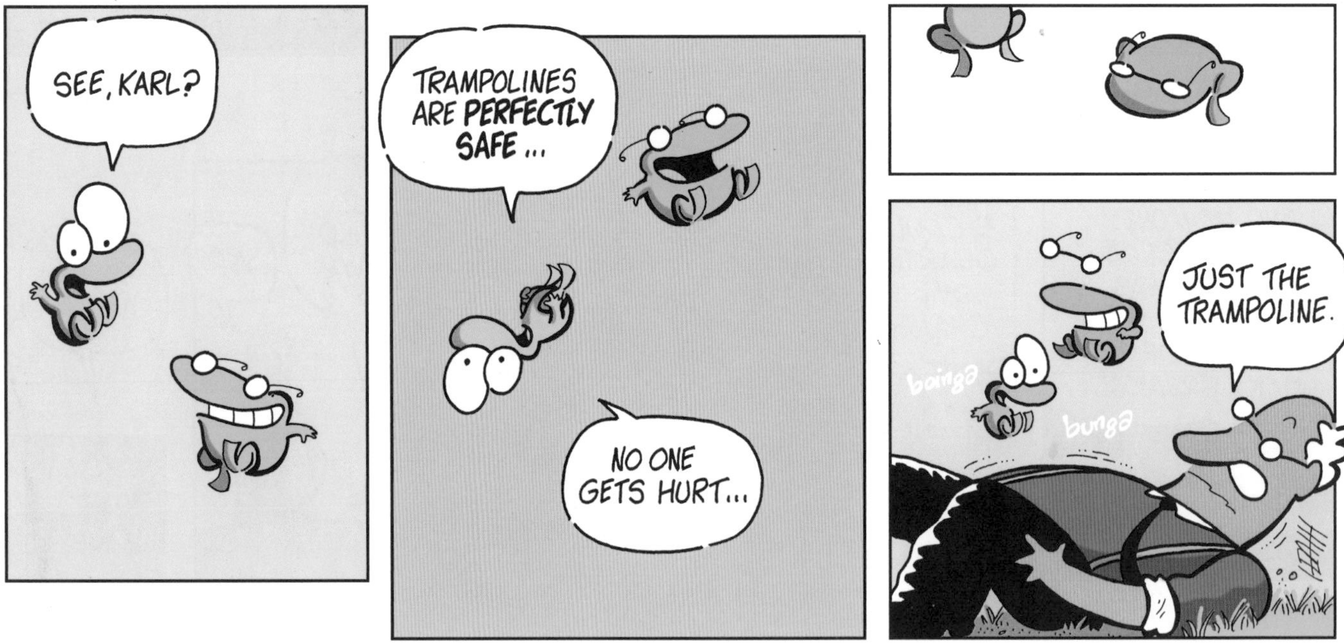
SEE, KARL?
TRAMPOLINES ARE PERFECTLY SAFE...
NO ONE GETS HURT...
boinga
bunga
JUST THE TRAMPOLINE.

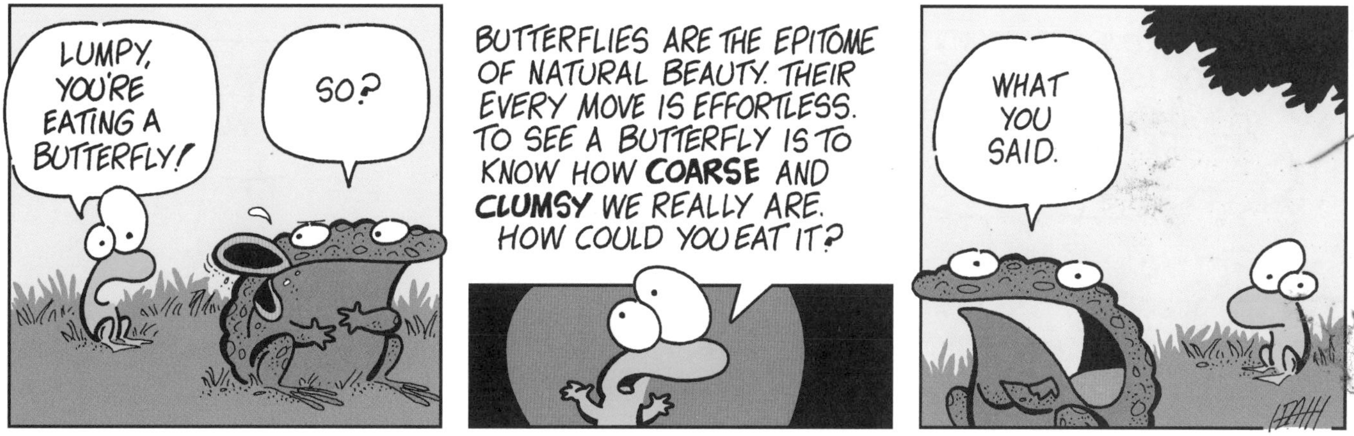
LUMPY, YOU'RE EATING A BUTTERFLY!
SO?
BUTTERFLIES ARE THE EPITOME OF NATURAL BEAUTY. THEIR EVERY MOVE IS EFFORTLESS. TO SEE A BUTTERFLY IS TO KNOW HOW COARSE AND CLUMSY WE REALLY ARE. HOW COULD YOU EAT IT?
WHAT YOU SAID.

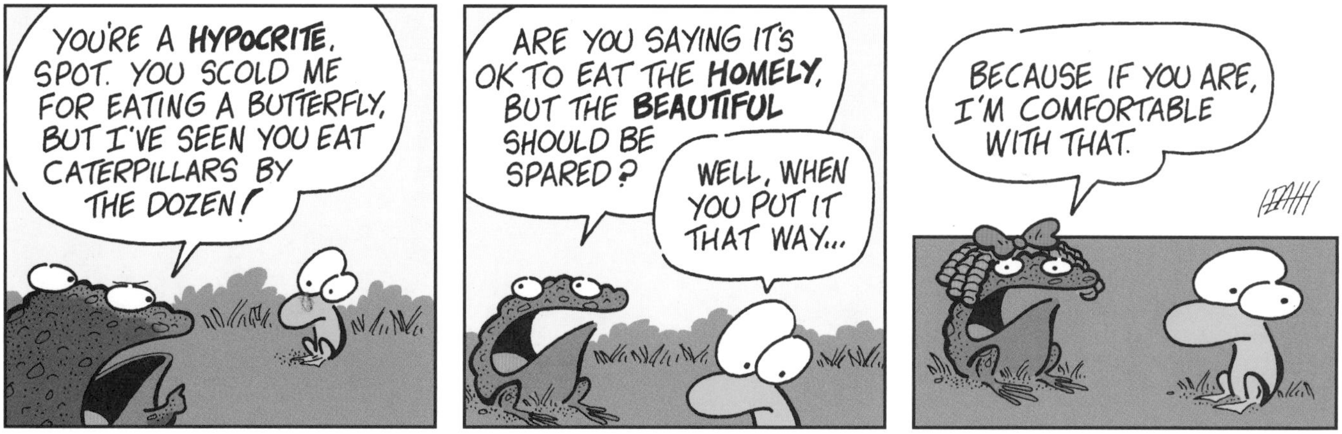
YOU'RE A HYPOCRITE, SPOT. YOU SCOLD ME FOR EATING A BUTTERFLY, BUT I'VE SEEN YOU EAT CATERPILLARS BY THE DOZEN!
ARE YOU SAYING IT'S OK TO EAT THE HOMELY, BUT THE BEAUTIFUL SHOULD BE SPARED?
WELL, WHEN YOU PUT IT THAT WAY...
BECAUSE IF YOU ARE, I'M COMFORTABLE WITH THAT.

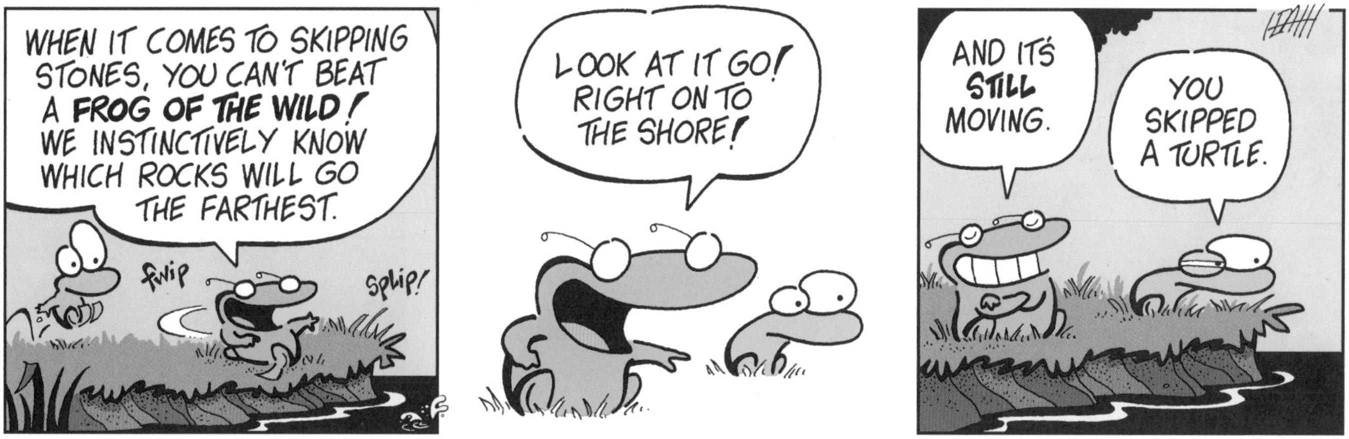
WHEN IT COMES TO SKIPPING STONES, YOU CAN'T BEAT A FROG OF THE WILD! WE INSTINCTIVELY KNOW WHICH ROCKS WILL GO THE FARTHEST.
fwip
splip!
LOOK AT IT GO! RIGHT ON TO THE SHORE!
AND IT'S STILL MOVING.
YOU SKIPPED A TURTLE.

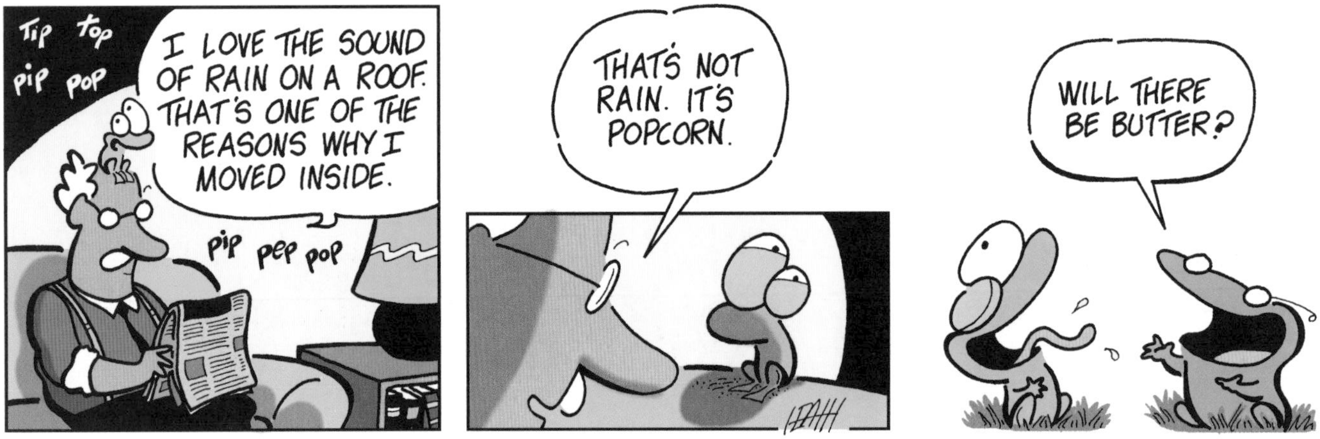
Tip top
pip pop
I LOVE THE SOUND OF RAIN ON A ROOF. THAT'S ONE OF THE REASONS WHY I MOVED INSIDE.
pip pep pop
THAT'S NOT RAIN. IT'S POPCORN.
WILL THERE BE BUTTER?

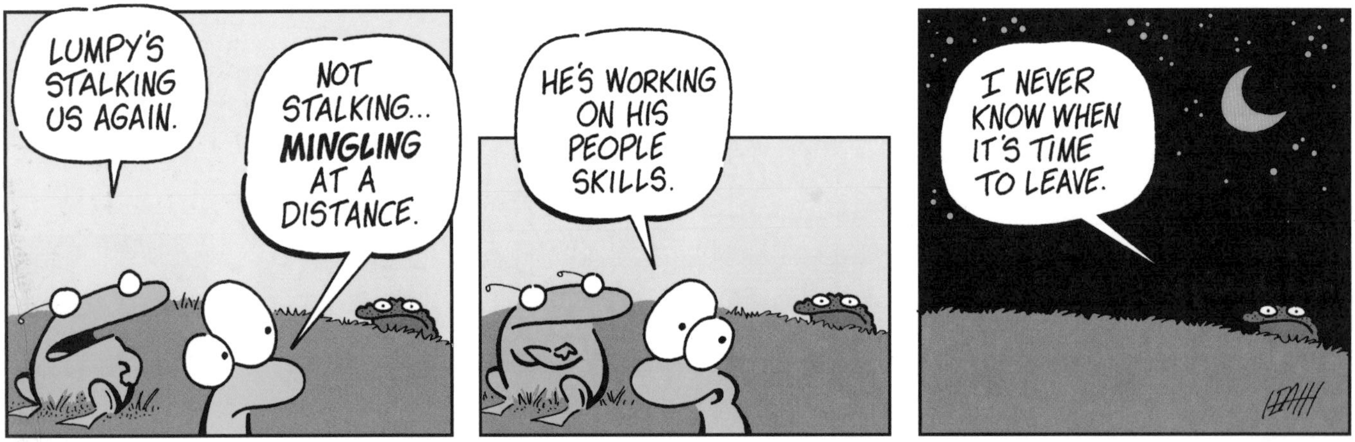
LUMPY'S STALKING US AGAIN.
NOT STALKING... **MINGLING** AT A DISTANCE.
HE'S WORKING ON HIS PEOPLE SKILLS.
I NEVER KNOW WHEN IT'S TIME TO LEAVE.

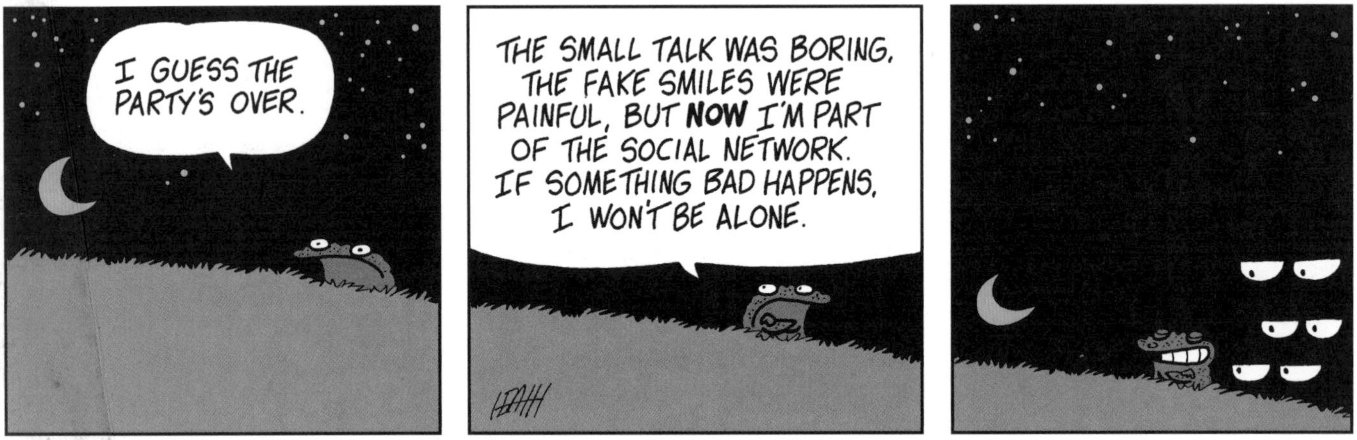
I GUESS THE PARTY'S OVER.
THE SMALL TALK WAS BORING. THE FAKE SMILES WERE PAINFUL, BUT **NOW** I'M PART OF THE SOCIAL NETWORK. IF SOMETHING BAD HAPPENS, I WON'T BE ALONE.

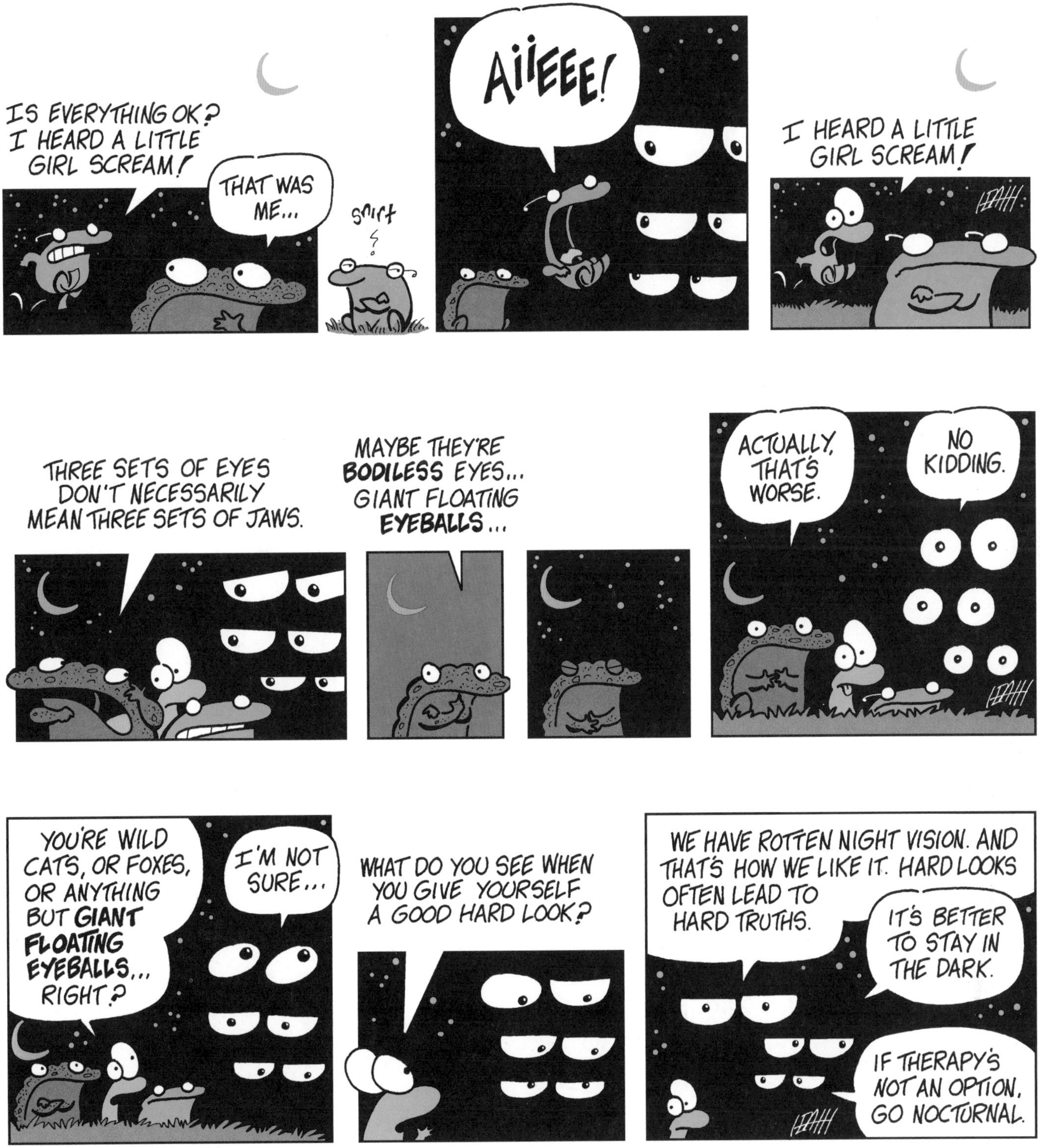
IS EVERYTHING OK? I HEARD A LITTLE GIRL SCREAM!
THAT WAS ME...
sniff
AiiEEE!
I HEARD A LITTLE GIRL SCREAM!
THREE SETS OF EYES DON'T NECESSARILY MEAN THREE SETS OF JAWS.
MAYBE THEY'RE **BODILESS** EYES... GIANT FLOATING **EYEBALLS**...
ACTUALLY, THAT'S WORSE.
NO KIDDING.
YOU'RE WILD CATS, OR FOXES, OR ANYTHING BUT **GIANT FLOATING EYEBALLS**... RIGHT?
I'M NOT SURE...
WHAT DO YOU SEE WHEN YOU GIVE YOURSELF A GOOD HARD LOOK?
WE HAVE ROTTEN NIGHT VISION. AND THAT'S HOW WE LIKE IT. HARD LOOKS OFTEN LEAD TO HARD TRUTHS.
IT'S BETTER TO STAY IN THE DARK.
IF THERAPY'S NOT AN OPTION, GO NOCTURNAL.

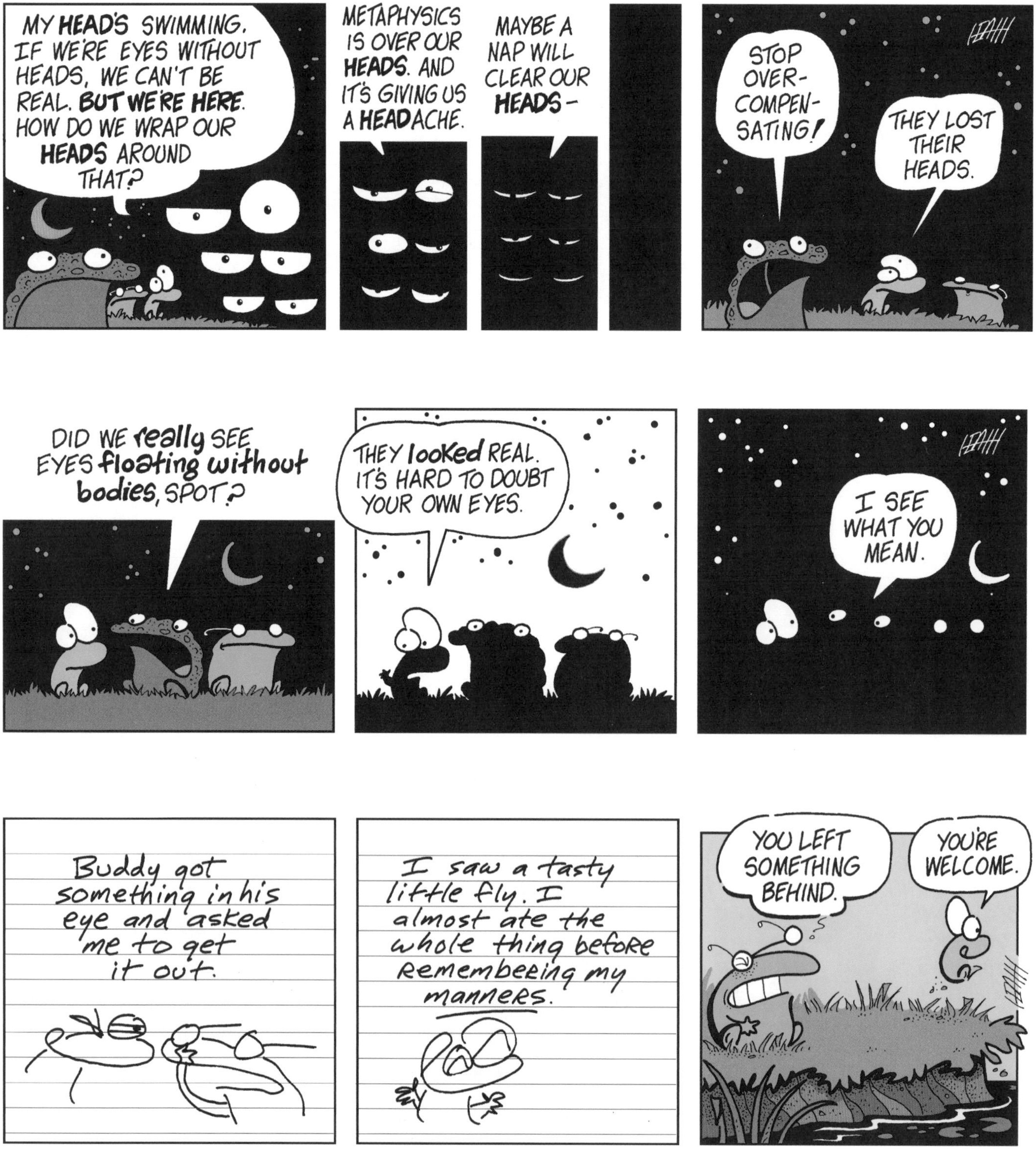
MY HEAD'S SWIMMING. IF WE'RE EYES WITHOUT HEADS, WE CAN'T BE REAL. BUT WE'RE HERE. HOW DO WE WRAP OUR HEADS AROUND THAT?
METAPHYSICS IS OVER OUR HEADS. AND IT'S GIVING US A HEADACHE.
MAYBE A NAP WILL CLEAR OUR HEADS –
STOP OVER-COMPEN-SATING!
THEY LOST THEIR HEADS.
DID WE really SEE EYES floating without bodies, SPOT?
THEY looked REAL. IT'S HARD TO DOUBT YOUR OWN EYES.
I SEE WHAT YOU MEAN.
Buddy got something in his eye and asked me to get it out.
I saw a tasty little fly. I almost ate the whole thing before remembering my manners.
YOU LEFT SOMETHING BEHIND.
YOU'RE WELCOME.

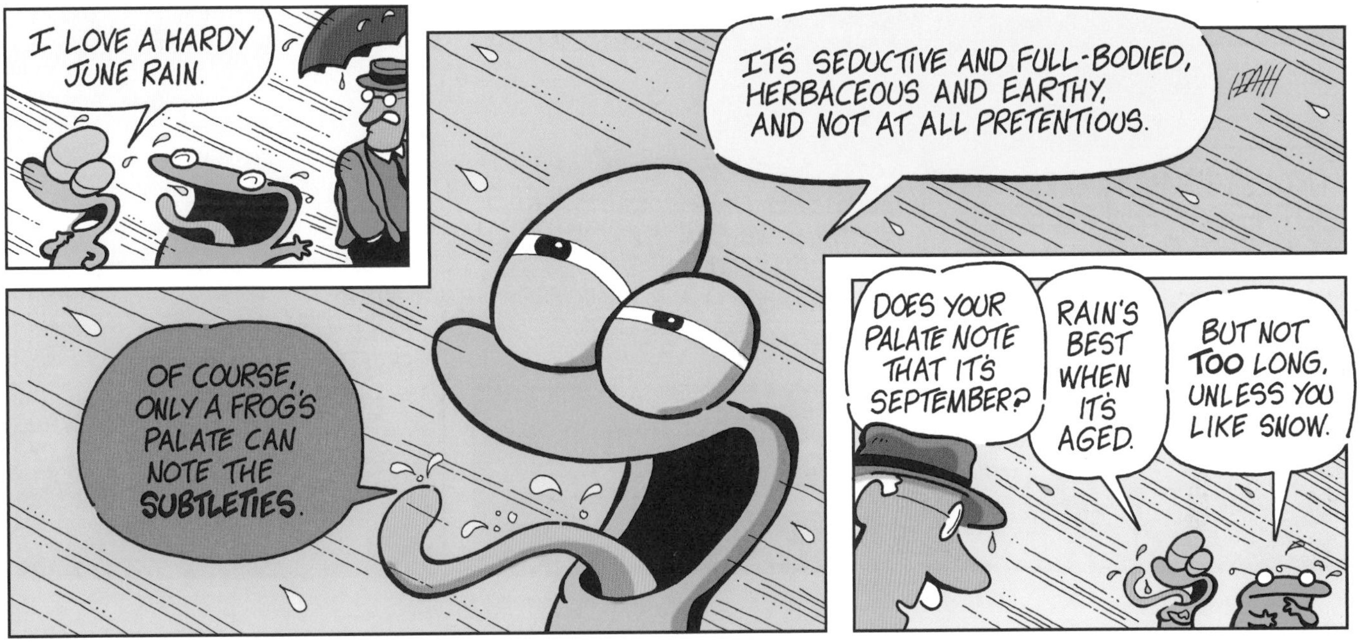
I LOVE A HARDY JUNE RAIN.
IT'S SEDUCTIVE AND FULL-BODIED, HERBACEOUS AND EARTHY, AND NOT AT ALL PRETENTIOUS.
OF COURSE, ONLY A FROG'S PALATE CAN NOTE THE **SUBTLETIES**.
DOES YOUR PALATE NOTE THAT IT'S SEPTEMBER?
RAIN'S BEST WHEN IT'S AGED.
BUT NOT **TOO** LONG, UNLESS YOU LIKE SNOW.

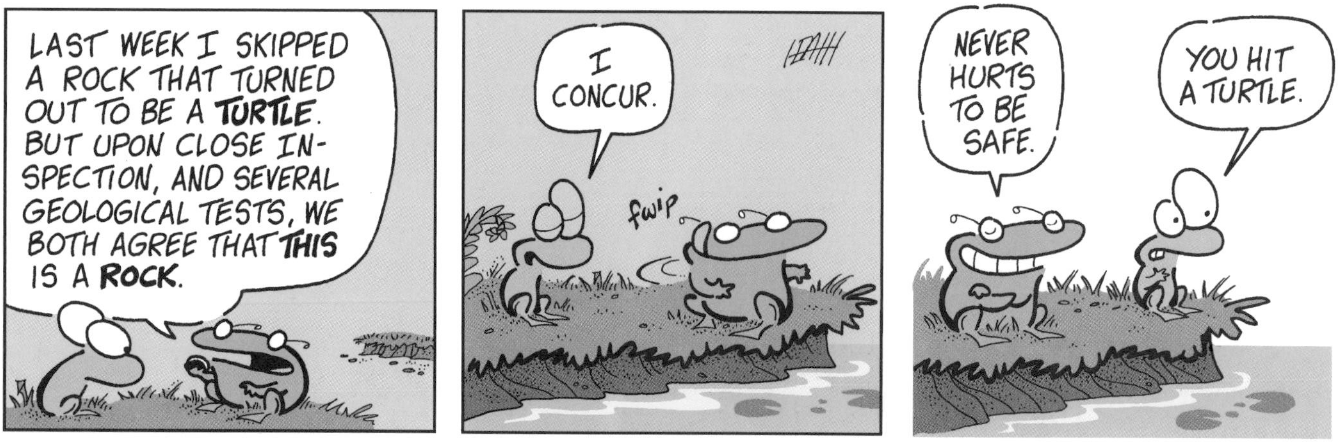
LAST WEEK I SKIPPED A ROCK THAT TURNED OUT TO BE A **TURTLE**. BUT UPON CLOSE IN-SPECTION, AND SEVERAL GEOLOGICAL TESTS, WE BOTH AGREE THAT **THIS** IS A **ROCK**.
I CONCUR.
fwip
NEVER HURTS TO BE SAFE.
YOU HIT A TURTLE.

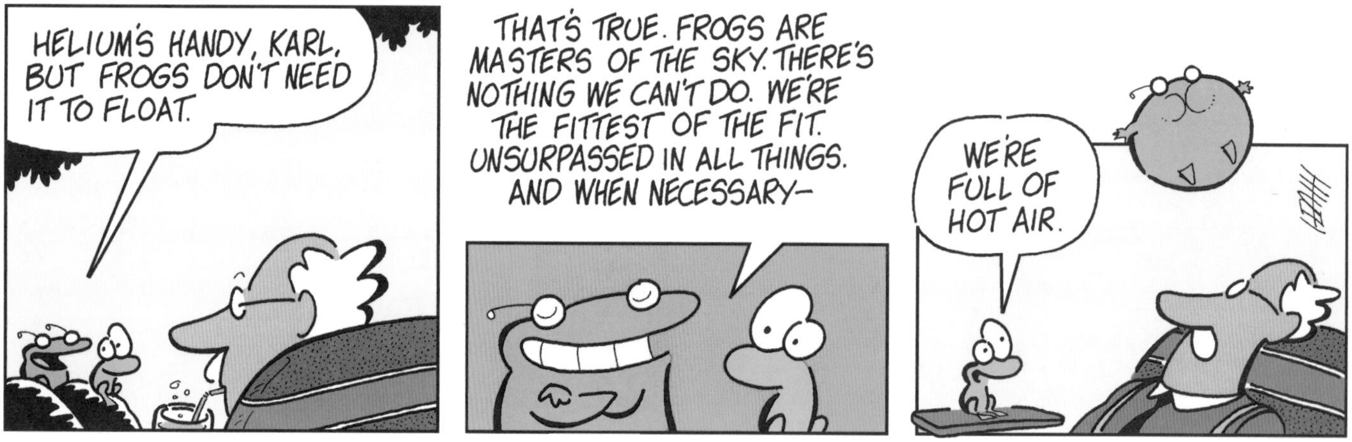
HELIUM'S HANDY, KARL, BUT FROGS DON'T NEED IT TO FLOAT.
THAT'S TRUE. FROGS ARE MASTERS OF THE SKY. THERE'S NOTHING WE CAN'T DO. WE'RE THE FITTEST OF THE FIT. UNSURPASSED IN ALL THINGS. AND WHEN NECESSARY—
WE'RE FULL OF HOT AIR.

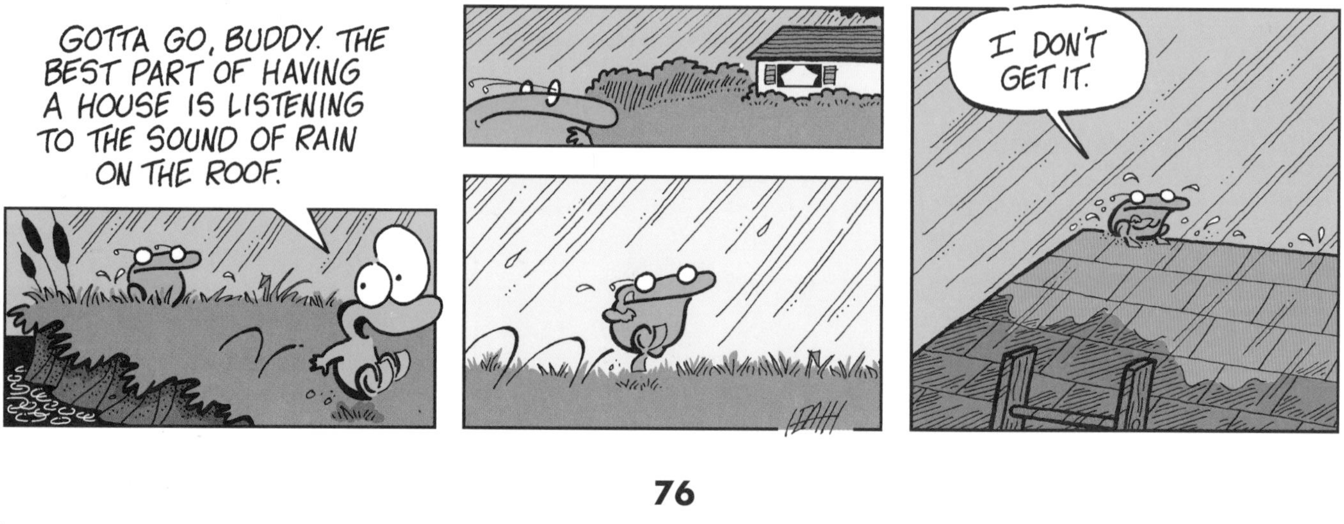
GOTTA GO, BUDDY. THE BEST PART OF HAVING A HOUSE IS LISTENING TO THE SOUND OF RAIN ON THE ROOF.
I DON'T GET IT.

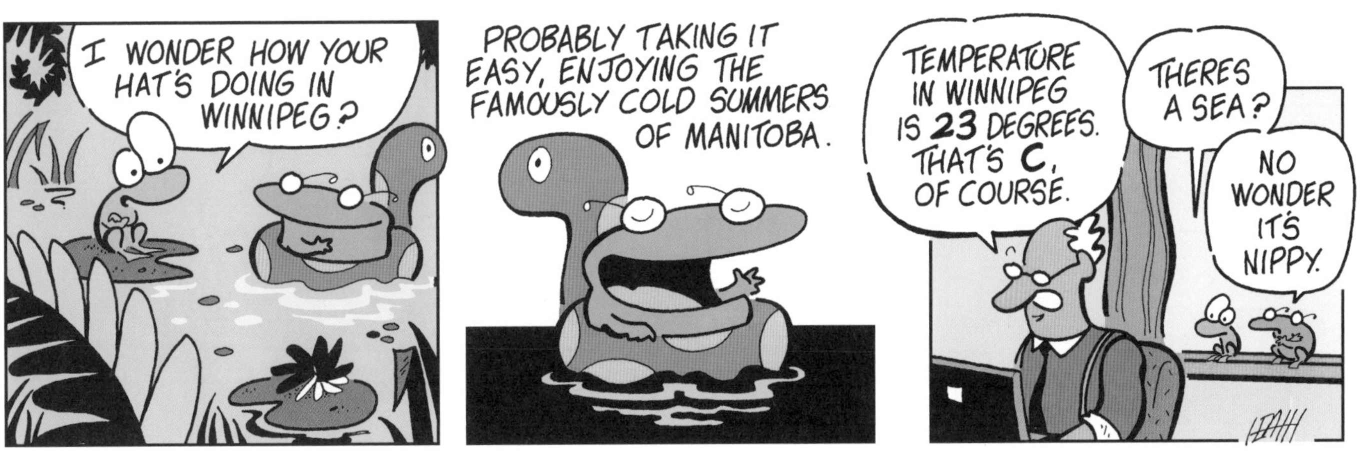
I WONDER HOW YOUR HAT'S DOING IN WINNIPEG?
PROBABLY TAKING IT EASY, ENJOYING THE FAMOUSLY COLD SUMMERS OF MANITOBA.
TEMPERATURE IN WINNIPEG IS **23** DEGREES. THAT'S **C**, OF COURSE.
THERES A SEA?
NO WONDER IT'S NIPPY.

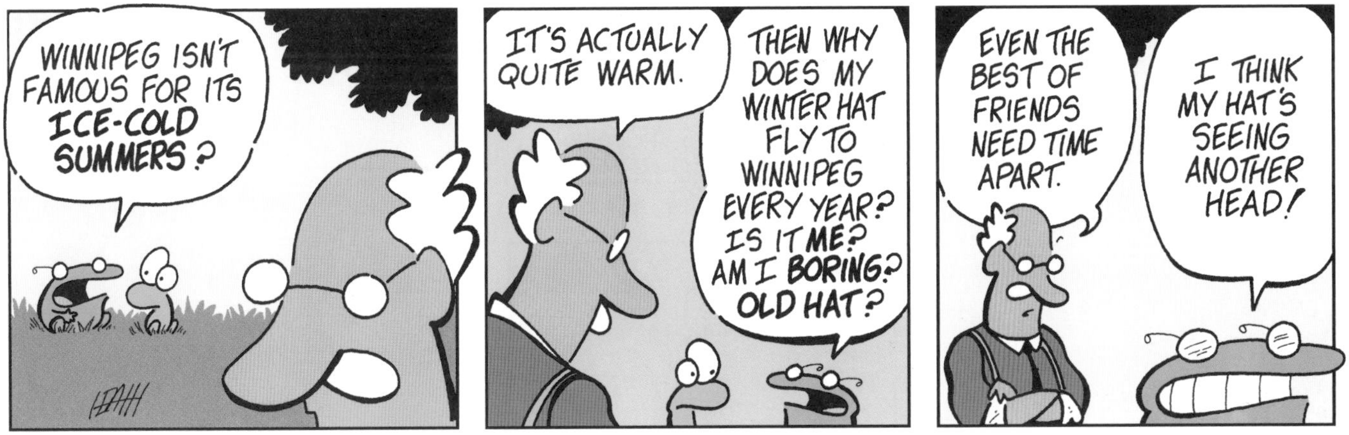
WINNIPEG ISN'T FAMOUS FOR ITS **ICE-COLD SUMMERS**?
IT'S ACTUALLY QUITE WARM.
THEN WHY DOES MY WINTER HAT FLY TO WINNIPEG EVERY YEAR? IS IT **ME**? AM I **BORING**? **OLD HAT**?
EVEN THE BEST OF FRIENDS NEED TIME APART.
I THINK MY HAT'S SEEING ANOTHER HEAD!

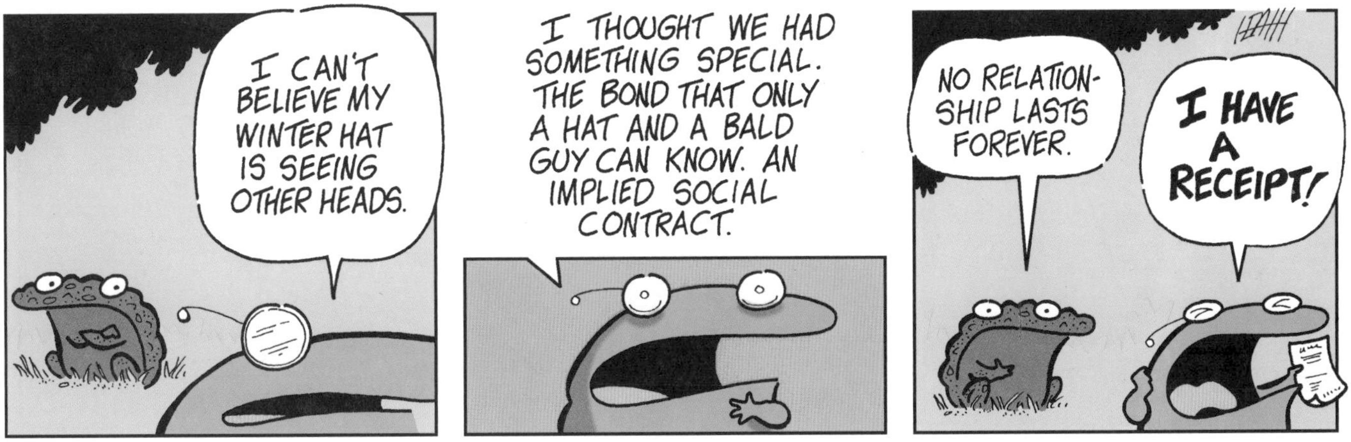
I CAN'T BELIEVE MY WINTER HAT IS SEEING OTHER HEADS.
I THOUGHT WE HAD SOMETHING SPECIAL. THE BOND THAT ONLY A HAT AND A BALD GUY CAN KNOW. AN IMPLIED SOCIAL CONTRACT.
NO RELATION-SHIP LASTS FOREVER.
I HAVE A RECEIPT!

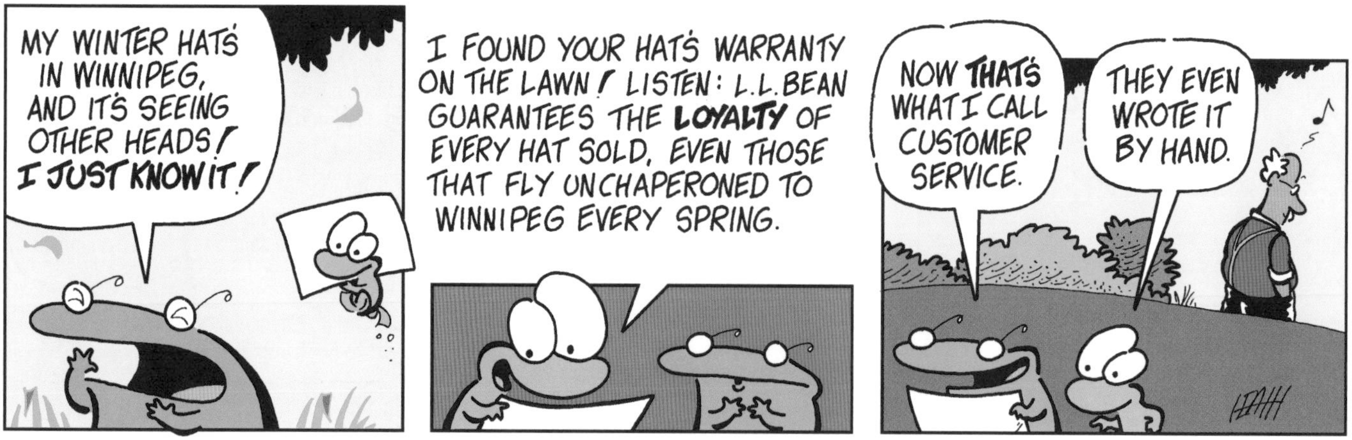
MY WINTER HAT'S IN WINNIPEG, AND IT'S SEEING OTHER HEADS! I JUST KNOW IT!
I FOUND YOUR HAT'S WARRANTY ON THE LAWN! LISTEN: L.L. BEAN GUARANTEES THE LOYALTY OF EVERY HAT SOLD, EVEN THOSE THAT FLY UNCHAPERONED TO WINNIPEG EVERY SPRING.
NOW THAT'S WHAT I CALL CUSTOMER SERVICE.
THEY EVEN WROTE IT BY HAND.

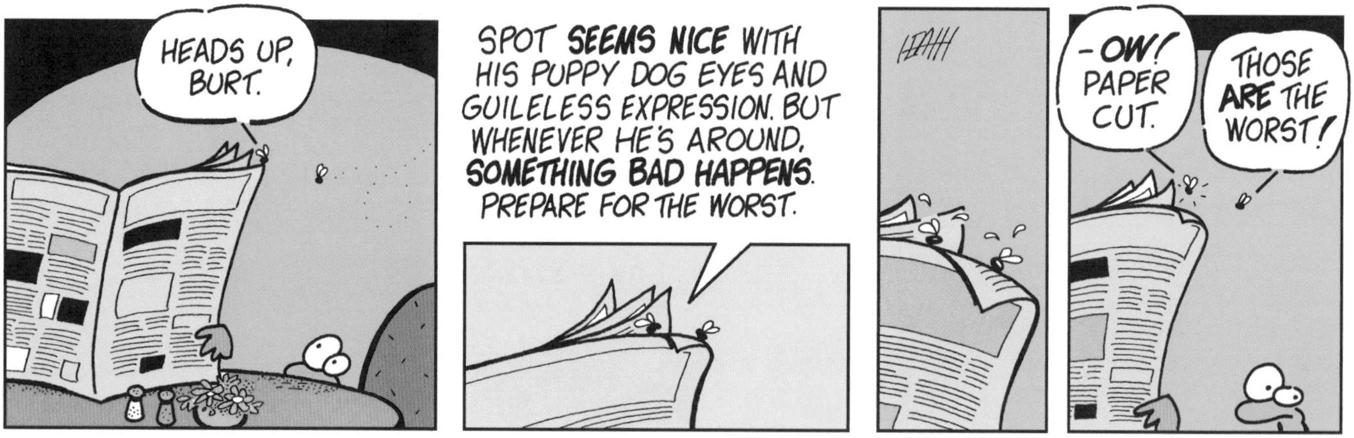
HEADS UP, BURT.
SPOT SEEMS NICE WITH HIS PUPPY DOG EYES AND GUILELESS EXPRESSION. BUT WHENEVER HE'S AROUND, SOMETHING BAD HAPPENS. PREPARE FOR THE WORST.
-OW! PAPER CUT.
THOSE ARE THE WORST!

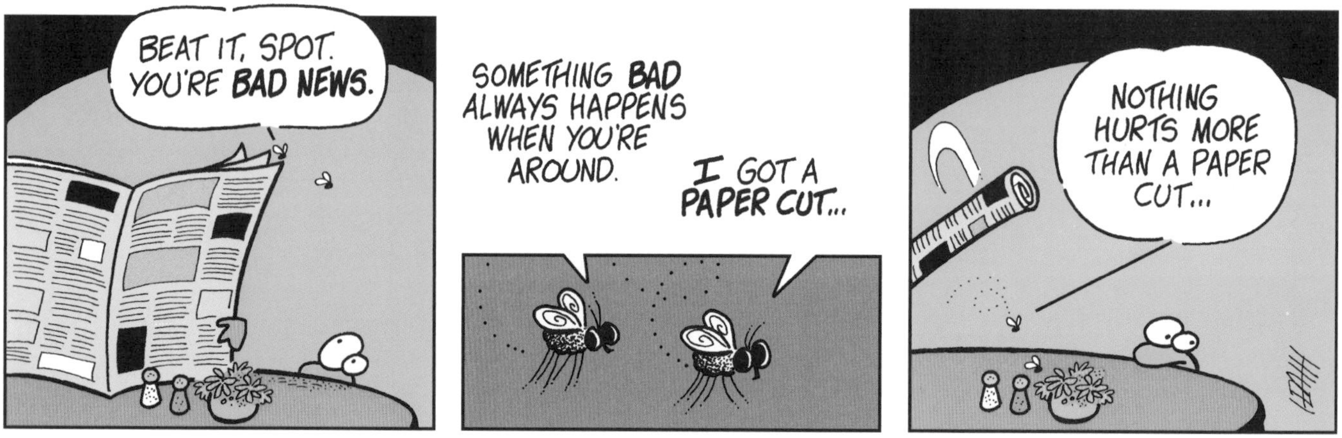
BEAT IT, SPOT. YOU'RE BAD NEWS.
SOMETHING BAD ALWAYS HAPPENS WHEN YOU'RE AROUND.
I GOT A PAPER CUT...
NOTHING HURTS MORE THAN A PAPER CUT...

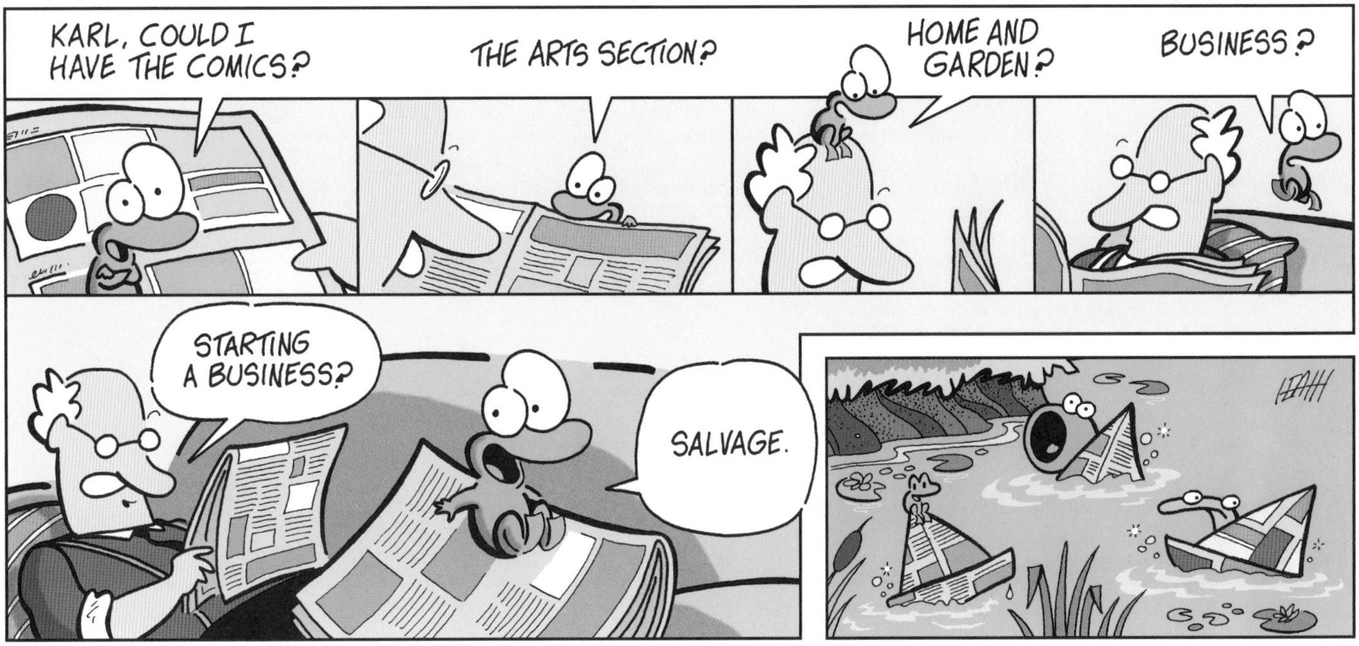
KARL, COULD I HAVE THE COMICS?
THE ARTS SECTION?
HOME AND GARDEN?
BUSINESS?
STARTING A BUSINESS?
SALVAGE.

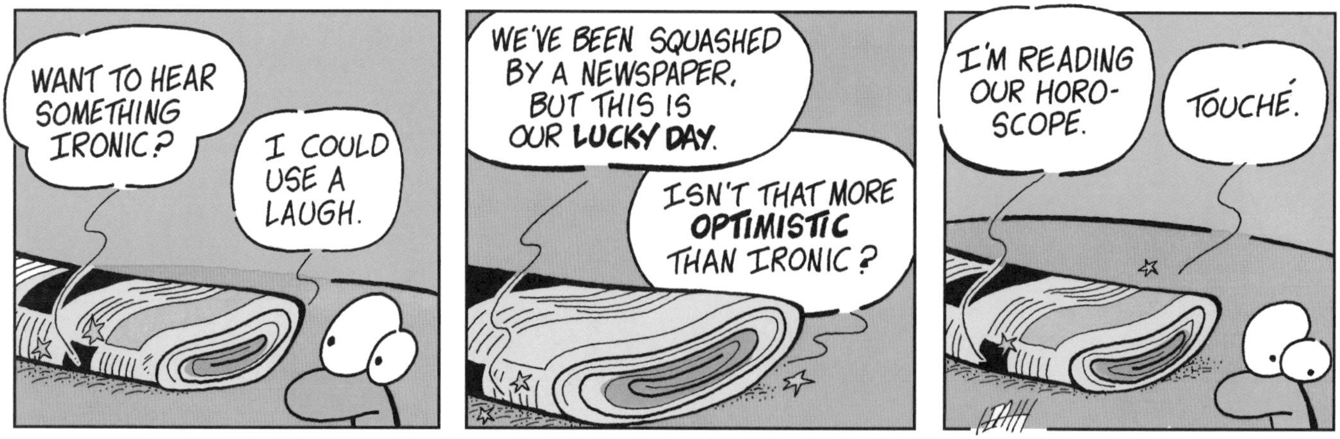
WANT TO HEAR SOMETHING IRONIC?
I COULD USE A LAUGH.
WE'VE BEEN SQUASHED BY A NEWSPAPER, BUT THIS IS OUR **LUCKY DAY**.
ISN'T THAT MORE **OPTIMISTIC** THAN IRONIC?
I'M READING OUR HORO-SCOPE.
TOUCHÉ.

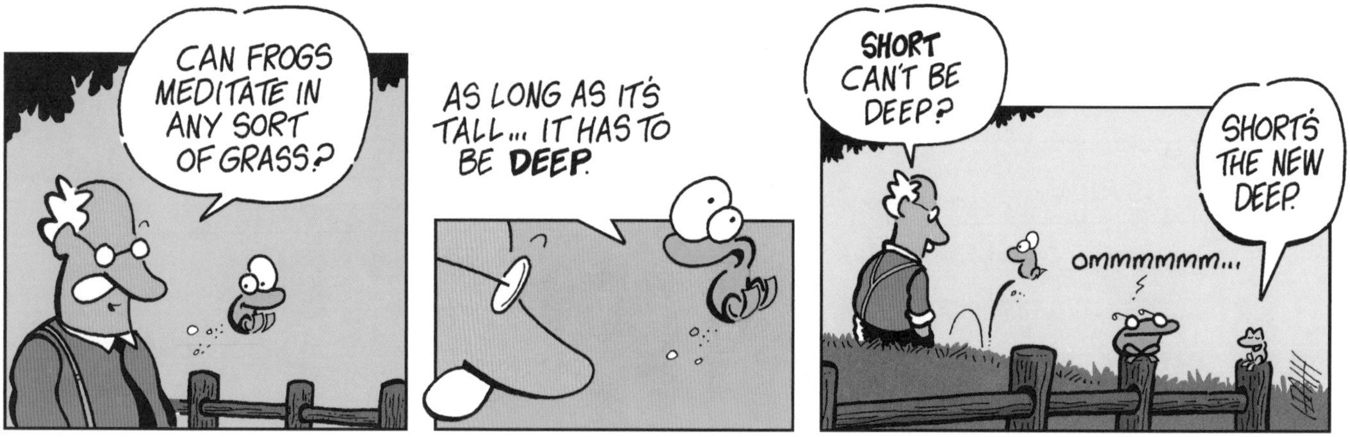
CAN FROGS MEDITATE IN ANY SORT OF GRASS?
AS LONG AS IT'S TALL... IT HAS TO BE **DEEP**.
SHORT CAN'T BE DEEP?
OMMMMMM...
SHORT'S THE NEW DEEP.

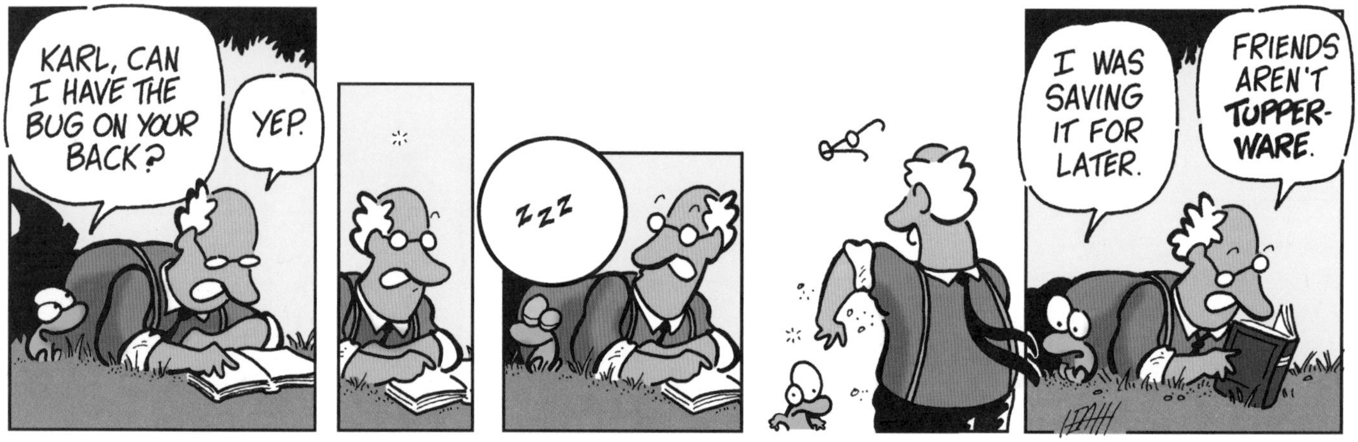
KARL, CAN I HAVE THE BUG ON YOUR BACK?
YEP.
ZZZ
I WAS SAVING IT FOR LATER.
FRIENDS AREN'T **TUPPER-WARE**.

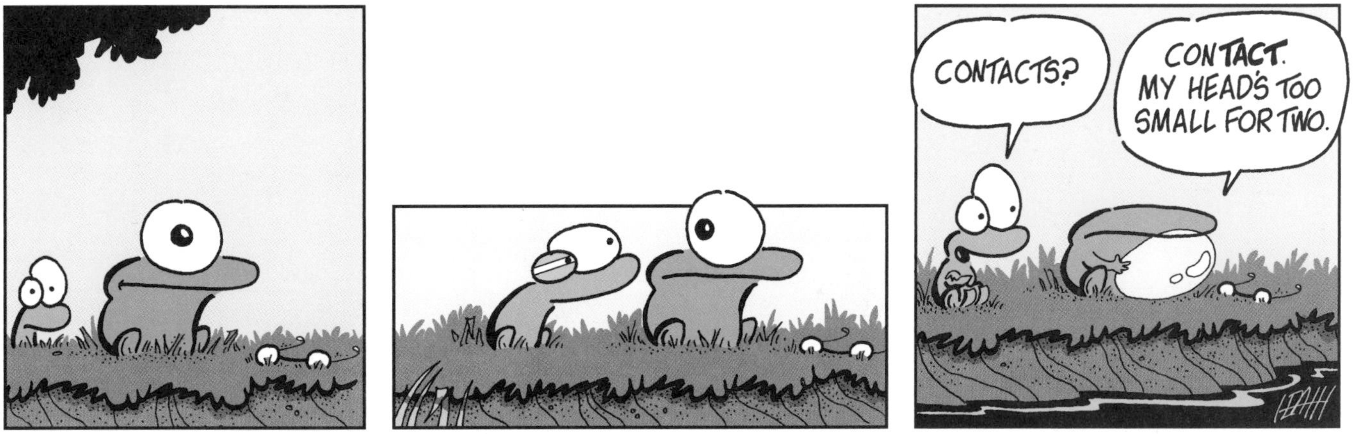
CONTACTS?
CONTACT. MY HEAD'S TOO SMALL FOR TWO.

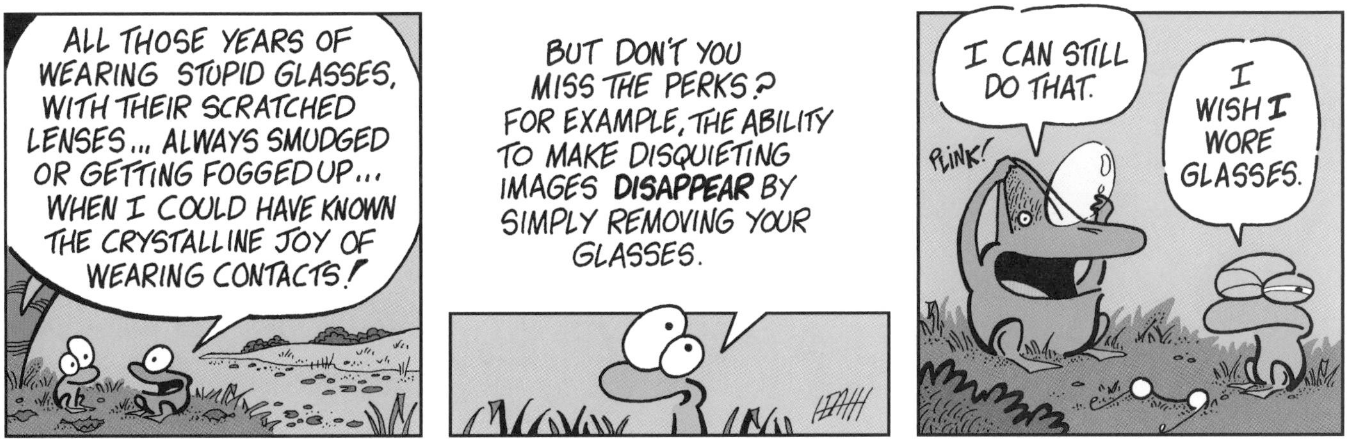
ALL THOSE YEARS OF WEARING STUPID GLASSES, WITH THEIR SCRATCHED LENSES... ALWAYS SMUDGED OR GETTING FOGGED UP... WHEN I COULD HAVE KNOWN THE CRYSTALLINE JOY OF WEARING CONTACTS!
BUT DON'T YOU MISS THE PERKS? FOR EXAMPLE, THE ABILITY TO MAKE DISQUIETING IMAGES DISAPPEAR BY SIMPLY REMOVING YOUR GLASSES.
PLINK!
I CAN STILL DO THAT.
I WISH I WORE GLASSES.

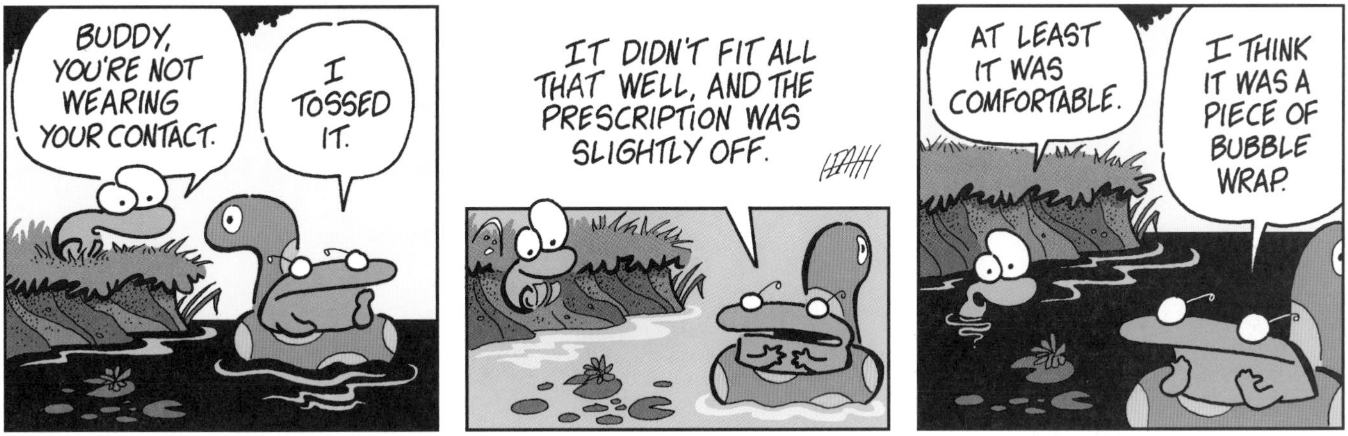
BUDDY, YOU'RE NOT WEARING YOUR CONTACT.
I TOSSED IT.
IT DIDN'T FIT ALL THAT WELL, AND THE PRESCRIPTION WAS SLIGHTLY OFF.
AT LEAST IT WAS COMFORTABLE.
I THINK IT WAS A PIECE OF BUBBLE WRAP.

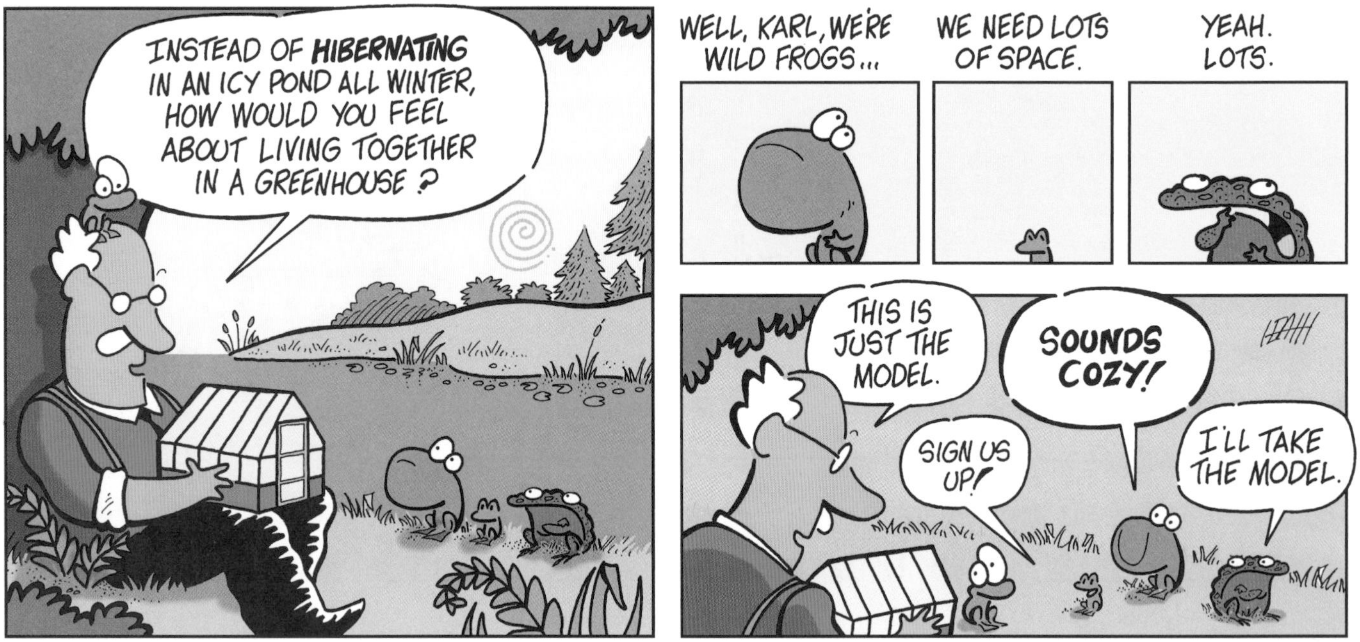

INSTEAD OF HIBERNATING IN AN ICY POND ALL WINTER, HOW WOULD YOU FEEL ABOUT LIVING TOGETHER IN A GREENHOUSE?
WELL, KARL, WE'RE WILD FROGS...
WE NEED LOTS OF SPACE.
YEAH. LOTS.
THIS IS JUST THE MODEL.
SOUNDS COZY!
SIGN US UP!
I'LL TAKE THE MODEL.

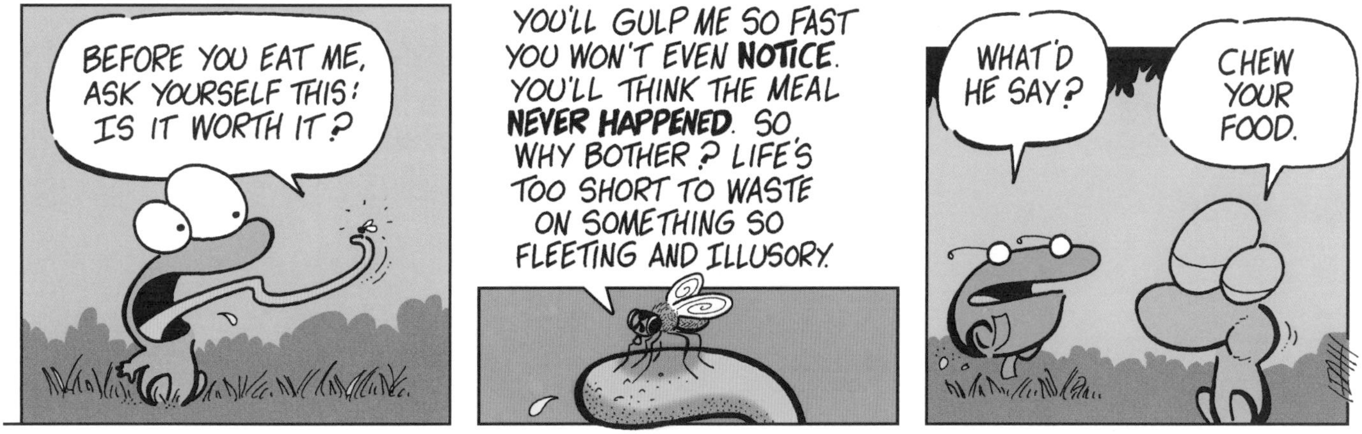
BEFORE YOU EAT ME, ASK YOURSELF THIS: IS IT WORTH IT?
YOU'LL GULP ME SO FAST YOU WON'T EVEN **NOTICE**. YOU'LL THINK THE MEAL **NEVER HAPPENED**. SO WHY BOTHER? LIFE'S TOO SHORT TO WASTE ON SOMETHING SO FLEETING AND ILLUSORY.
WHAT'D HE SAY?
CHEW YOUR FOOD.

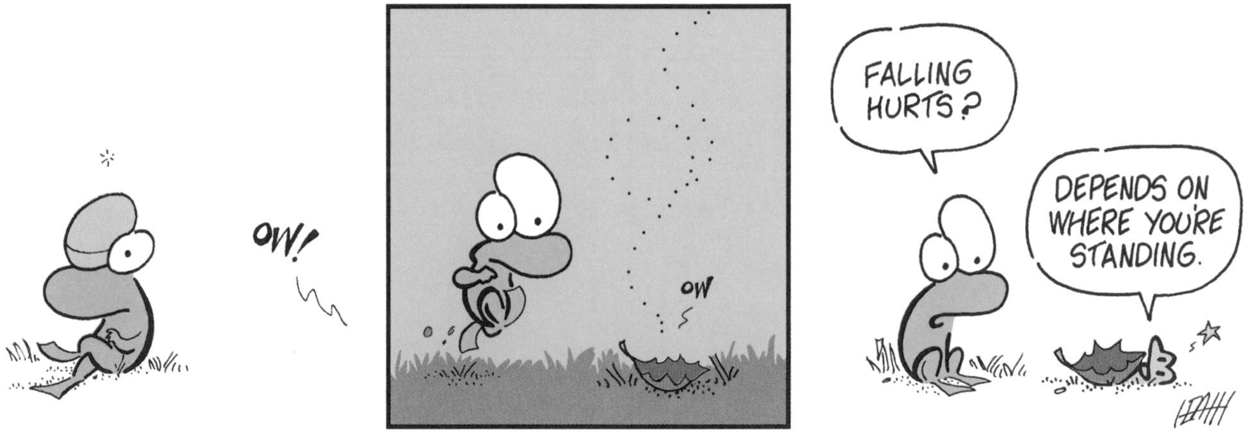
OW!
OW
FALLING HURTS?
DEPENDS ON WHERE YOU'RE STANDING.

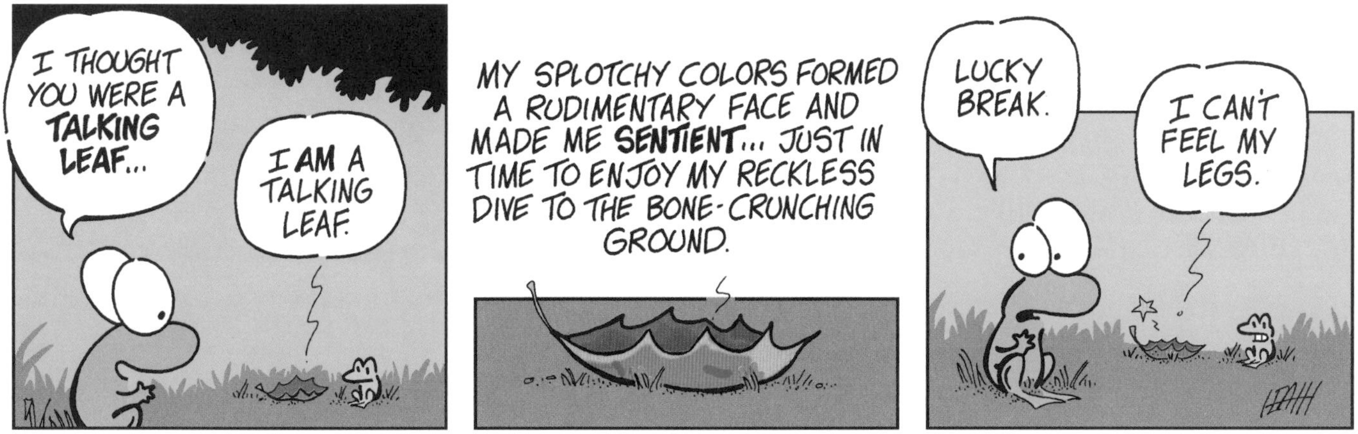
I THOUGHT YOU WERE A **TALKING LEAF**...
I **AM** A TALKING LEAF.
MY SPLOTCHY COLORS FORMED A RUDIMENTARY FACE AND MADE ME **SENTIENT**... JUST IN TIME TO ENJOY MY RECKLESS DIVE TO THE BONE-CRUNCHING GROUND.
LUCKY BREAK.
I CAN'T FEEL MY LEGS.

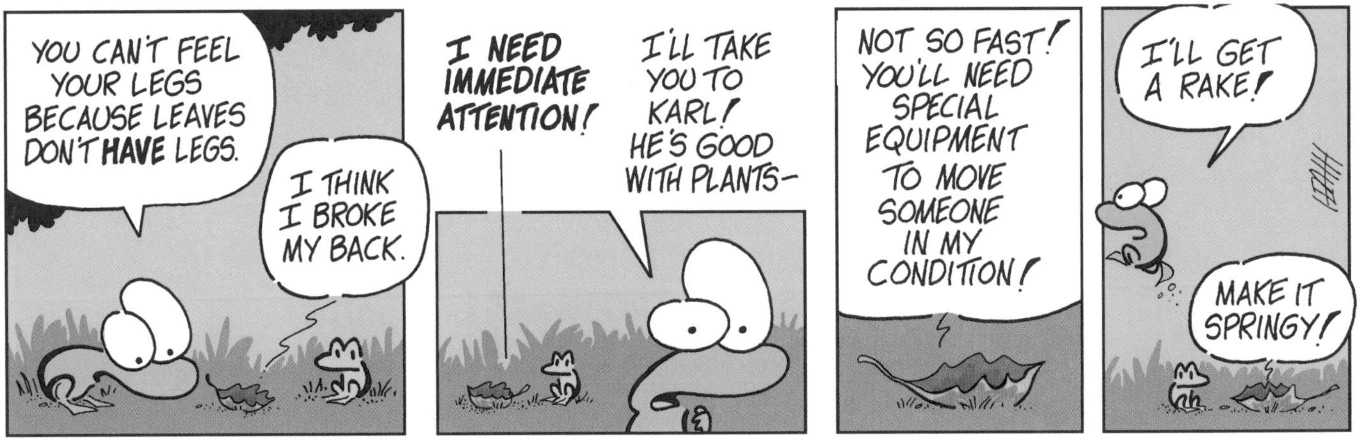
YOU CAN'T FEEL YOUR LEGS BECAUSE LEAVES DON'T **HAVE** LEGS.
I THINK I BROKE MY BACK.
I NEED IMMEDIATE ATTENTION!
I'LL TAKE YOU TO KARL! HE'S GOOD WITH PLANTS-
NOT SO FAST! YOU'LL NEED SPECIAL EQUIPMENT TO MOVE SOMEONE IN MY CONDITION!
I'LL GET A RAKE!
MAKE IT SPRINGY!

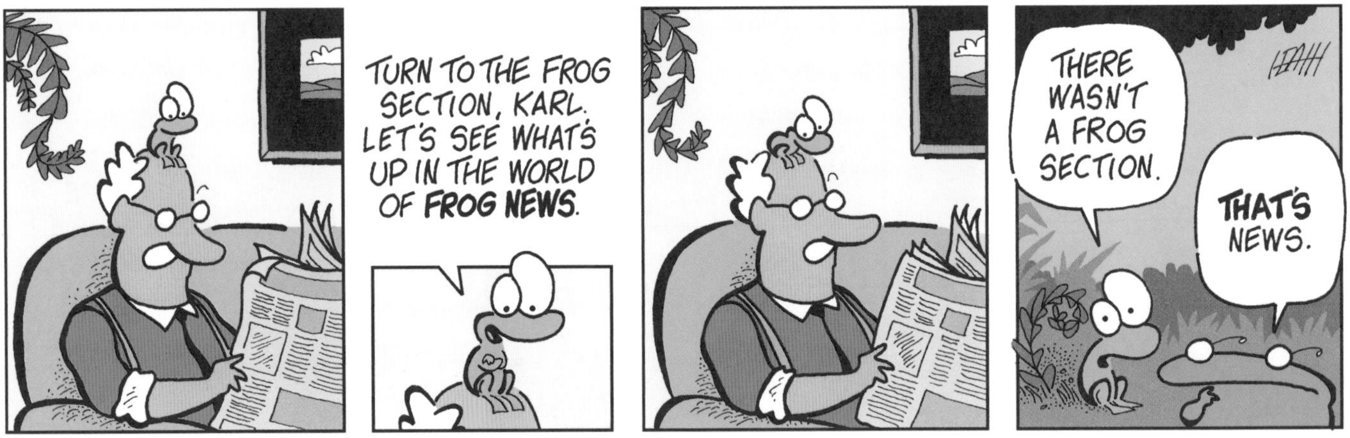
TURN TO THE FROG SECTION, KARL. LET'S SEE WHAT'S UP IN THE WORLD OF **FROG NEWS**.
THERE WASN'T A FROG SECTION.
THAT'S NEWS.

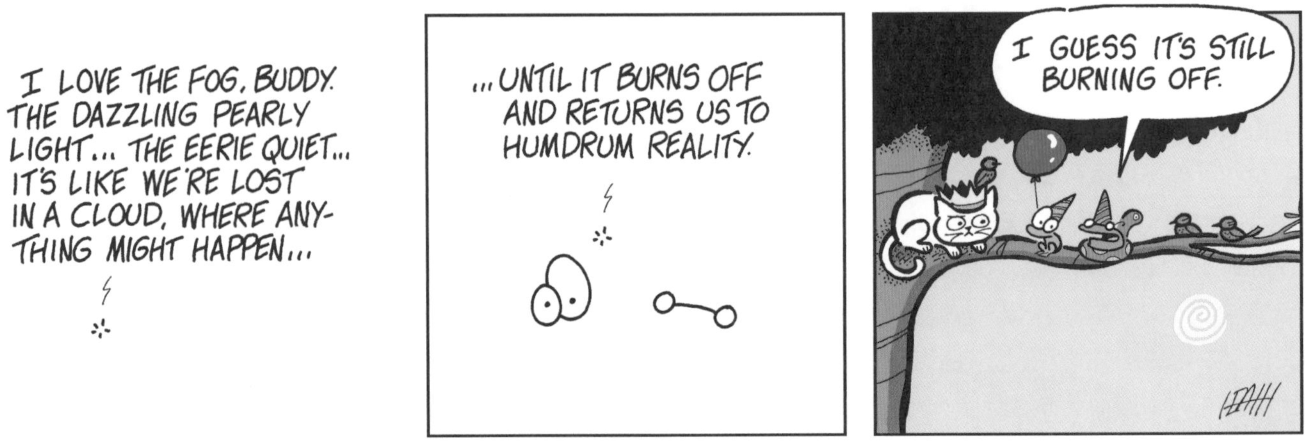
I LOVE THE FOG, BUDDY. THE DAZZLING PEARLY LIGHT... THE EERIE QUIET... IT'S LIKE WE'RE LOST IN A CLOUD, WHERE ANY-THING MIGHT HAPPEN...
...UNTIL IT BURNS OFF AND RETURNS US TO HUMDRUM REALITY.
I GUESS IT'S STILL BURNING OFF.

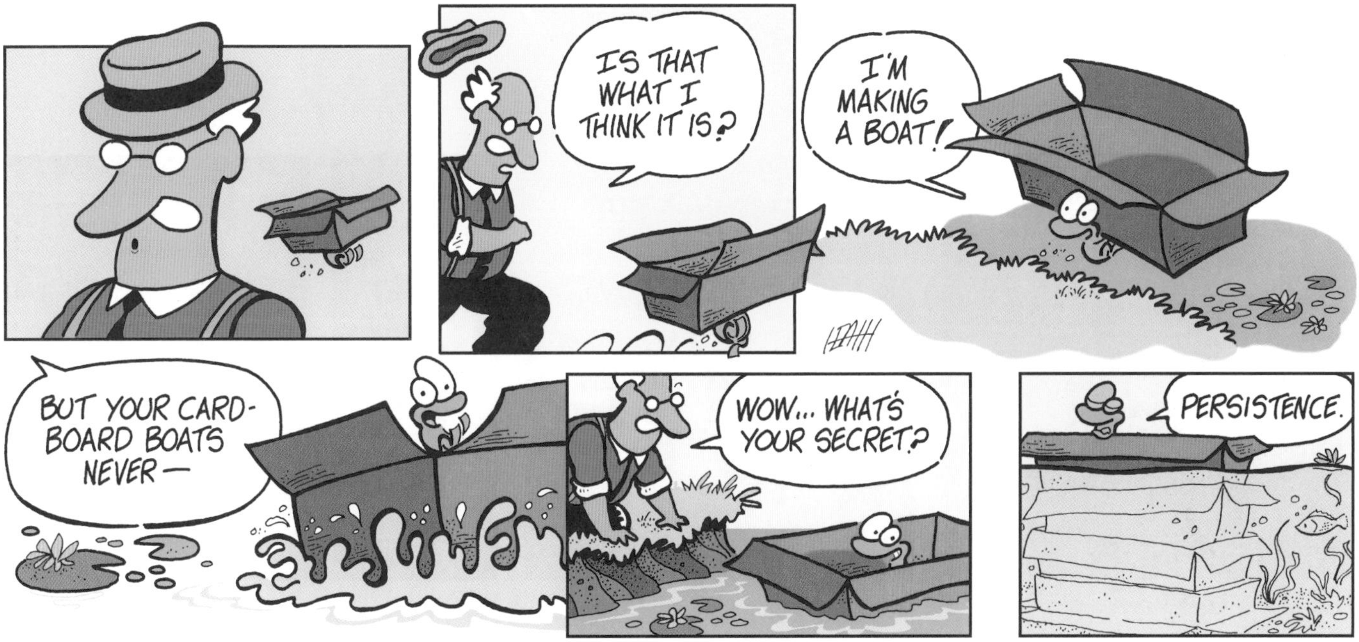
I'S THAT WHAT I THINK IT IS?
I'M MAKING A BOAT!
BUT YOUR CARD-BOARD BOATS NEVER—
WOW... WHAT'S YOUR SECRET?
PERSISTENCE.

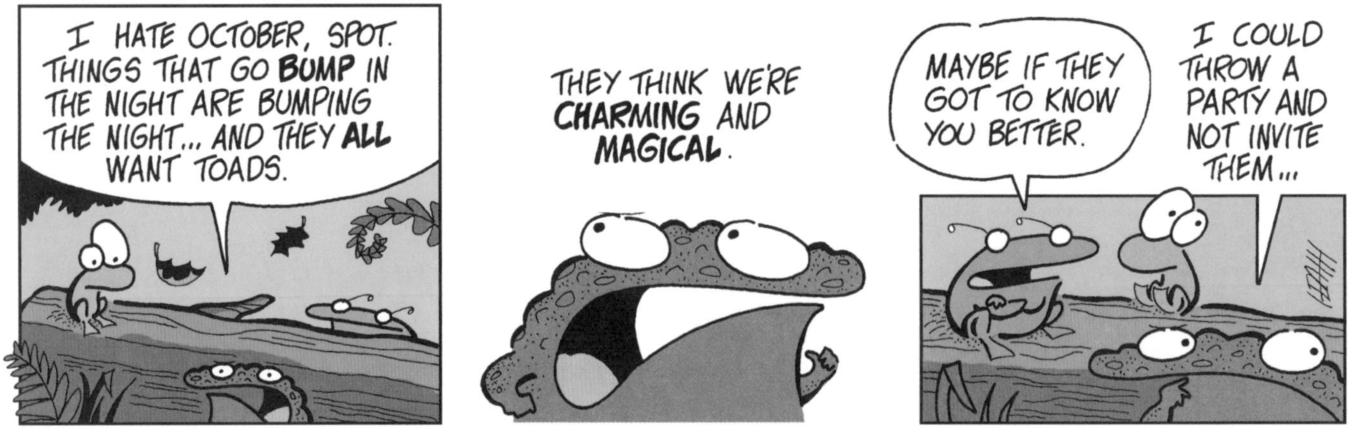
I HATE OCTOBER, SPOT. THINGS THAT GO **BUMP** IN THE NIGHT ARE BUMPING THE NIGHT... AND THEY **ALL** WANT TOADS.
THEY THINK WE'RE **CHARMING** AND **MAGICAL**.
MAYBE IF THEY GOT TO KNOW YOU BETTER.
I COULD THROW A PARTY AND NOT INVITE THEM...

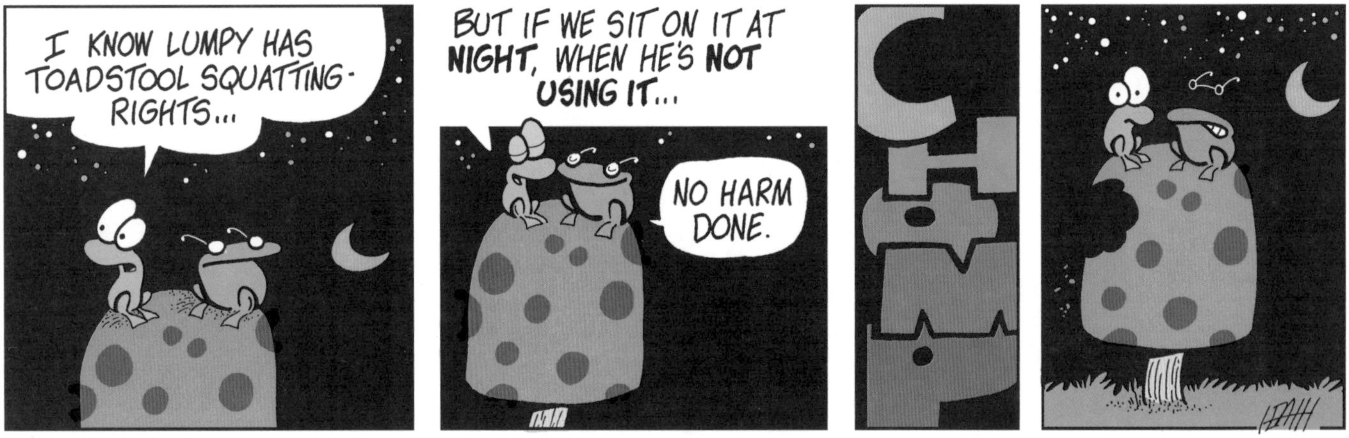
I KNOW LUMPY HAS TOADSTOOL SQUATTING-RIGHTS...
BUT IF WE SIT ON IT AT **NIGHT**, WHEN HE'S **NOT USING IT**...
NO HARM DONE.
CHOMP

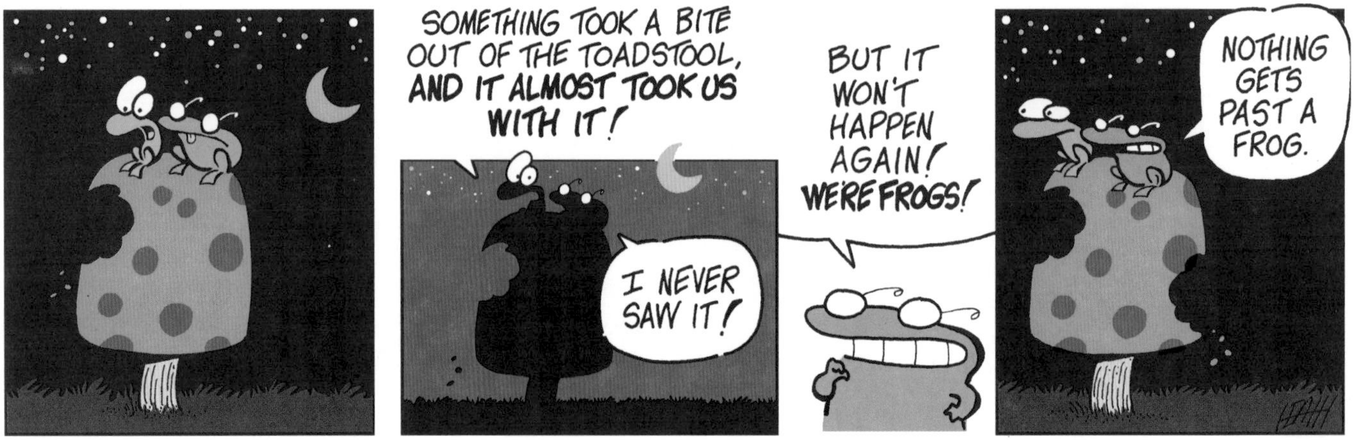
SOMETHING TOOK A BITE OUT OF THE TOADSTOOL, **AND IT ALMOST TOOK US WITH IT!**
I NEVER SAW IT!
BUT IT WON'T HAPPEN AGAIN! **WE'RE FROGS!**
NOTHING GETS PAST A FROG.

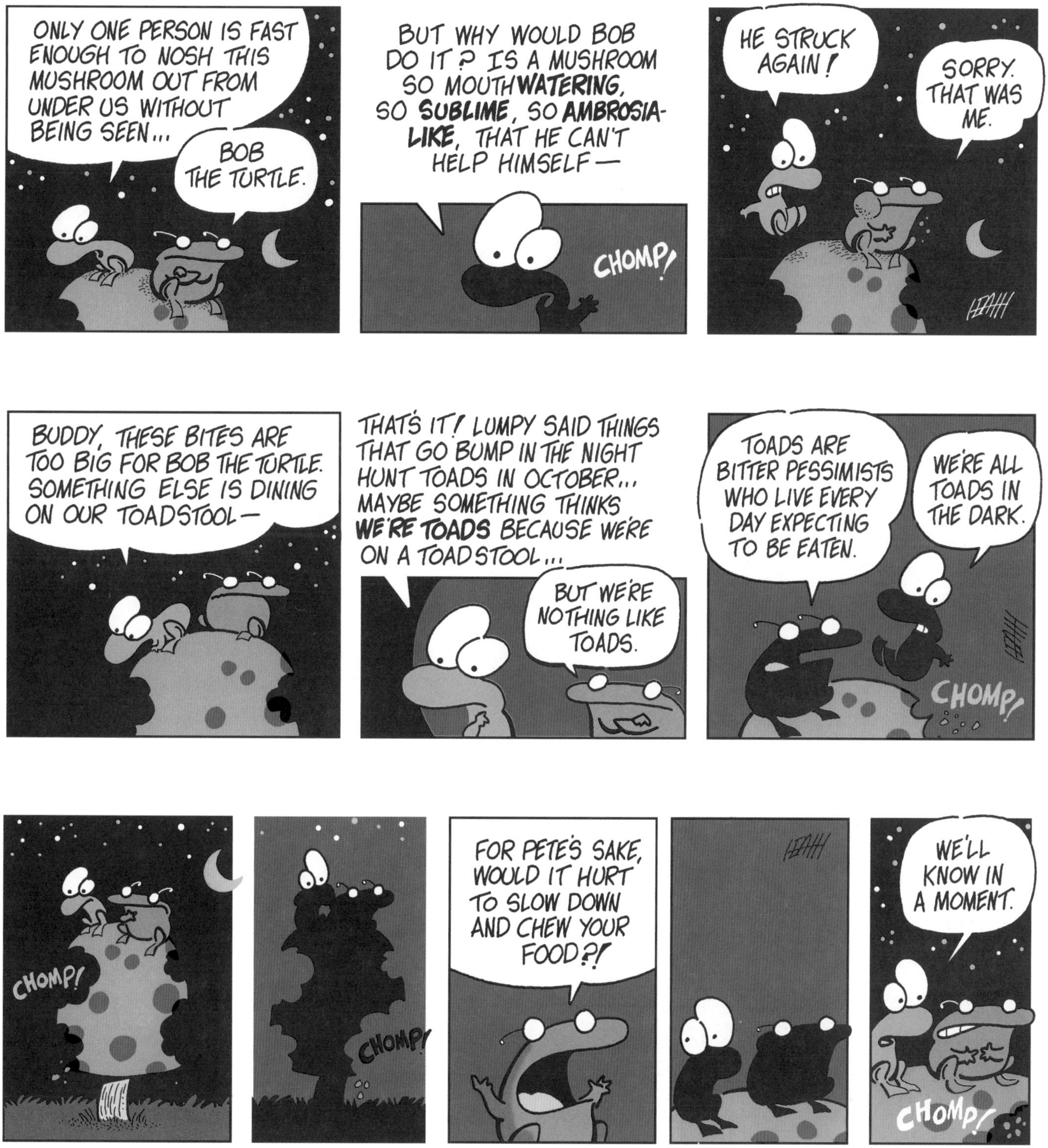
ONLY ONE PERSON IS FAST ENOUGH TO NOSH THIS MUSHROOM OUT FROM UNDER US WITHOUT BEING SEEN...
BOB THE TURTLE.
BUT WHY WOULD BOB DO IT? IS A MUSHROOM SO MOUTHWATERING, SO SUBLIME, SO AMBROSIA-LIKE, THAT HE CAN'T HELP HIMSELF—
CHOMP!
HE STRUCK AGAIN!
SORRY. THAT WAS ME.
BUDDY, THESE BITES ARE TOO BIG FOR BOB THE TURTLE. SOMETHING ELSE IS DINING ON OUR TOADSTOOL—
THAT'S IT! LUMPY SAID THINGS THAT GO BUMP IN THE NIGHT HUNT TOADS IN OCTOBER... MAYBE SOMETHING THINKS WE'RE TOADS BECAUSE WE'RE ON A TOADSTOOL...
BUT WE'RE NOTHING LIKE TOADS.
TOADS ARE BITTER PESSIMISTS WHO LIVE EVERY DAY EXPECTING TO BE EATEN.
WE'RE ALL TOADS IN THE DARK.
CHOMP!
CHOMP!
CHOMP!
FOR PETE'S SAKE, WOULD IT HURT TO SLOW DOWN AND CHEW YOUR FOOD?!
WE'LL KNOW IN A MOMENT.
CHOMP!

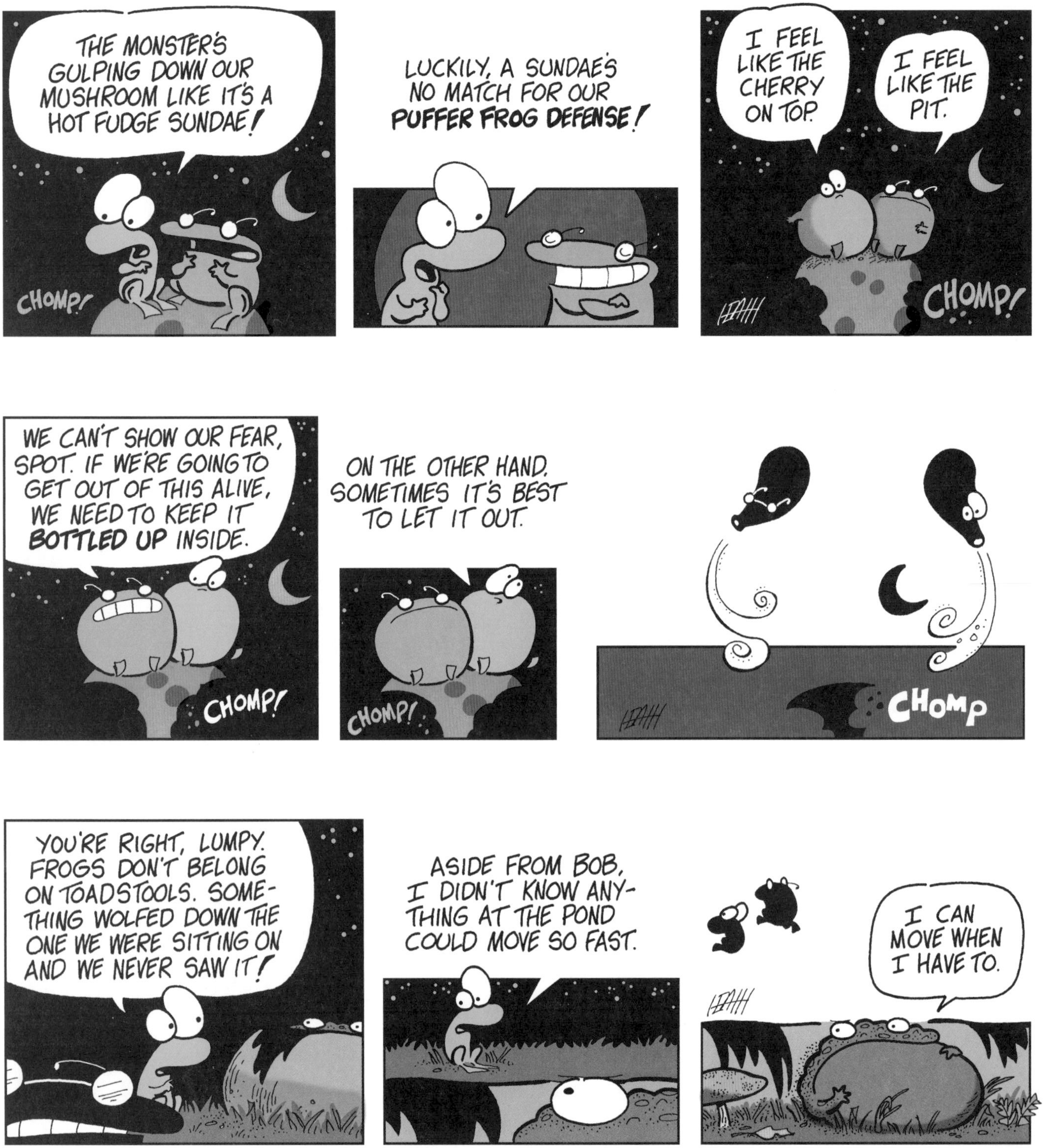

THE MONSTER'S GULPING DOWN OUR MUSHROOM LIKE IT'S A HOT FUDGE SUNDAE!
CHOMP!
LUCKILY, A SUNDAE'S NO MATCH FOR OUR **PUFFER FROG DEFENSE**!
I FEEL LIKE THE CHERRY ON TOP.
I FEEL LIKE THE PIT.
CHOMP!
WE CAN'T SHOW OUR FEAR, SPOT. IF WE'RE GOING TO GET OUT OF THIS ALIVE, WE NEED TO KEEP IT **BOTTLED UP** INSIDE.
CHOMP!
ON THE OTHER HAND. SOMETIMES IT'S BEST TO LET IT OUT.
CHOMP!
CHOMP
YOU'RE RIGHT, LUMPY. FROGS DON'T BELONG ON TOADSTOOLS. SOMETHING WOLFED DOWN THE ONE WE WERE SITTING ON AND WE NEVER SAW IT!
ASIDE FROM BOB, I DIDN'T KNOW ANYTHING AT THE POND COULD MOVE SO FAST.
I CAN MOVE WHEN I HAVE TO.

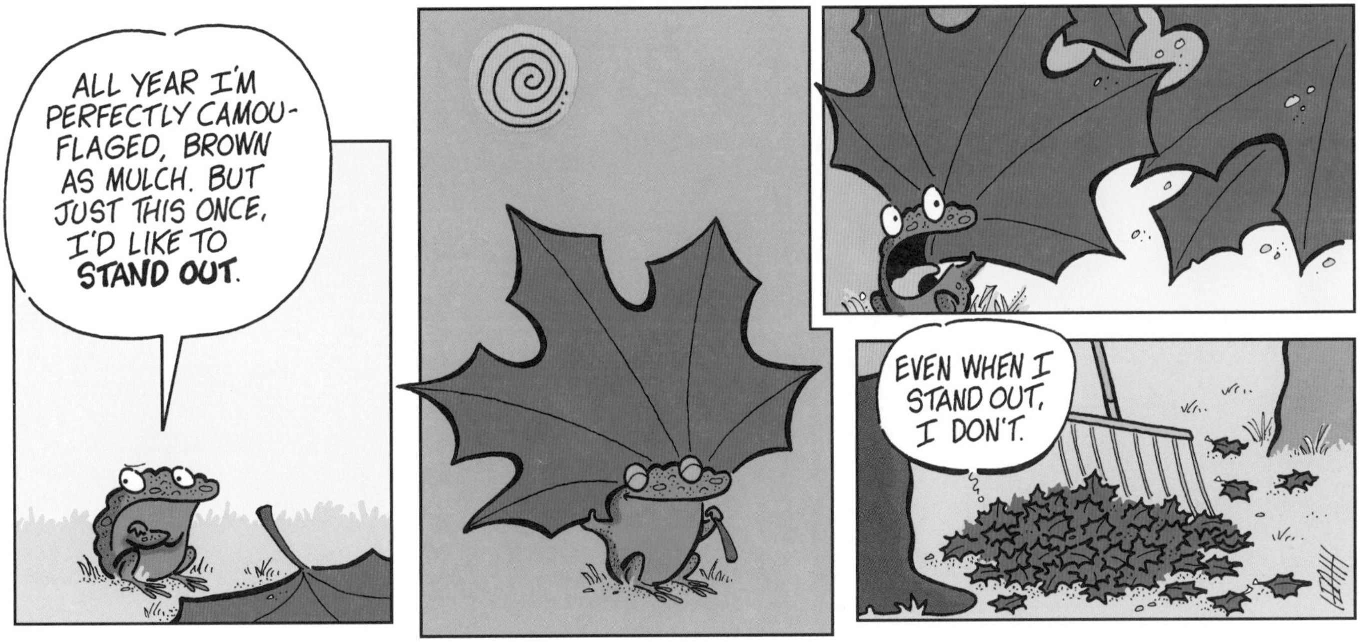
ALL YEAR I'M PERFECTLY CAMOU-FLAGED, BROWN AS MULCH. BUT JUST THIS ONCE, I'D LIKE TO **STAND OUT**.
EVEN WHEN I STAND OUT, I DON'T.

ARE YOU PULLING MY LEG? THERE'S A GUY CALLED **SPIDER-MAN**? **AND HE FIGHTS CRIME**?! INSTEAD OF HANGING AROUND AND STUFFING MY FACE, I COULD BE **STRIKING FEAR** IN THE HEARTS OF CRIMINALS?!
WOW.
DOES HE SCARE THEM BY CRAWLING OUT OF SINK DRAINS? THAT'S WHAT I'D DO.
PROBABLY. I HAVEN'T SEEN ALL THE MOVIES.

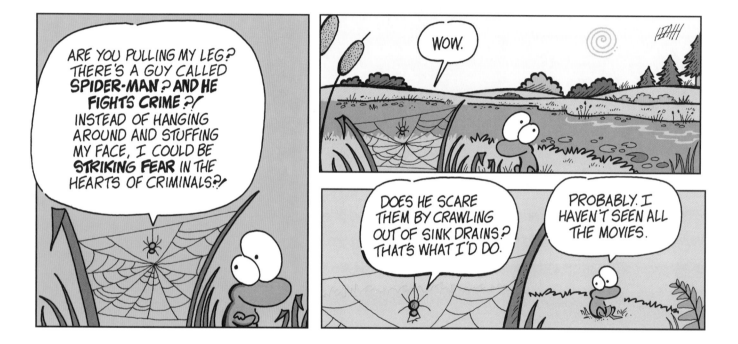

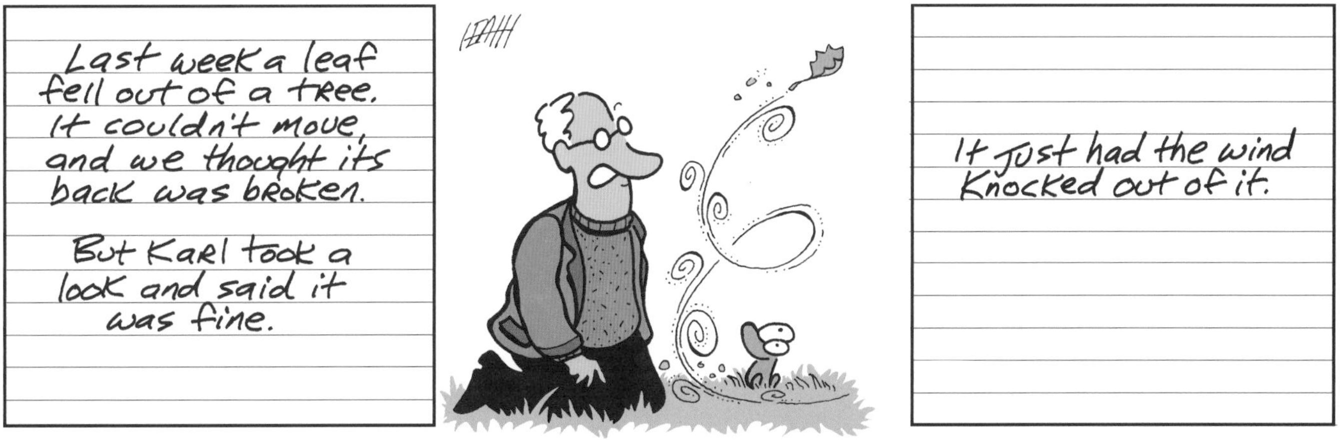
Last week a leaf fell out of a tree. It couldn't move, and we thought its back was broken.
But Karl took a look and said it was fine.
It just had the wind knocked out of it.

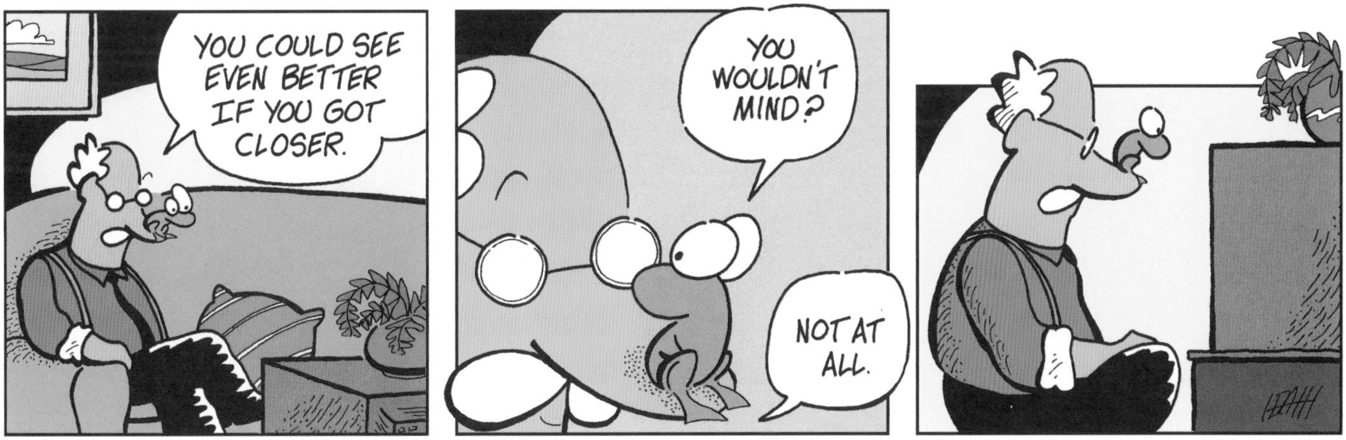
YOU COULD SEE EVEN BETTER IF YOU GOT CLOSER.
YOU WOULDN'T MIND?
NOT AT ALL.

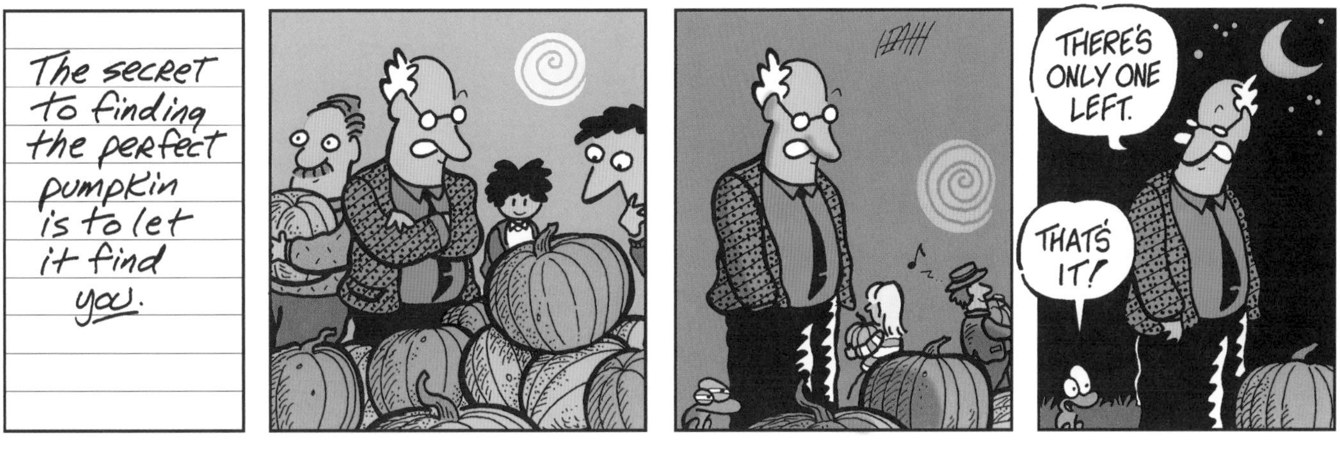
The secret to finding the perfect pumpkin is to let it find you.
THERE'S ONLY ONE LEFT.
THAT'S IT!

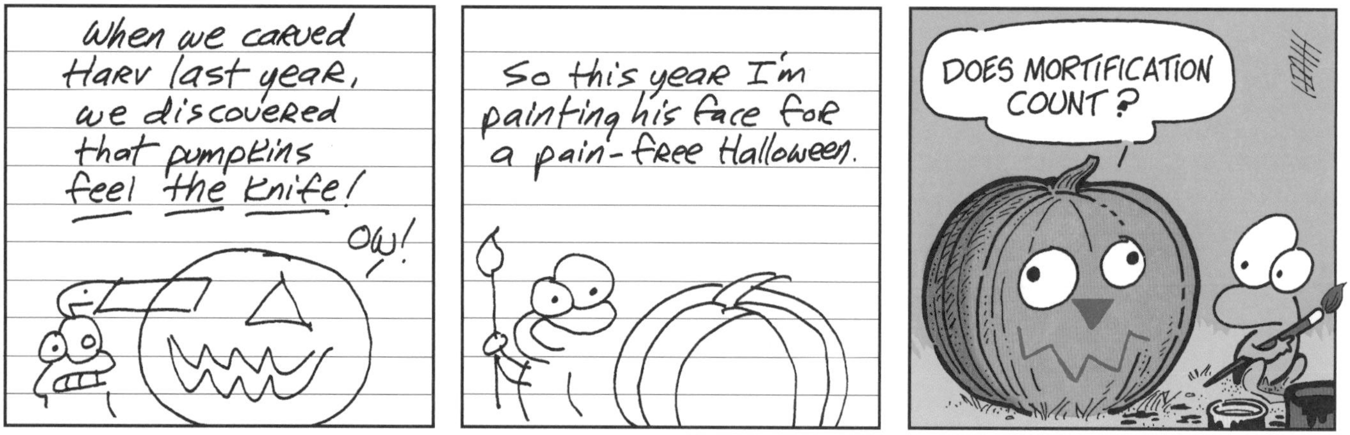
When we carved Harv last year, we discovered that pumpkins feel the knife!
OW!
So this year I'm painting his face for a pain-free Halloween.
DOES MORTIFICATION COUNT?

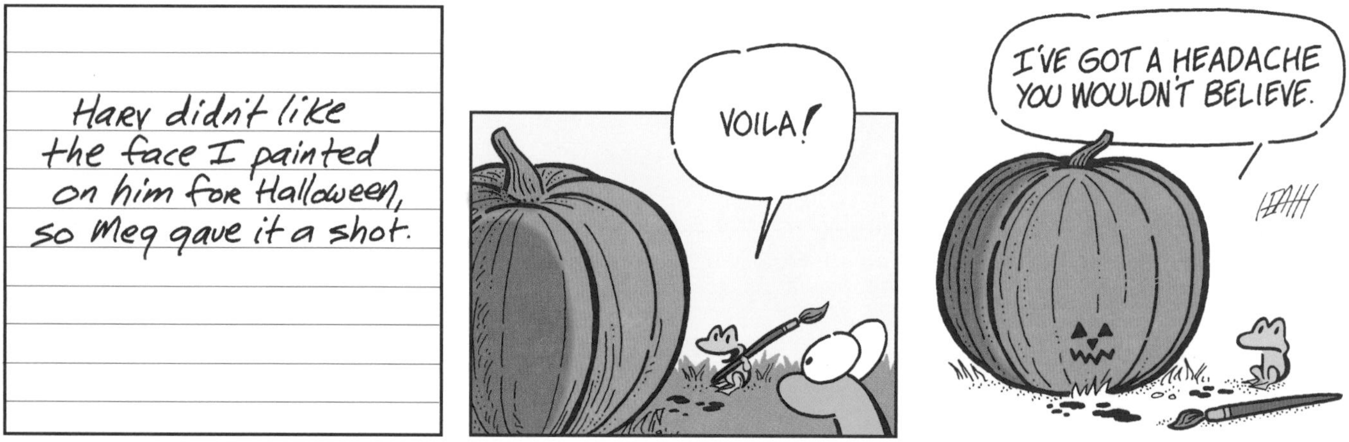
Harv didn't like the face I painted on him for Halloween, so Meg gave it a shot.
VOILA!
I'VE GOT A HEADACHE YOU WOULDN'T BELIEVE.

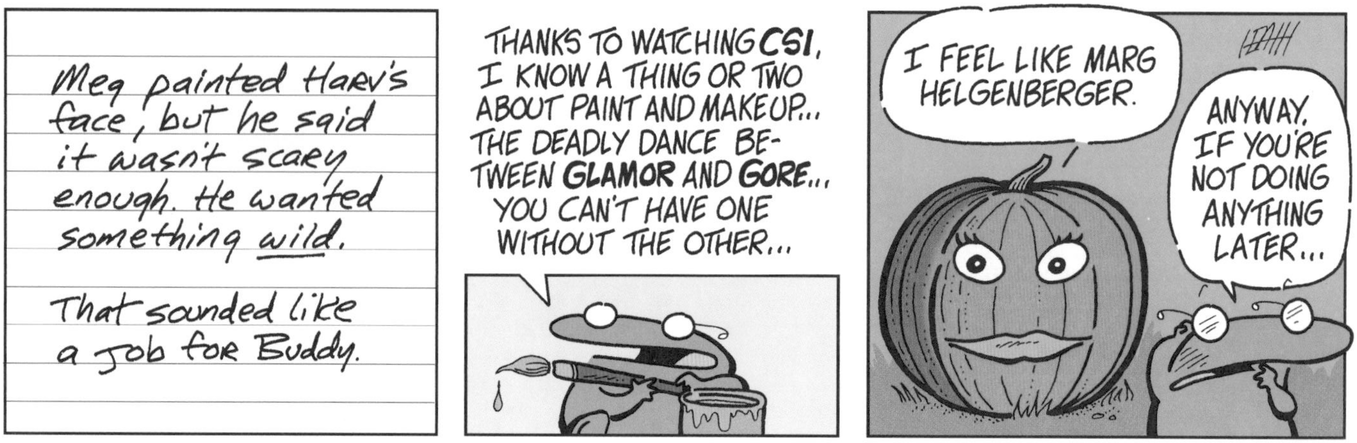
Meg painted Harv's face, but he said it wasn't scary enough. He wanted something wild.
That sounded like a job for Buddy.
THANKS TO WATCHING CSI, I KNOW A THING OR TWO ABOUT PAINT AND MAKEUP... THE DEADLY DANCE BETWEEN GLAMOR AND GORE... YOU CAN'T HAVE ONE WITHOUT THE OTHER...
I FEEL LIKE MARG HELGENBERGER.
ANYWAY, IF YOU'RE NOT DOING ANYTHING LATER...

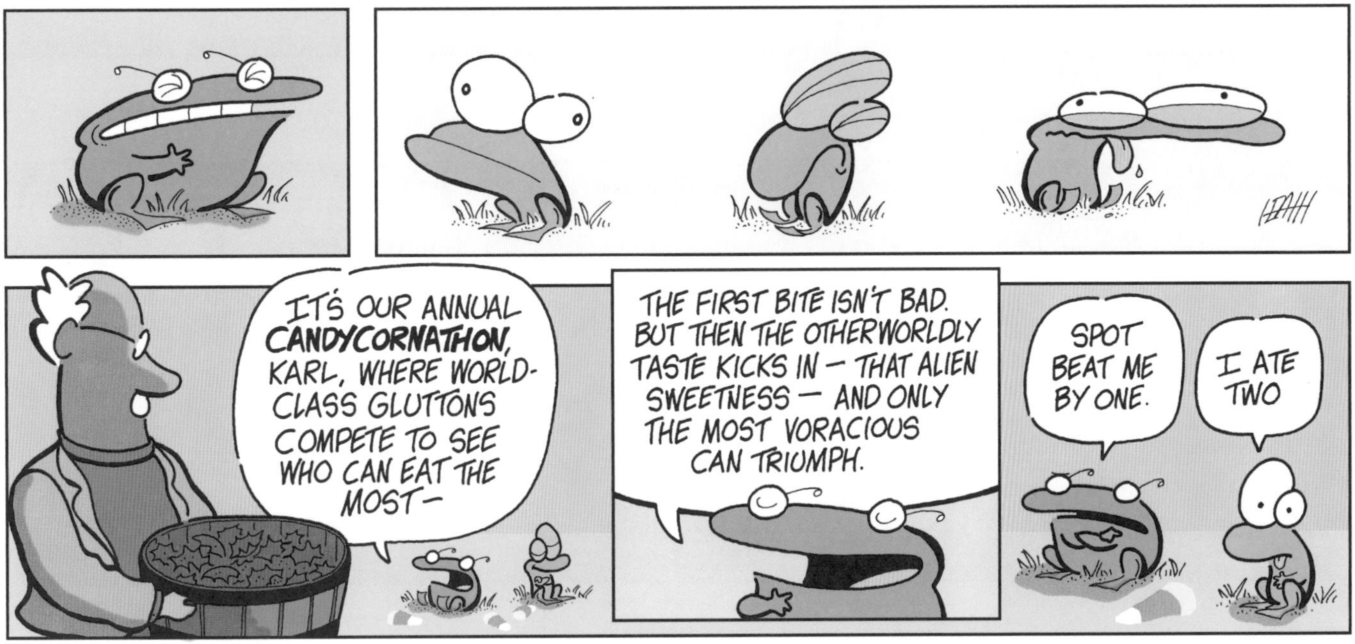
IT'S OUR ANNUAL **CANDYCORNATHON**, KARL, WHERE WORLD-CLASS GLUTTONS COMPETE TO SEE WHO CAN EAT THE MOST–
THE FIRST BITE ISN'T BAD. BUT THEN THE OTHERWORLDLY TASTE KICKS IN – THAT ALIEN SWEETNESS – AND ONLY THE MOST VORACIOUS CAN TRIUMPH.
SPOT BEAT ME BY ONE.
I ATE TWO

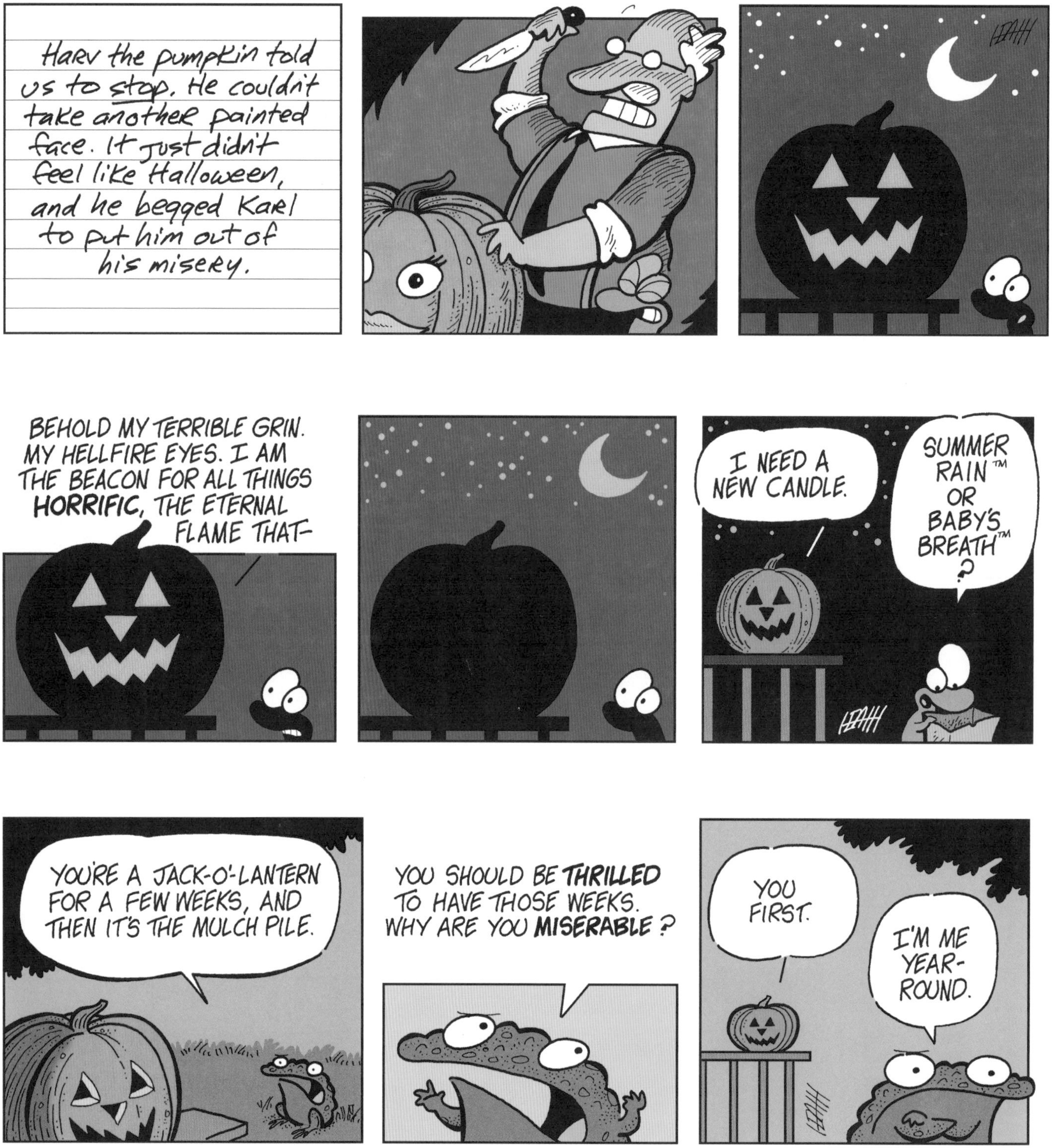
Harv the pumpkin told us to stop. He couldn't take another painted face. It just didn't feel like Halloween, and he begged Karl to put him out of his misery.
BEHOLD MY TERRIBLE GRIN. MY HELLFIRE EYES. I AM THE BEACON FOR ALL THINGS HORRIFIC, THE ETERNAL FLAME THAT-
I NEED A NEW CANDLE.
SUMMER RAIN™ OR BABY'S BREATH™?
YOU'RE A JACK-O'-LANTERN FOR A FEW WEEKS, AND THEN IT'S THE MULCH PILE.
YOU SHOULD BE THRILLED TO HAVE THOSE WEEKS. WHY ARE YOU MISERABLE?
YOU FIRST.
I'M ME YEAR-ROUND.

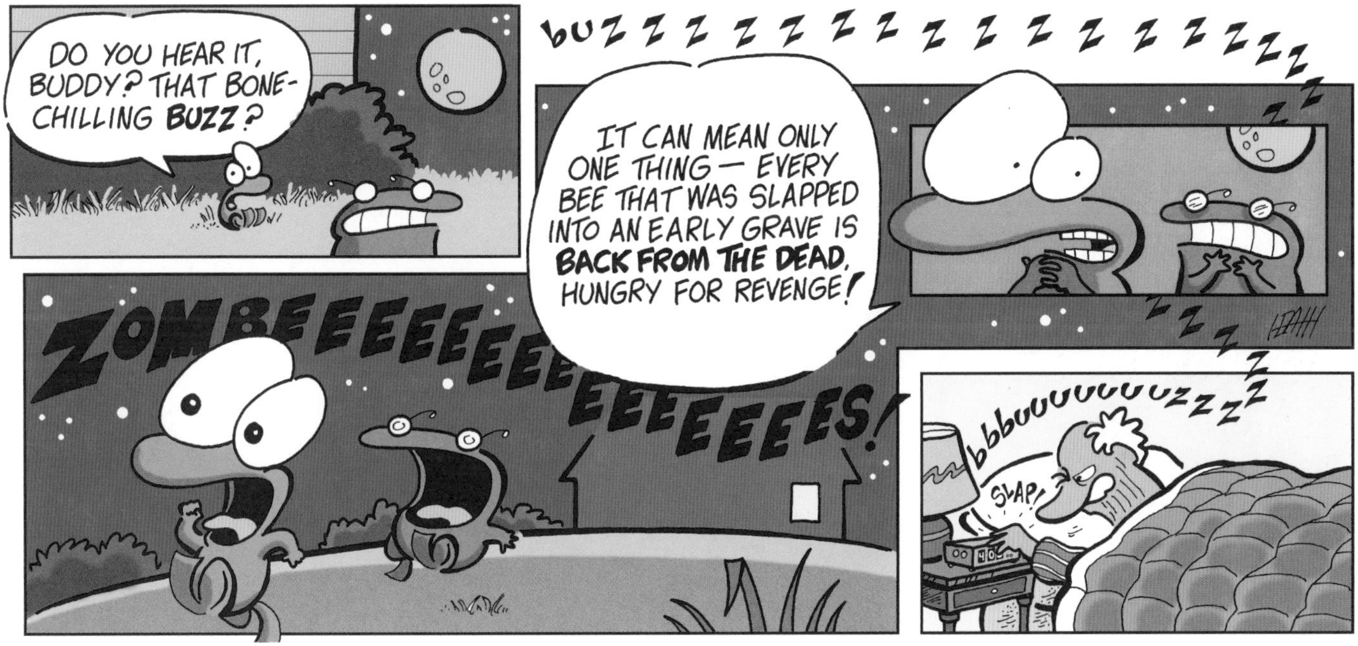
DO YOU HEAR IT, BUDDY? THAT BONE-CHILLING BUZZ?
buzzzzzzzzzzzzzzzzzzzzzz
IT CAN MEAN ONLY ONE THING— EVERY BEE THAT WAS SLAPPED INTO AN EARLY GRAVE IS BACK FROM THE DEAD, HUNGRY FOR REVENGE!
ZOMBEEEEEEEEEEEEEEEEES!
bbbuuuuuuuuzzzz
SLAP!

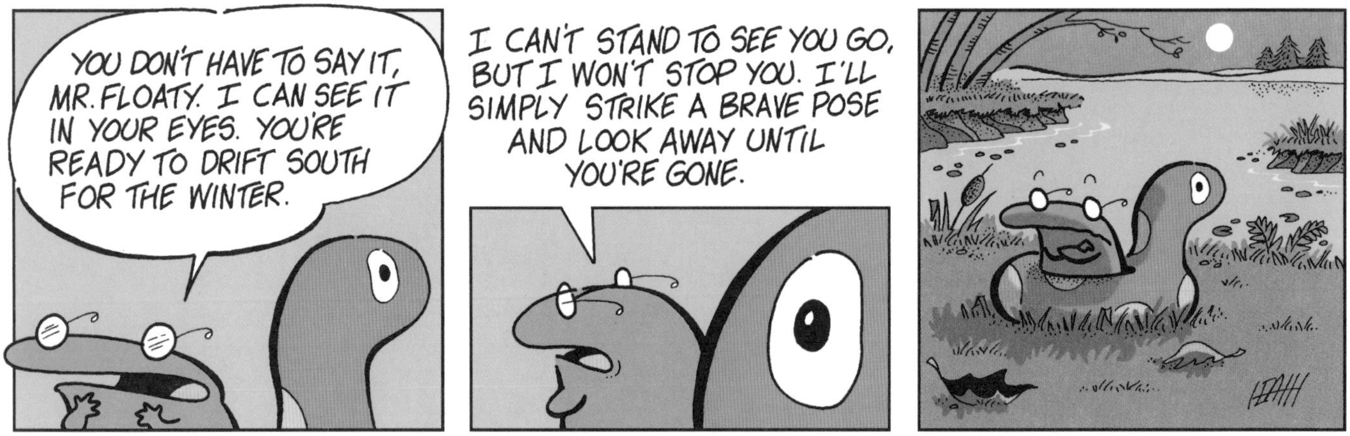
YOU DON'T HAVE TO SAY IT, MR. FLOATY. I CAN SEE IT IN YOUR EYES. YOU'RE READY TO DRIFT SOUTH FOR THE WINTER.
I CAN'T STAND TO SEE YOU GO, BUT I WON'T STOP YOU. I'LL SIMPLY STRIKE A BRAVE POSE AND LOOK AWAY UNTIL YOU'RE GONE.

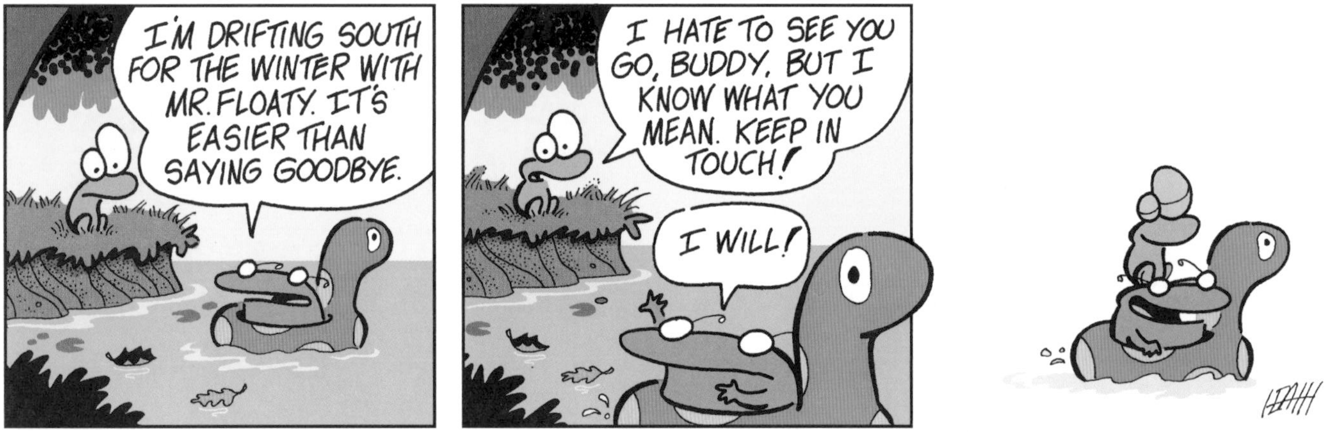
I'M DRIFTING SOUTH FOR THE WINTER WITH MR. FLOATY. IT'S EASIER THAN SAYING GOODBYE.
I HATE TO SEE YOU GO, BUDDY, BUT I KNOW WHAT YOU MEAN. KEEP IN TOUCH!
I WILL!

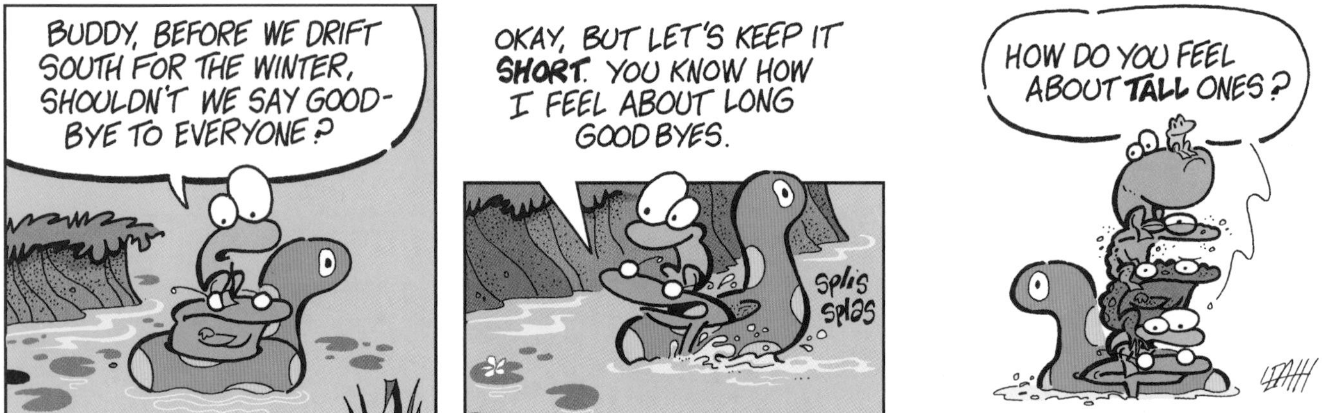
BUDDY, BEFORE WE DRIFT SOUTH FOR THE WINTER, SHOULDN'T WE SAY GOOD-BYE TO EVERYONE?
OKAY, BUT LET'S KEEP IT **SHORT**. YOU KNOW HOW I FEEL ABOUT LONG GOOD BYES.
splis
splas
HOW DO YOU FEEL ABOUT **TALL** ONES?

WE CAN'T LEAVE UNTIL WE'VE SAID GOODBYE TO EVERYONE, AND WE HAVEN'T—

ALL THESE GOODBYES ARE SLOWING US DOWN. BUT I GUESS ONE MORE CAN'T HURT...

HOLD IT, KARL—

I GET IT NOW. SOMETIMES A FRIEND SAYS GOODBYE TO A FRIEND BECAUSE ALL OF HIS FRIENDS WON'T FIT ON AN INFLATABLE TOY...

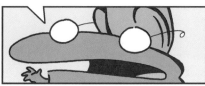

THAT'S GOOD THINKING.

IT JUST HIT ME OFF THE TOP OF YOUR HEAD.

SO LONG, MY PLASTIC FRIEND. I'LL MISS YOUR STURDY AND BUOYANT EMBRACE—

THIS CALLS FOR SOME COMFORT FOOD.

FOOD CAN **NEVER** REPLACE A HUG, KARL.

I STAND CORRECTED.

DO BAGELS FLOAT?

I CAN FEEL IT, SPOT. MY WINTER HAT'S IN THE AIR...
...FLYING HOME FROM WINNIPEG.
ARE YOU **SURE**?
A **FROG OF THE WILD** ALWAYS KNOWS. BEFORE THE SUN SETS, I'LL HAVE A HAT ON MY HEAD!

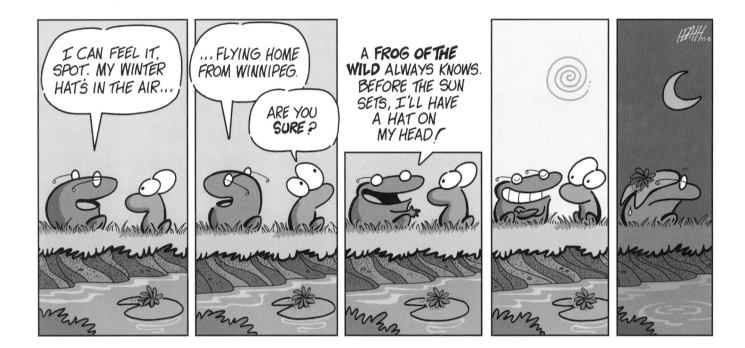

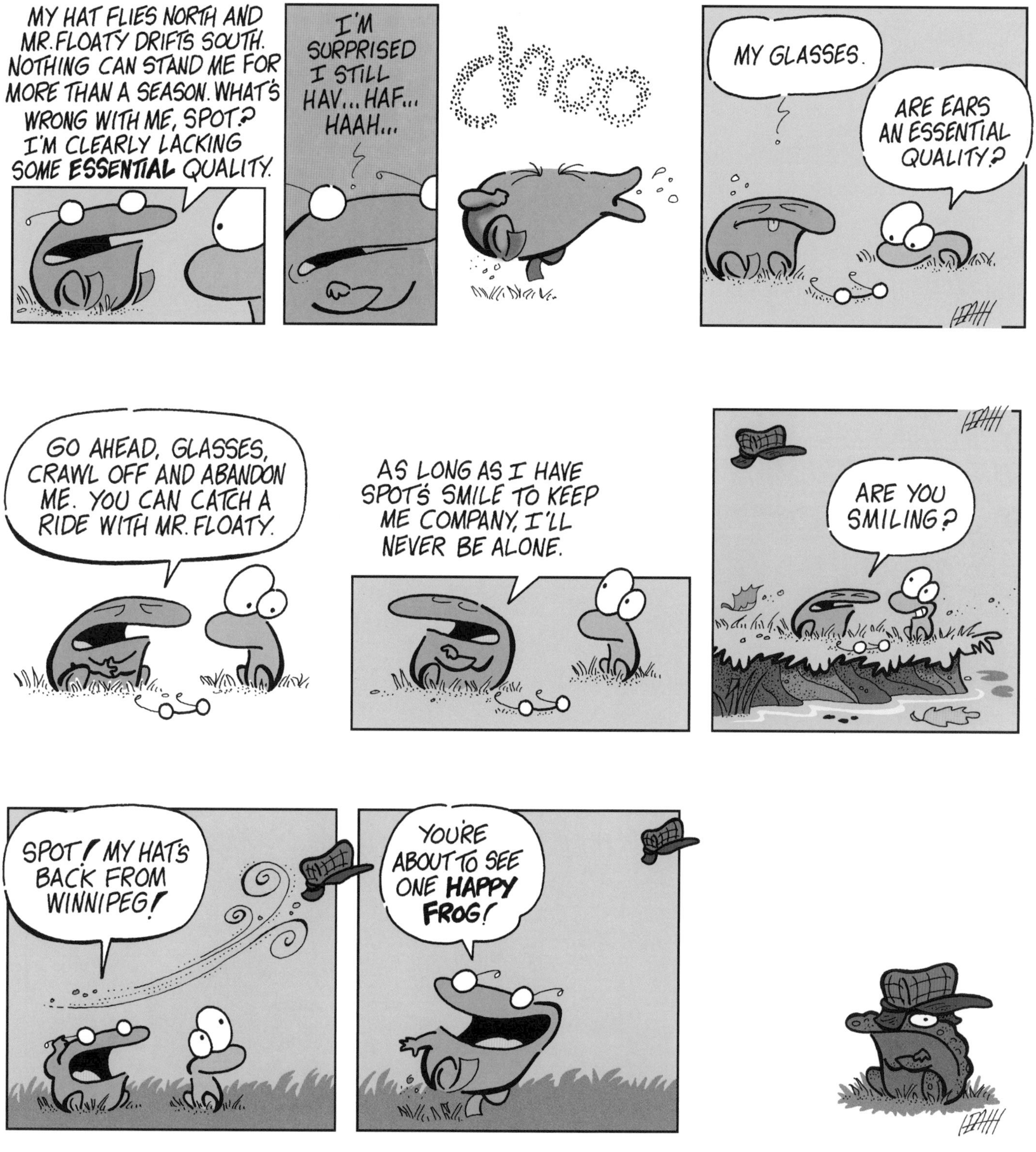
MY HAT FLIES NORTH AND MR. FLOATY DRIFTS SOUTH. NOTHING CAN STAND ME FOR MORE THAN A SEASON. WHAT'S WRONG WITH ME, SPOT? I'M CLEARLY LACKING SOME **ESSENTIAL** QUALITY.
I'M SURPRISED I STILL HAV... HAF... HAAH...
CHOO
MY GLASSES.
ARE EARS AN ESSENTIAL QUALITY?
GO AHEAD, GLASSES, CRAWL OFF AND ABANDON ME. YOU CAN CATCH A RIDE WITH MR. FLOATY.
AS LONG AS I HAVE SPOT'S SMILE TO KEEP ME COMPANY, I'LL NEVER BE ALONE.
ARE YOU SMILING?
SPOT! MY HAT'S BACK FROM WINNIPEG!
YOU'RE ABOUT TO SEE ONE **HAPPY FROG**!

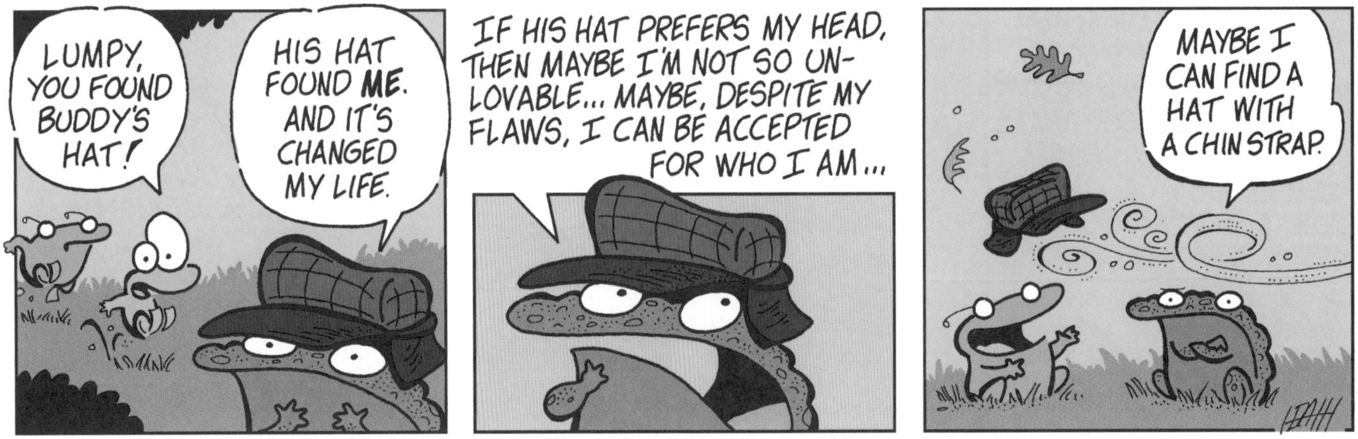
LUMPY, YOU FOUND BUDDY'S HAT!
HIS HAT FOUND **ME**. AND IT'S CHANGED MY LIFE.
IF HIS HAT PREFERS MY HEAD, THEN MAYBE I'M NOT SO UN-LOVABLE... MAYBE, DESPITE MY FLAWS, I CAN BE ACCEPTED FOR WHO I AM...
MAYBE I CAN FIND A HAT WITH A CHIN STRAP.

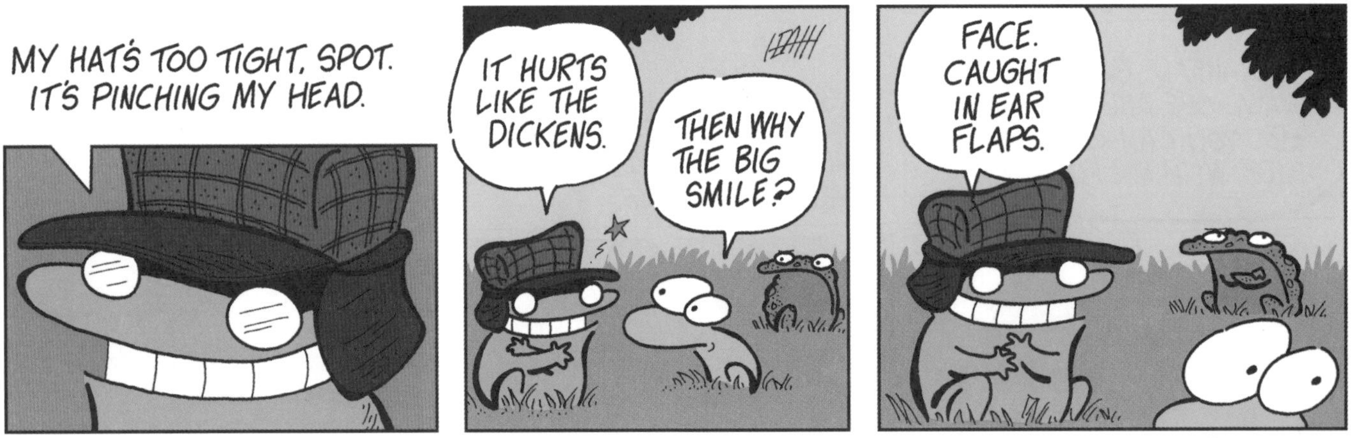
MY HAT'S TOO TIGHT, SPOT. IT'S PINCHING MY HEAD.
IT HURTS LIKE THE DICKENS.
THEN WHY THE BIG SMILE?
FACE. CAUGHT IN EAR FLAPS.

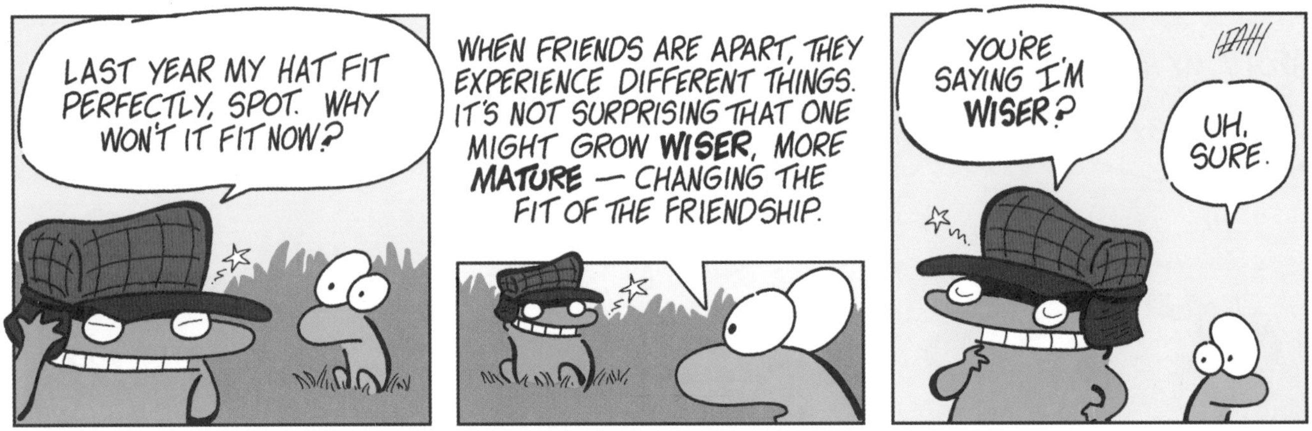
LAST YEAR MY HAT FIT PERFECTLY, SPOT. WHY WON'T IT FIT NOW?
WHEN FRIENDS ARE APART, THEY EXPERIENCE DIFFERENT THINGS. IT'S NOT SURPRISING THAT ONE MIGHT GROW **WISER**, MORE **MATURE** — CHANGING THE FIT OF THE FRIENDSHIP.
YOU'RE SAYING I'M **WISER**?
UH, SURE.

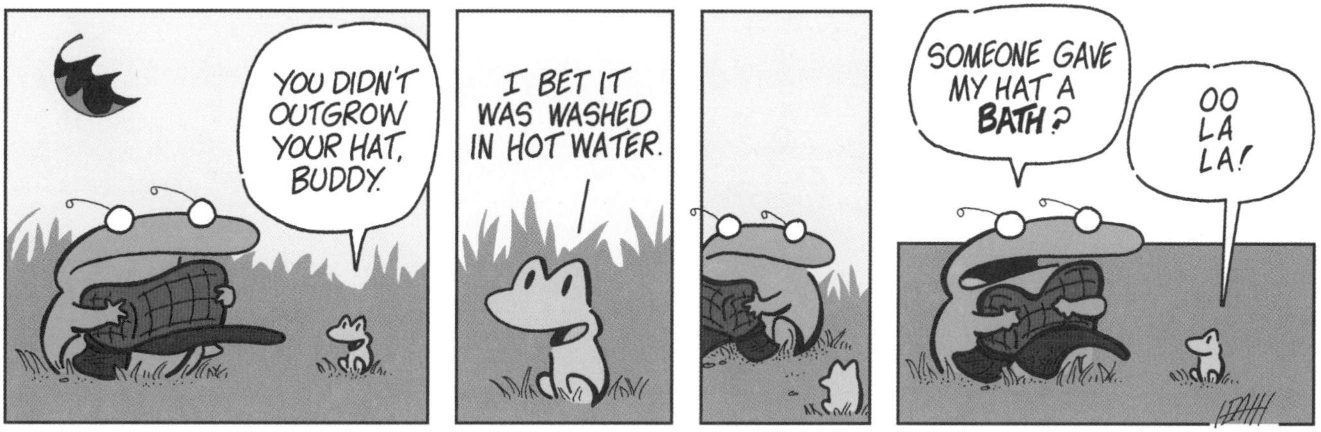
YOU DIDN'T OUTGROW YOUR HAT, BUDDY.
I BET IT WAS WASHED IN HOT WATER.
SOMEONE GAVE MY HAT A **BATH**?
OO LA LA!

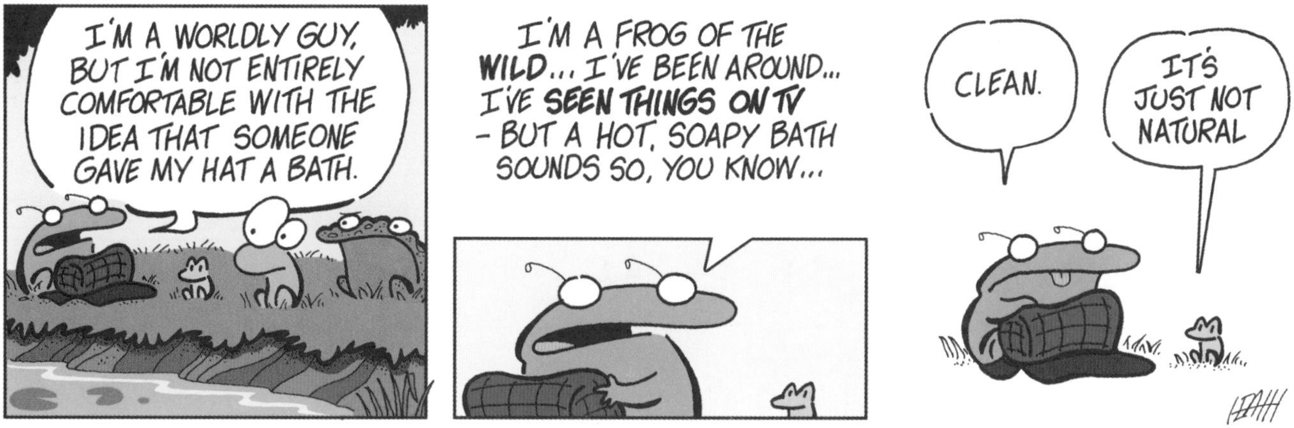
I'M A WORLDLY GUY, BUT I'M NOT ENTIRELY COMFORTABLE WITH THE IDEA THAT SOMEONE GAVE MY HAT A BATH.
I'M A FROG OF THE **WILD**... I'VE BEEN AROUND... I'VE **SEEN THINGS ON TV** - BUT A HOT, SOAPY BATH SOUNDS SO, YOU KNOW...
CLEAN.
IT'S JUST NOT NATURAL

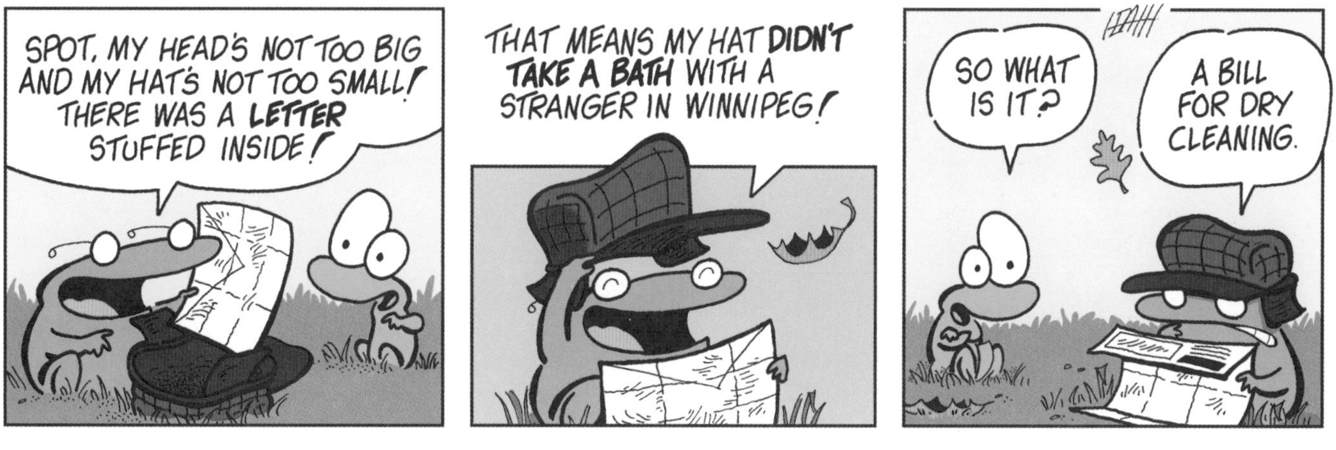
SPOT, MY HEAD'S NOT TOO BIG AND MY HAT'S NOT TOO SMALL! THERE WAS A **LETTER** STUFFED INSIDE!
THAT MEANS MY HAT **DIDN'T TAKE A BATH** WITH A STRANGER IN WINNIPEG!
SO WHAT IS IT?
A BILL FOR DRY CLEANING.

CLOUD WATCHING'S MORE AGREEABLE WHEN YOU'RE **WARM**. MAYBE IT'S TIME FOR YOUR WINTER HAT...
IT'S STILL **FALL**, KARL. WEARING MY **WINTER** HAT WOULD BE RUDE TO THE SEASON.
HOW ABOUT YOUR SLEEPING BAG?

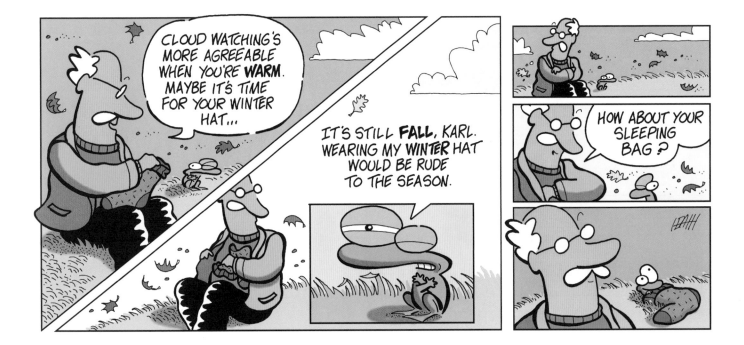

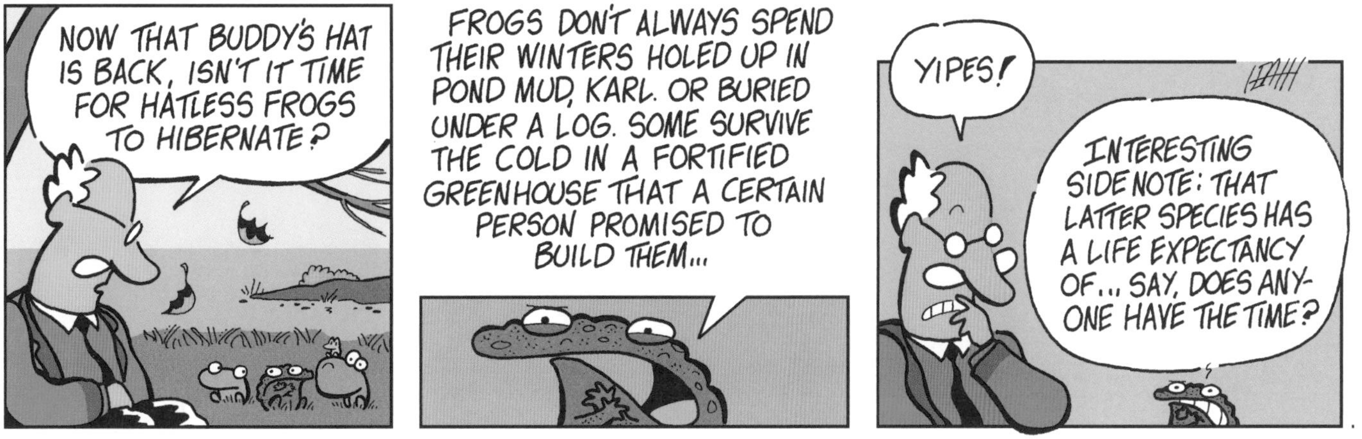
NOW THAT BUDDY'S HAT IS BACK, ISN'T IT TIME FOR HATLESS FROGS TO HIBERNATE?
FROGS DON'T ALWAYS SPEND THEIR WINTERS HOLED UP IN POND MUD, KARL. OR BURIED UNDER A LOG. SOME SURVIVE THE COLD IN A FORTIFIED GREENHOUSE THAT A CERTAIN PERSON PROMISED TO BUILD THEM...
YIPES!
INTERESTING SIDE NOTE: THAT LATTER SPECIES HAS A LIFE EXPECTANCY OF... SAY, DOES ANY-ONE HAVE THE TIME?

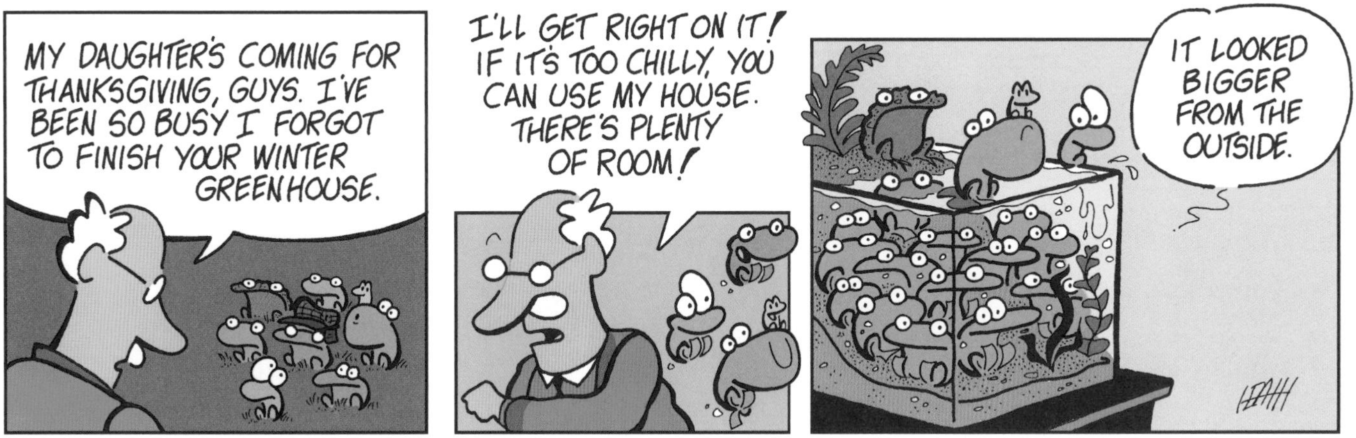
MY DAUGHTER'S COMING FOR THANKSGIVING, GUYS. I'VE BEEN SO BUSY I FORGOT TO FINISH YOUR WINTER GREENHOUSE.
I'LL GET RIGHT ON IT! IF IT'S TOO CHILLY, YOU CAN USE MY HOUSE. THERE'S PLENTY OF ROOM!
IT LOOKED BIGGER FROM THE OUTSIDE.

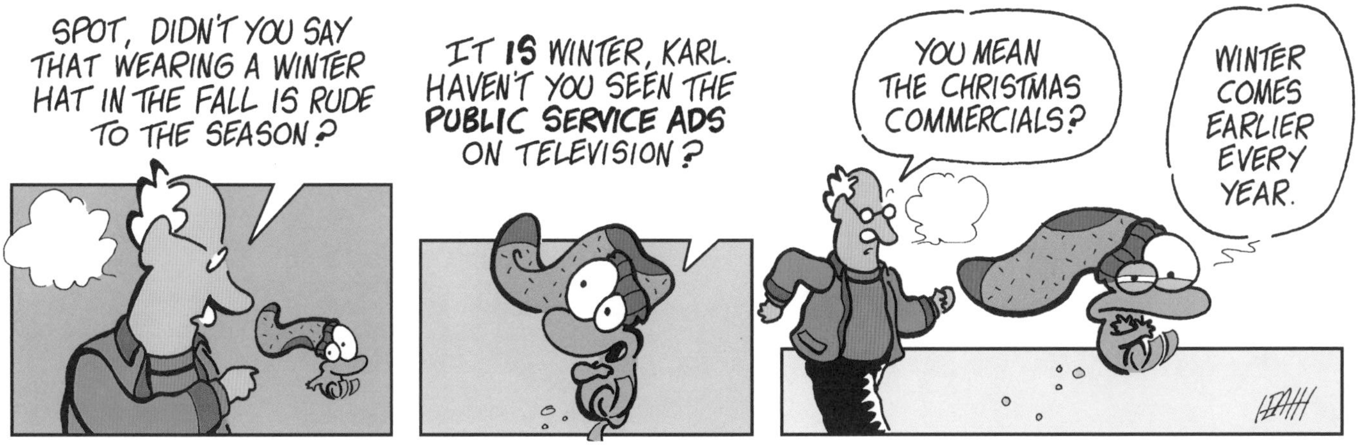
SPOT, DIDN'T YOU SAY THAT WEARING A WINTER HAT IN THE FALL IS RUDE TO THE SEASON?
IT **IS** WINTER, KARL. HAVEN'T YOU SEEN THE **PUBLIC SERVICE ADS** ON TELEVISION?
YOU MEAN THE CHRISTMAS COMMERCIALS?
WINTER COMES EARLIER EVERY YEAR.

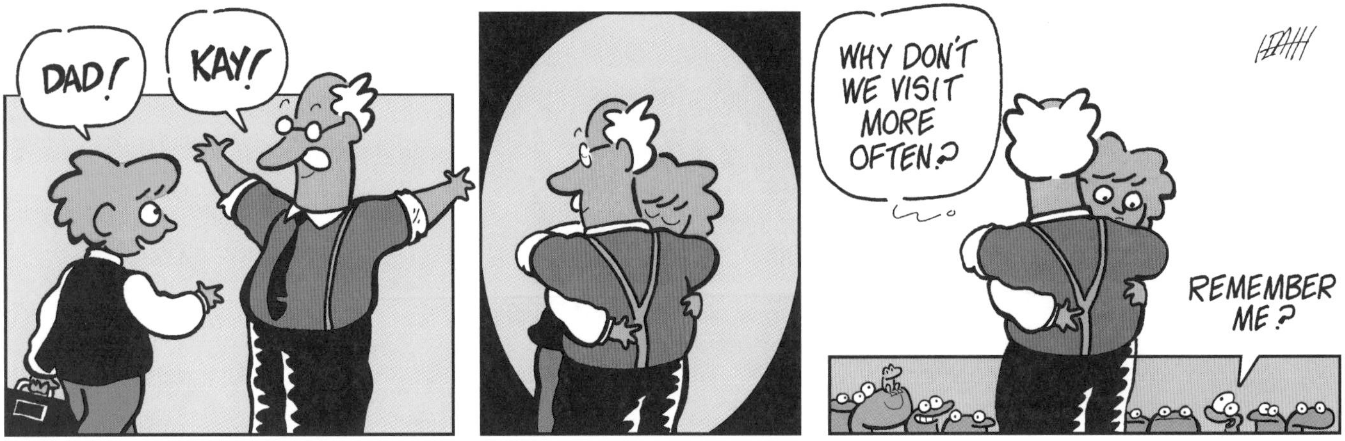
DAD!
KAY!
WHY DON'T WE VISIT MORE OFTEN?
REMEMBER ME?

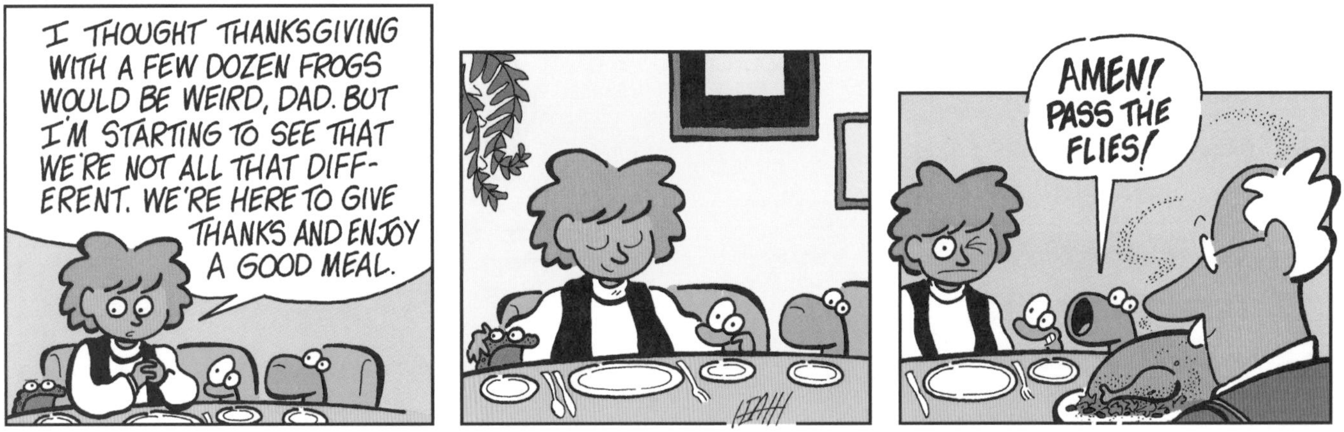
I THOUGHT THANKSGIVING WITH A FEW DOZEN FROGS WOULD BE WEIRD, DAD. BUT I'M STARTING TO SEE THAT WE'RE NOT ALL THAT DIFFERENT. WE'RE HERE TO GIVE THANKS AND ENJOY A GOOD MEAL.
AMEN! PASS THE FLIES!

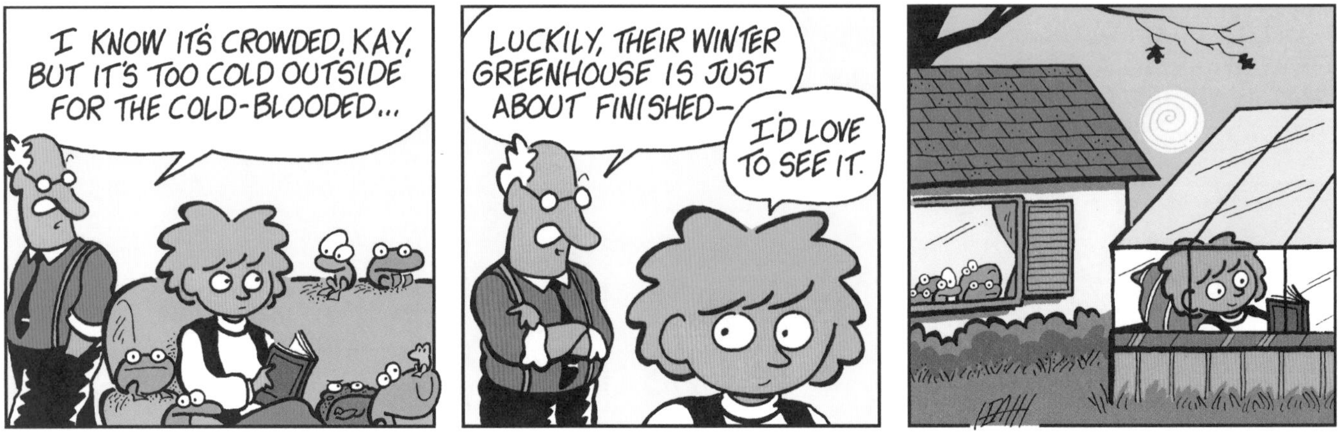
I KNOW IT'S CROWDED, KAY, BUT IT'S TOO COLD OUTSIDE FOR THE COLD-BLOODED...
LUCKILY, THEIR WINTER GREENHOUSE IS JUST ABOUT FINISHED–
I'D LOVE TO SEE IT.

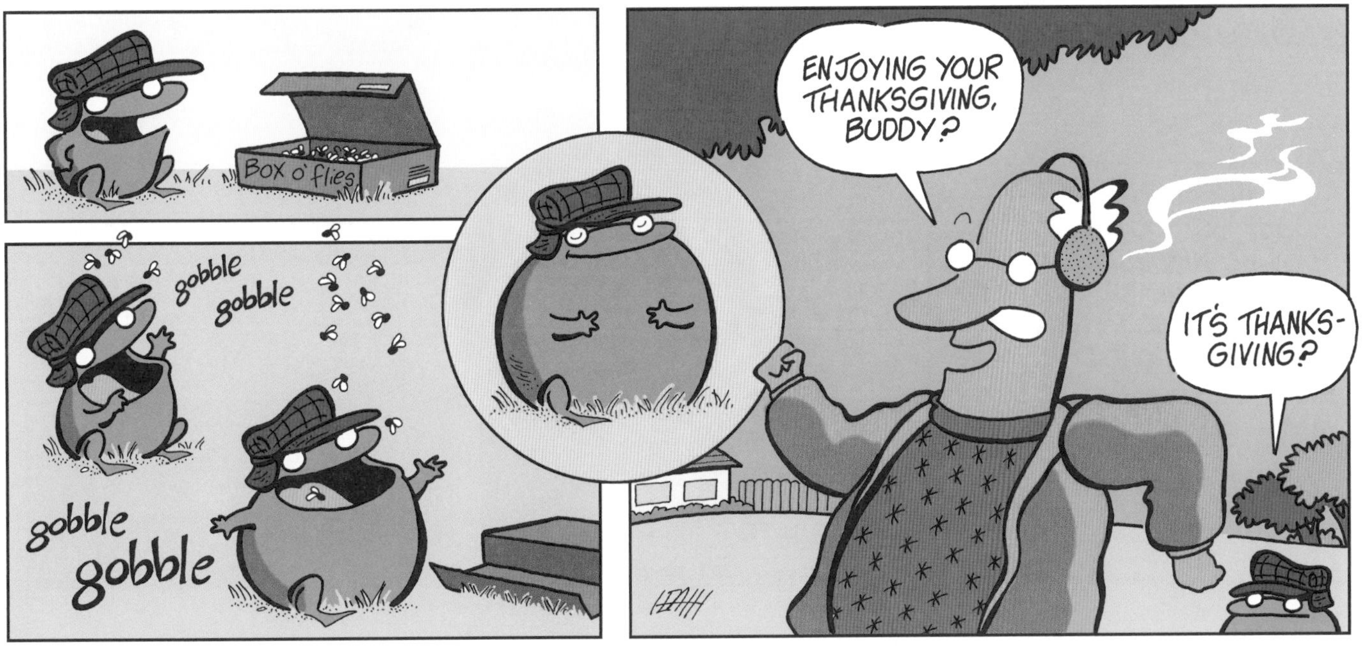
Box o' flies
gobble
gobble
gobble
gobble
ENJOYING YOUR THANKSGIVING, BUDDY?
IT'S THANKS-GIVING?

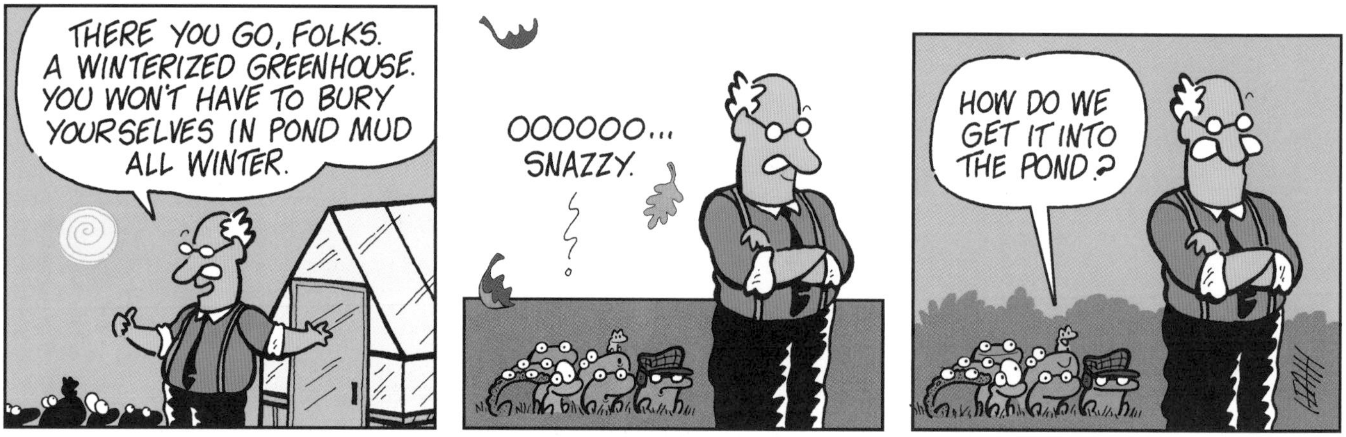
THERE YOU GO, FOLKS. A WINTERIZED GREENHOUSE. YOU WON'T HAVE TO BURY YOURSELVES IN POND MUD ALL WINTER.
OOOOOO... SNAZZY.
HOW DO WE GET IT INTO THE POND?

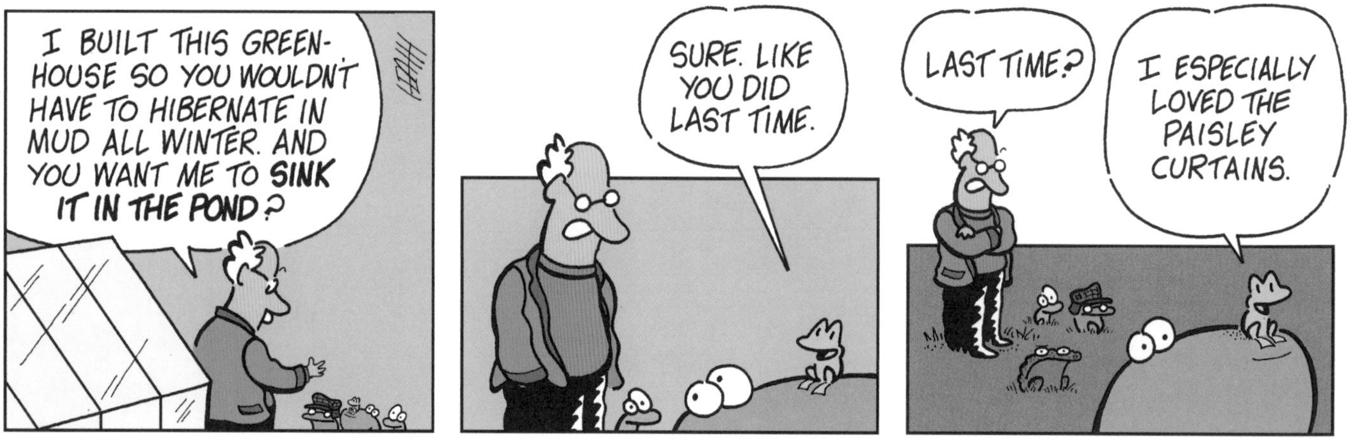
I BUILT THIS GREENHOUSE SO YOU WOULDN'T HAVE TO HIBERNATE IN MUD ALL WINTER. AND YOU WANT ME TO SINK IT IN THE POND?
SURE. LIKE YOU DID LAST TIME.
LAST TIME?
I ESPECIALLY LOVED THE PAISLEY CURTAINS.

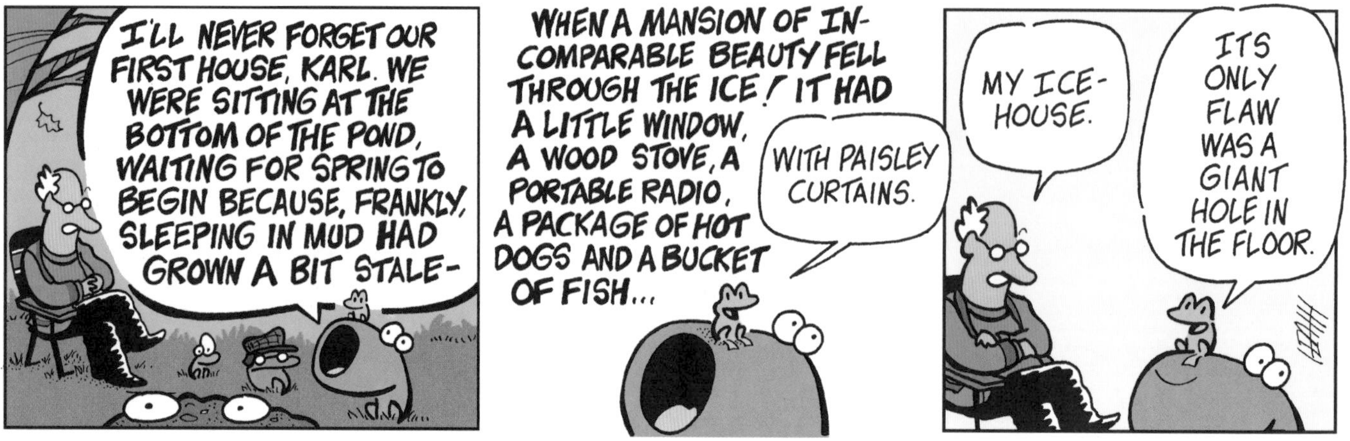
I'LL NEVER FORGET OUR FIRST HOUSE, KARL. WE WERE SITTING AT THE BOTTOM OF THE POND, WAITING FOR SPRING TO BEGIN BECAUSE, FRANKLY, SLEEPING IN MUD HAD GROWN A BIT STALE-
WHEN A MANSION OF INCOMPARABLE BEAUTY FELL THROUGH THE ICE! IT HAD A LITTLE WINDOW, A WOOD STOVE, A PORTABLE RADIO, A PACKAGE OF HOT DOGS AND A BUCKET OF FISH...
WITH PAISLEY CURTAINS.
MY ICE-HOUSE.
ITS ONLY FLAW WAS A GIANT HOLE IN THE FLOOR.

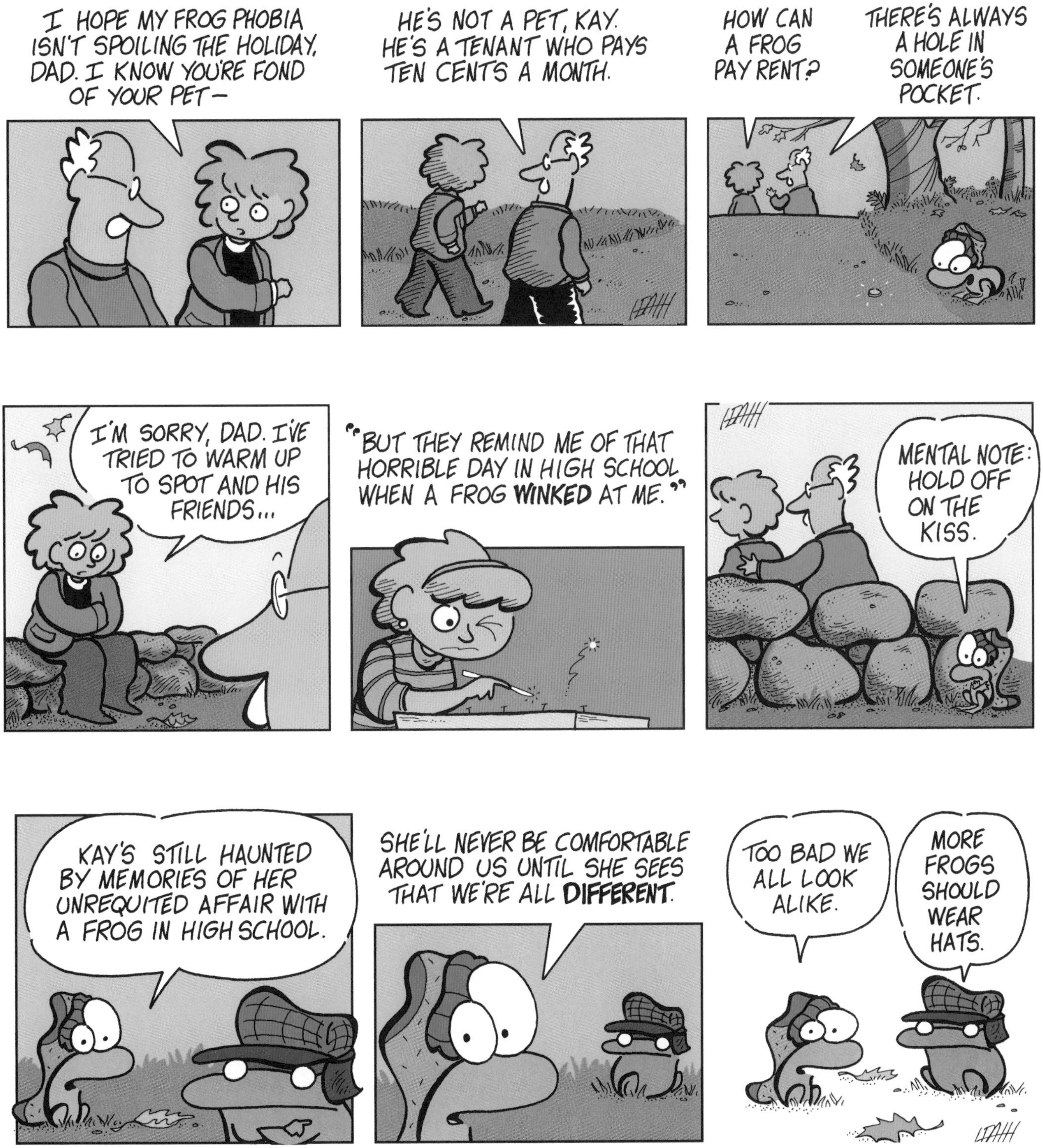
I HOPE MY FROG PHOBIA ISN'T SPOILING THE HOLIDAY, DAD. I KNOW YOU'RE FOND OF YOUR PET—
HE'S NOT A PET, KAY. HE'S A TENANT WHO PAYS TEN CENTS A MONTH.
HOW CAN A FROG PAY RENT?
THERE'S ALWAYS A HOLE IN SOMEONE'S POCKET.
I'M SORRY, DAD. I'VE TRIED TO WARM UP TO SPOT AND HIS FRIENDS...
"BUT THEY REMIND ME OF THAT HORRIBLE DAY IN HIGH SCHOOL WHEN A FROG **WINKED** AT ME."
MENTAL NOTE: HOLD OFF ON THE KISS.
KAY'S STILL HAUNTED BY MEMORIES OF HER UNREQUITED AFFAIR WITH A FROG IN HIGH SCHOOL.
SHE'LL NEVER BE COMFORTABLE AROUND US UNTIL SHE SEES THAT WE'RE ALL **DIFFERENT**.
TOO BAD WE ALL LOOK ALIKE.
MORE FROGS SHOULD WEAR HATS.

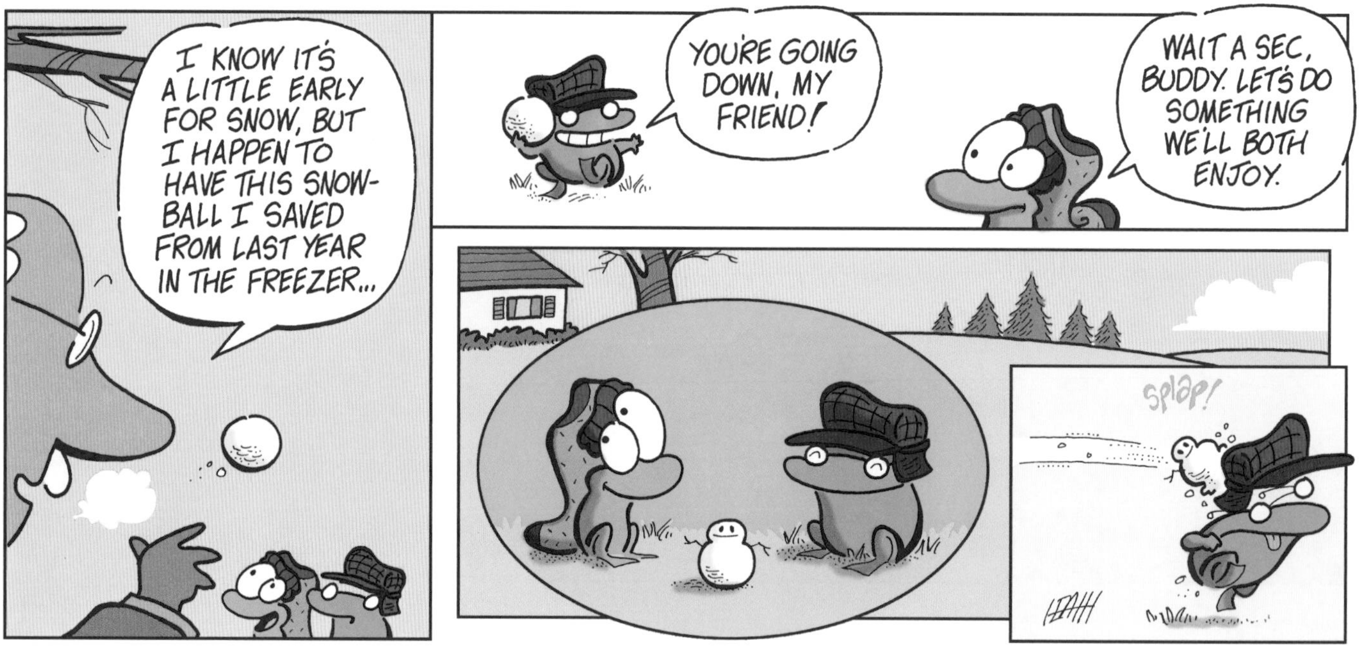
I KNOW IT'S A LITTLE EARLY FOR SNOW, BUT I HAPPEN TO HAVE THIS SNOW-BALL I SAVED FROM LAST YEAR IN THE FREEZER...
YOU'RE GOING DOWN, MY FRIEND!
WAIT A SEC, BUDDY. LET'S DO SOMETHING WE'LL BOTH ENJOY.
splap!

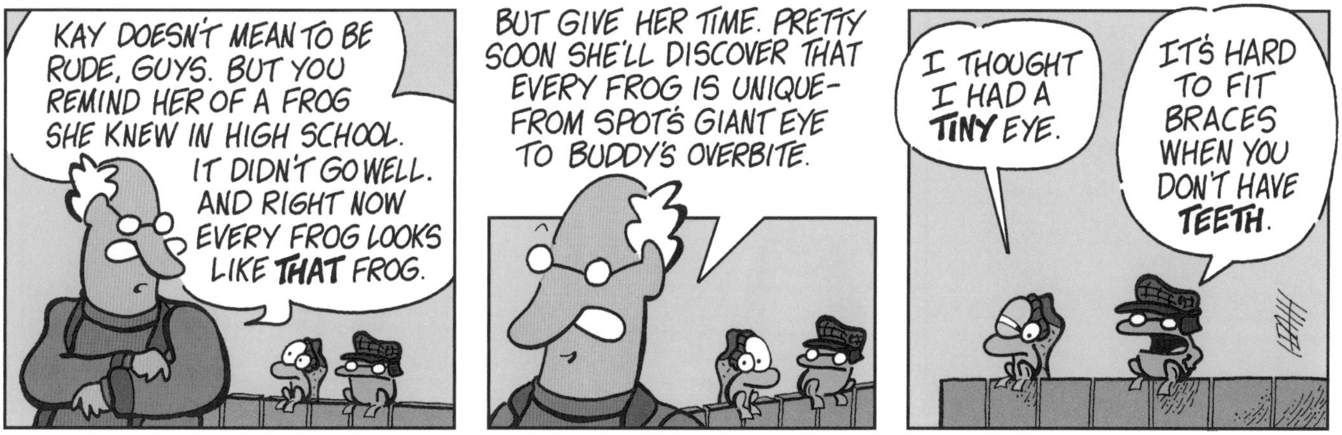
KAY DOESN'T MEAN TO BE RUDE, GUYS. BUT YOU REMIND HER OF A FROG SHE KNEW IN HIGH SCHOOL.
IT DIDN'T GO WELL. AND RIGHT NOW EVERY FROG LOOKS LIKE **THAT** FROG.
BUT GIVE HER TIME. PRETTY SOON SHE'LL DISCOVER THAT EVERY FROG IS UNIQUE- FROM SPOT'S GIANT EYE TO BUDDY'S OVERBITE.
I THOUGHT I HAD A **TINY** EYE.
IT'S HARD TO FIT BRACES WHEN YOU DON'T HAVE **TEETH**.

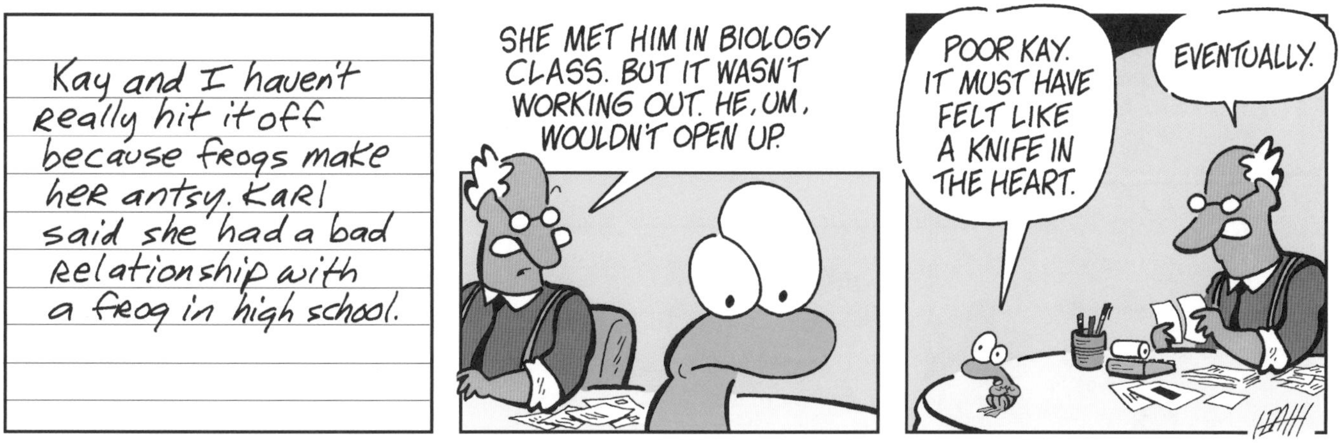
Kay and I haven't really hit it off because frogs make her antsy. Karl said she had a bad relationship with a frog in high school.
SHE MET HIM IN BIOLOGY CLASS. BUT IT WASN'T WORKING OUT. HE, UM, WOULDN'T OPEN UP.
POOR KAY. IT MUST HAVE FELT LIKE A KNIFE IN THE HEART.
EVENTUALLY.

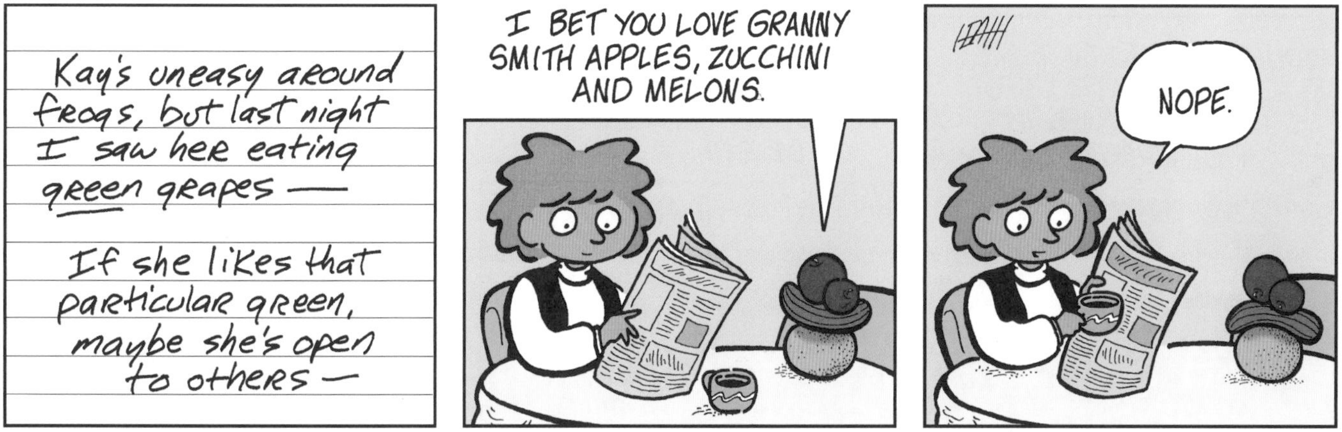
Kay's uneasy around frogs, but last night I saw her eating green grapes —
If she likes that particular green, maybe she's open to others —
I BET YOU LOVE GRANNY SMITH APPLES, ZUCCHINI AND MELONS.
NOPE.

I just had a brain-storm. I'll remind Kay that frogs are as green and life-affirming as plants.

Everyone loves plants.

I'M STYMIED, BUDDY. HOW CAN I SHOW KAY THAT FROGS ARE JUST AS HUMAN AS ANYONE ELSE?

ACCORDING TO TV, HUMANS SIMULTANEOUSLY YEARN TO BE UNIQUE AND **NOT** UNIQUE. TO STAND OUT IN A CROWD **WITHOUT** STANDING OUT...

YOU'RE SAYING I SHOULD GET TATTOOED?

OR CLONED. WHATEVER'S HIP WITH THE KIDS THESE DAYS.

YOU'VE COME TO THE RIGHT PLACE FOR A TATTOO, SPOT. I HAVE THE EQUIPMENT RIGHT HERE —

I HAVE DELICATE SKIN. T-ZONES. I THINK I'M AN AUTUMN. DO YOU HAVE SOMETHING TO EASE THE STING?

ABSOLUTELY. JUST BREATHE THE FUMES AND YOU WON'T FEEL A THING...

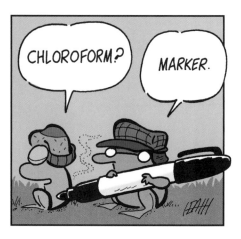

CHLOROFORM?

MARKER.

WHEN I SPENT MY WINTERS BURIED IN MUD AT THE BOTTOM OF THE POND, I'D DREAM OF GETTING THE BIGGEST CHRISTMAS TREE... BUT MY DREAM WAS TOO BIG FOR MY HOME.
SO NOW YOU LIVE HIGH AND DRY WITH PLENTY OF SPACE.
WHAT'S IT LIKE?
SKRIiiiiiiTCHHH
ABOUT THE SAME.

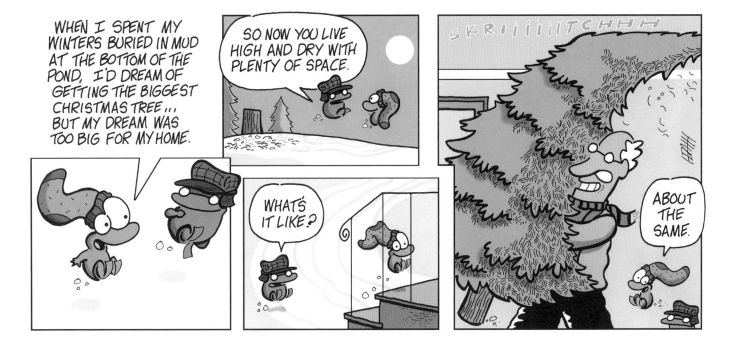

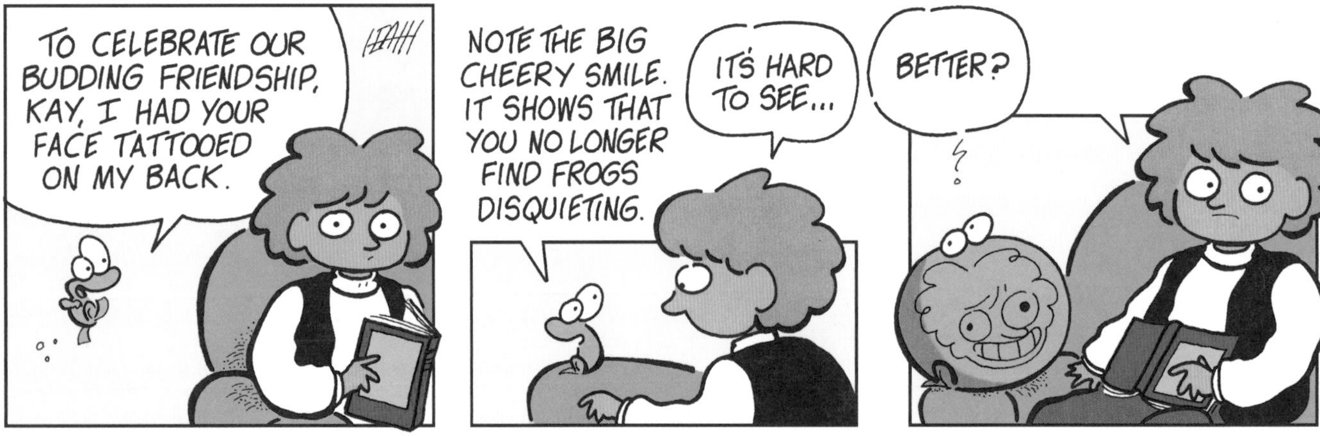
TO CELEBRATE OUR BUDDING FRIENDSHIP, KAY, I HAD YOUR FACE TATTOOED ON MY BACK.
NOTE THE BIG CHEERY SMILE. IT SHOWS THAT YOU NO LONGER FIND FROGS DISQUIETING.
IT'S HARD TO SEE...
BETTER?

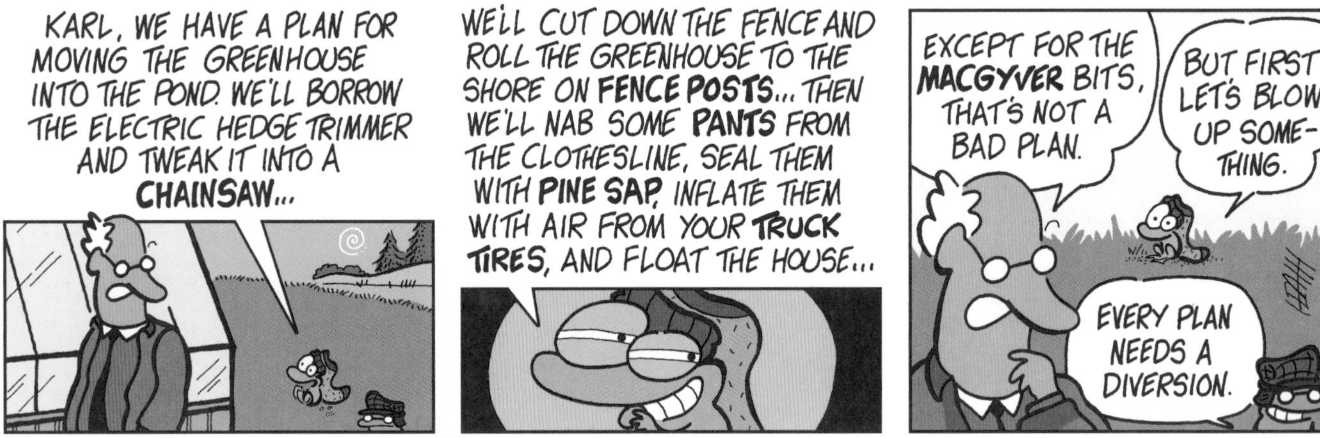
KARL, WE HAVE A PLAN FOR MOVING THE GREENHOUSE INTO THE POND. WE'LL BORROW THE ELECTRIC HEDGE TRIMMER AND TWEAK IT INTO A **CHAINSAW**...
WE'LL CUT DOWN THE FENCE AND ROLL THE GREENHOUSE TO THE SHORE ON **FENCE POSTS**... THEN WE'LL NAB SOME **PANTS** FROM THE CLOTHESLINE, SEAL THEM WITH **PINE SAP**, INFLATE THEM WITH AIR FROM YOUR **TRUCK TIRES**, AND FLOAT THE HOUSE...
EXCEPT FOR THE **MACGYVER** BITS, THAT'S NOT A BAD PLAN.
BUT FIRST LET'S BLOW UP SOME-THING.
EVERY PLAN NEEDS A DIVERSION.

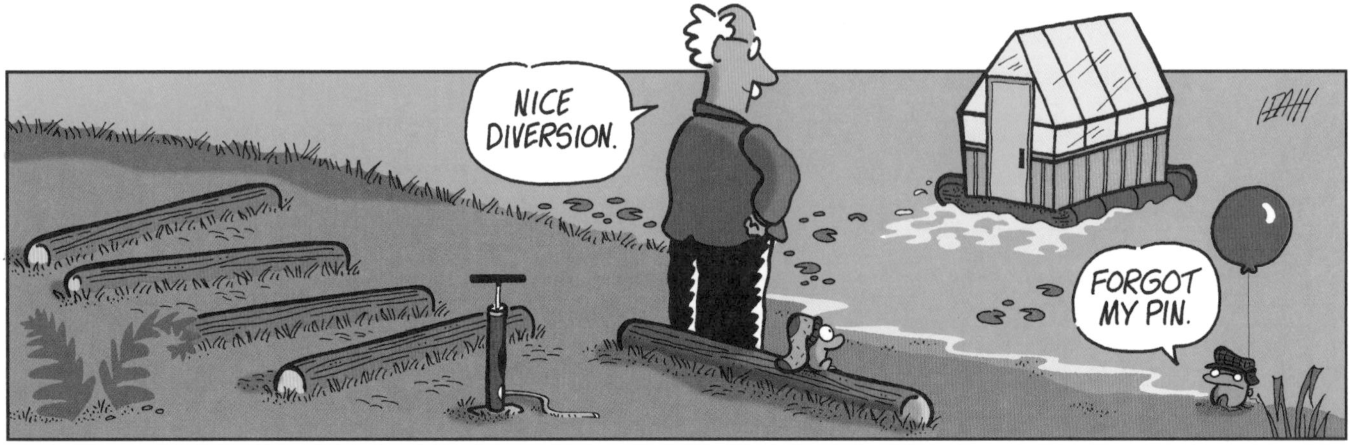
NICE DIVERSION.
FORGOT MY PIN.

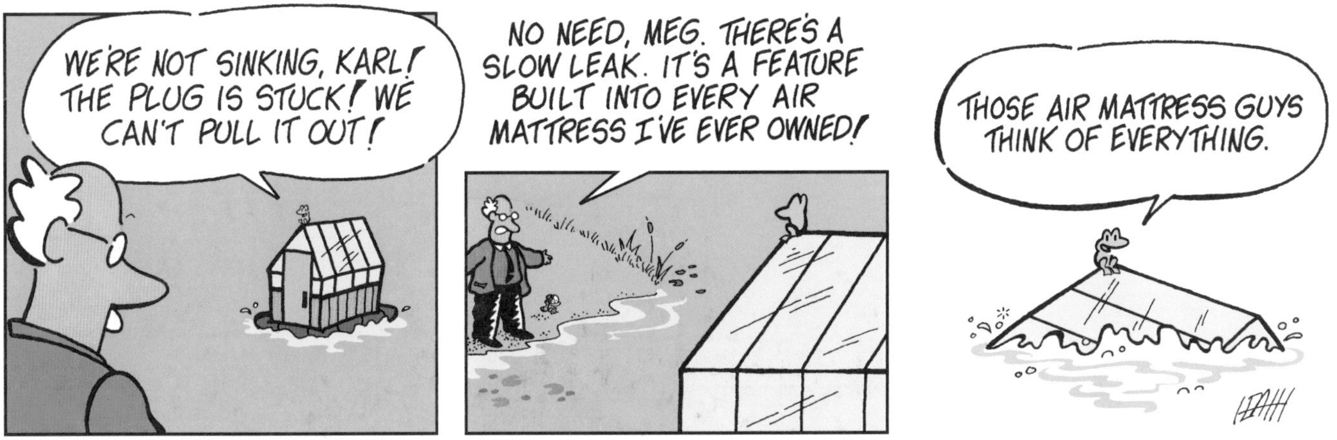
WE'RE NOT SINKING, KARL! THE PLUG IS STUCK! WE CAN'T PULL IT OUT!
NO NEED, MEG. THERE'S A SLOW LEAK. IT'S A FEATURE BUILT INTO EVERY AIR MATTRESS I'VE EVER OWNED!
THOSE AIR MATTRESS GUYS THINK OF EVERYTHING.

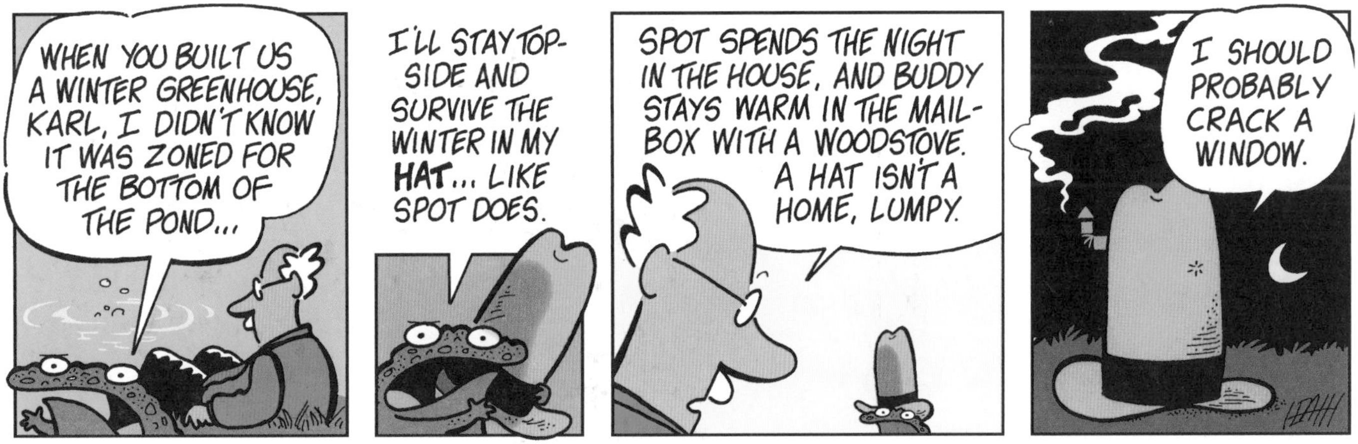
WHEN YOU BUILT US A WINTER GREENHOUSE, KARL, I DIDN'T KNOW IT WAS ZONED FOR THE BOTTOM OF THE POND...
I'LL STAY TOP-SIDE AND SURVIVE THE WINTER IN MY **HAT**... LIKE SPOT DOES.
SPOT SPENDS THE NIGHT IN THE HOUSE, AND BUDDY STAYS WARM IN THE MAIL-BOX WITH A WOODSTOVE.
A HAT ISN'T A HOME, LUMPY.
I SHOULD PROBABLY CRACK A WINDOW.

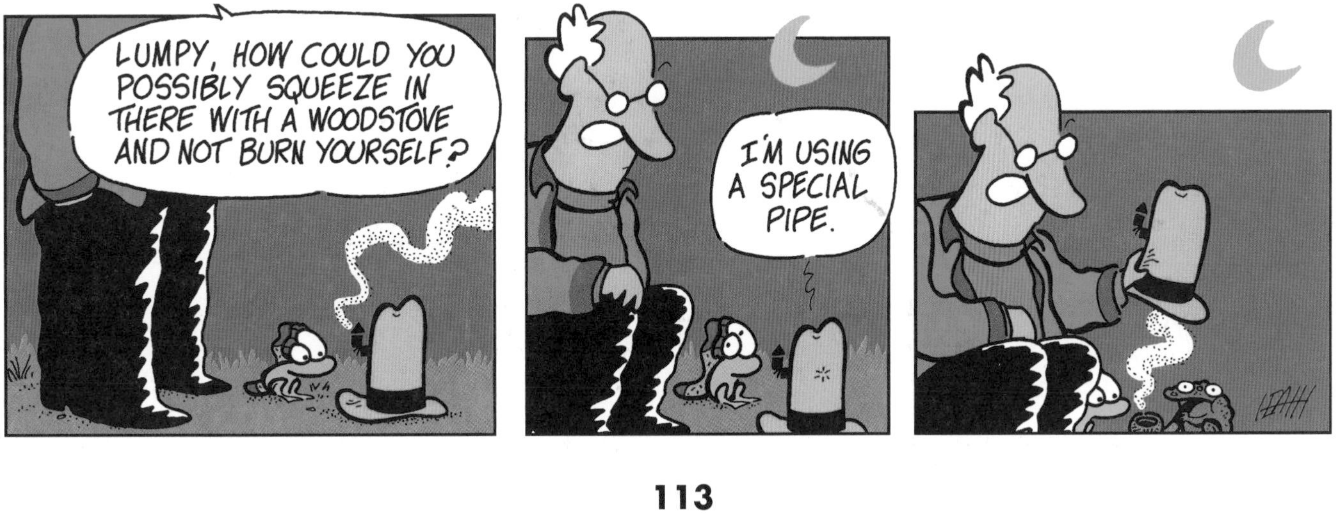
LUMPY, HOW COULD YOU POSSIBLY SQUEEZE IN THERE WITH A WOODSTOVE AND NOT BURN YOURSELF?
I'M USING A SPECIAL PIPE.

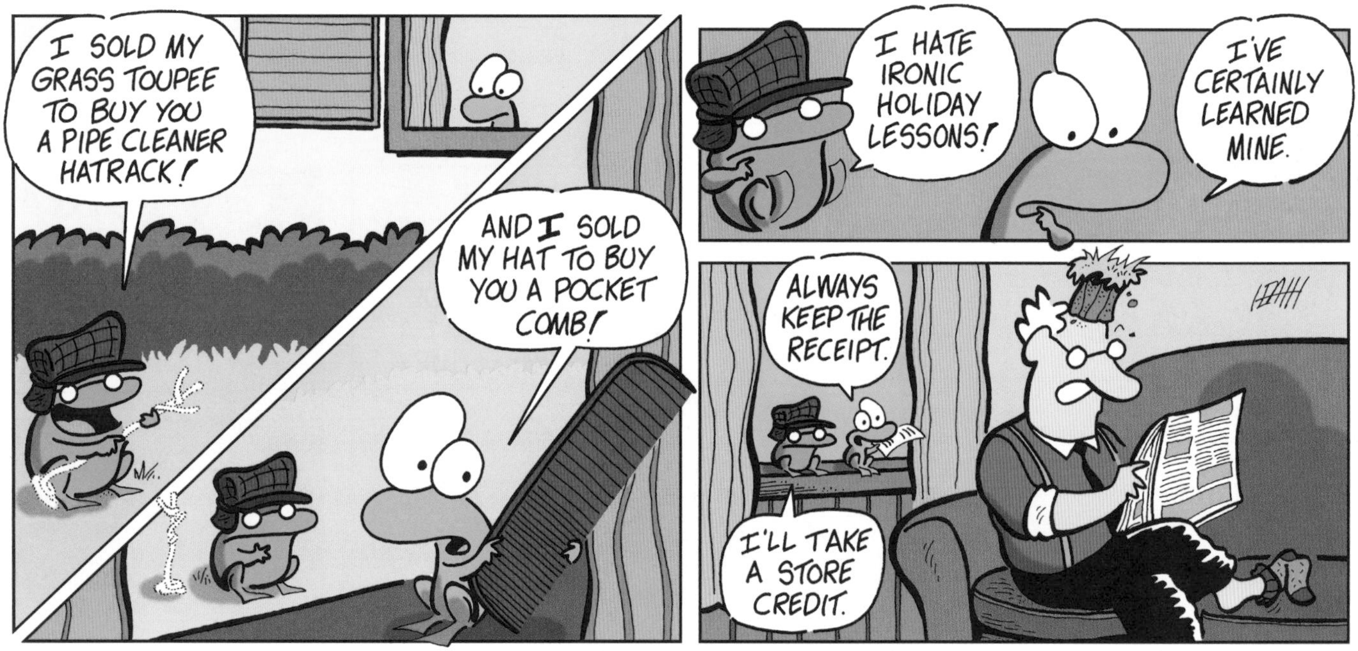
I SOLD MY GRASS TOUPEE TO BUY YOU A PIPE CLEANER HATRACK!
AND I SOLD MY HAT TO BUY YOU A POCKET COMB!
I HATE IRONIC HOLIDAY LESSONS!
I'VE CERTAINLY LEARNED MINE.
ALWAYS KEEP THE RECEIPT.
I'LL TAKE A STORE CREDIT.

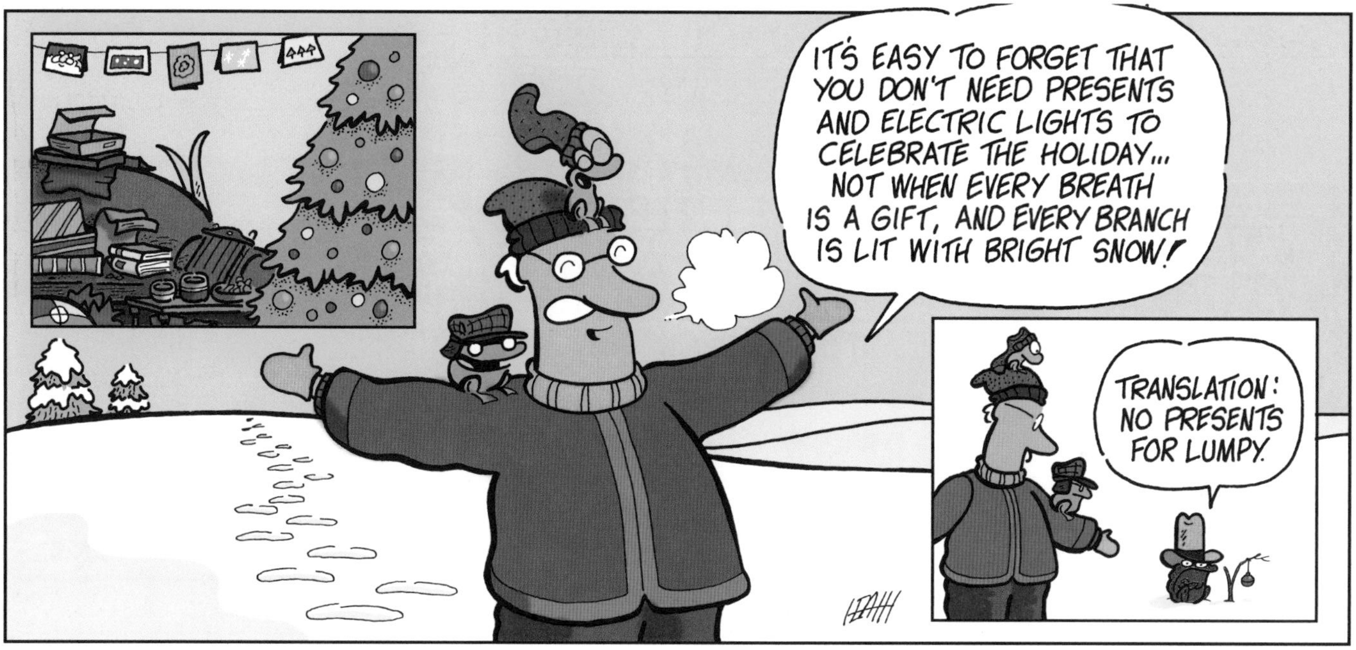
IT'S EASY TO FORGET THAT YOU DON'T NEED PRESENTS AND ELECTRIC LIGHTS TO CELEBRATE THE HOLIDAY... NOT WHEN EVERY BREATH IS A GIFT, AND EVERY BRANCH IS LIT WITH BRIGHT SNOW!
TRANSLATION: NO PRESENTS FOR LUMPY.

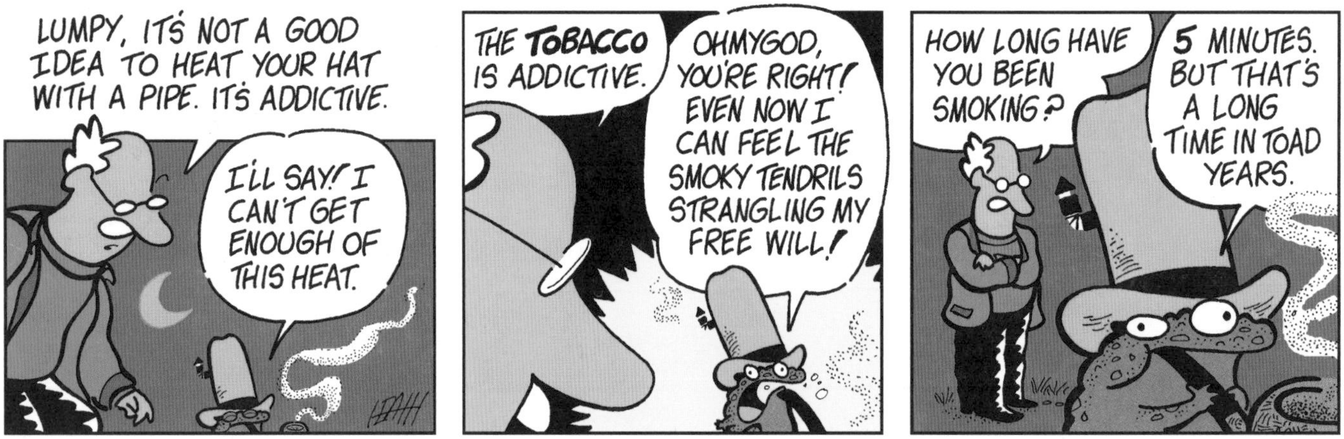
LUMPY, IT'S NOT A GOOD IDEA TO HEAT YOUR HAT WITH A PIPE. IT'S ADDICTIVE.
I'LL SAY! I CAN'T GET ENOUGH OF THIS HEAT.
THE **TOBACCO** IS ADDICTIVE.
OHMYGOD, YOU'RE RIGHT! EVEN NOW I CAN FEEL THE SMOKY TENDRILS STRANGLING MY FREE WILL!
HOW LONG HAVE YOU BEEN SMOKING?
5 MINUTES. BUT THAT'S A LONG TIME IN TOAD YEARS.

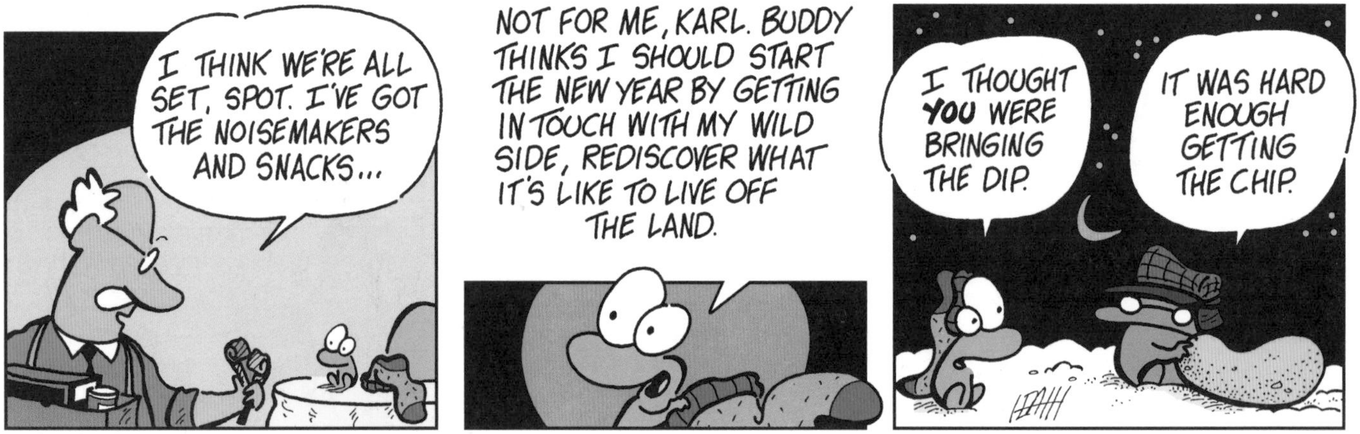
I THINK WE'RE ALL SET, SPOT. I'VE GOT THE NOISEMAKERS AND SNACKS...
NOT FOR ME, KARL. BUDDY THINKS I SHOULD START THE NEW YEAR BY GETTING IN TOUCH WITH MY WILD SIDE, REDISCOVER WHAT IT'S LIKE TO LIVE OFF THE LAND.
I THOUGHT **YOU** WERE BRINGING THE DIP.
IT WAS HARD ENOUGH GETTING THE CHIP.

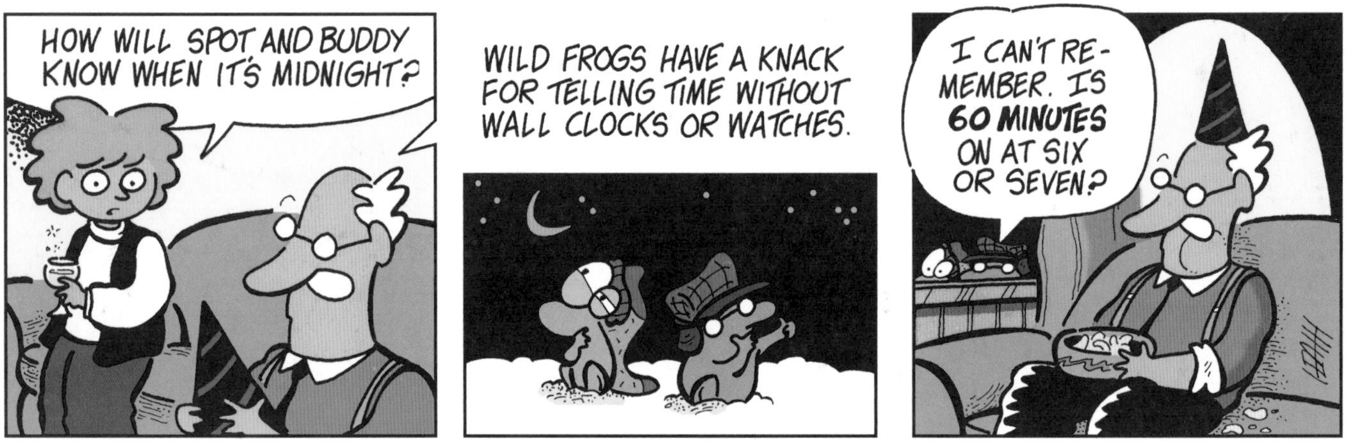
HOW WILL SPOT AND BUDDY KNOW WHEN IT'S MIDNIGHT?
WILD FROGS HAVE A KNACK FOR TELLING TIME WITHOUT WALL CLOCKS OR WATCHES.
I CAN'T RE-MEMBER. IS **60 MINUTES** ON AT SIX OR SEVEN?

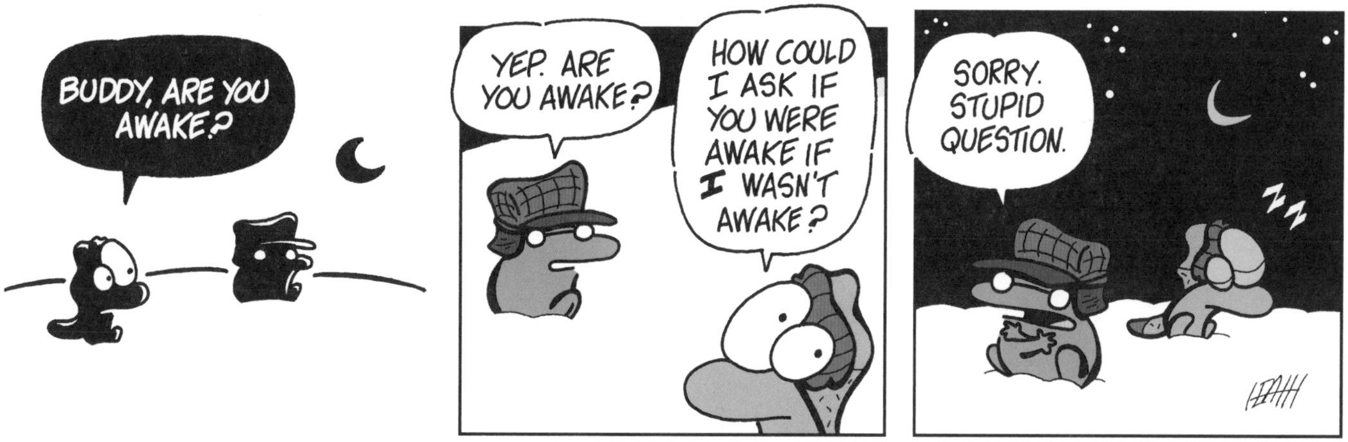
BUDDY, ARE YOU AWAKE?
YEP. ARE YOU AWAKE?
HOW COULD I ASK IF YOU WERE AWAKE IF I WASN'T AWAKE?
SORRY. STUPID QUESTION.
Z Z

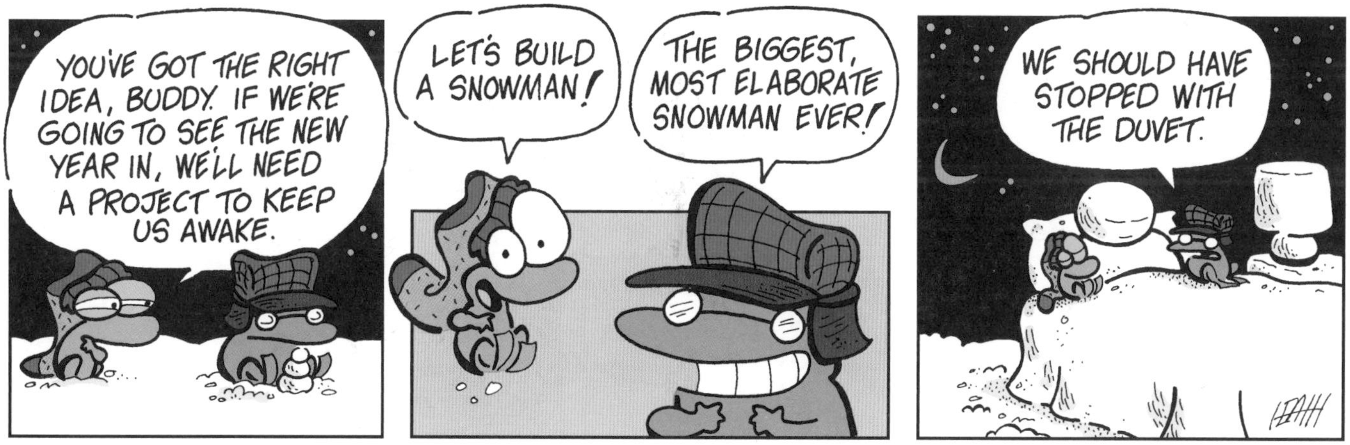
YOU'VE GOT THE RIGHT IDEA, BUDDY. IF WE'RE GOING TO SEE THE NEW YEAR IN, WE'LL NEED A PROJECT TO KEEP US AWAKE.
LET'S BUILD A SNOWMAN!
THE BIGGEST, MOST ELABORATE SNOWMAN EVER!
WE SHOULD HAVE STOPPED WITH THE DUVET.

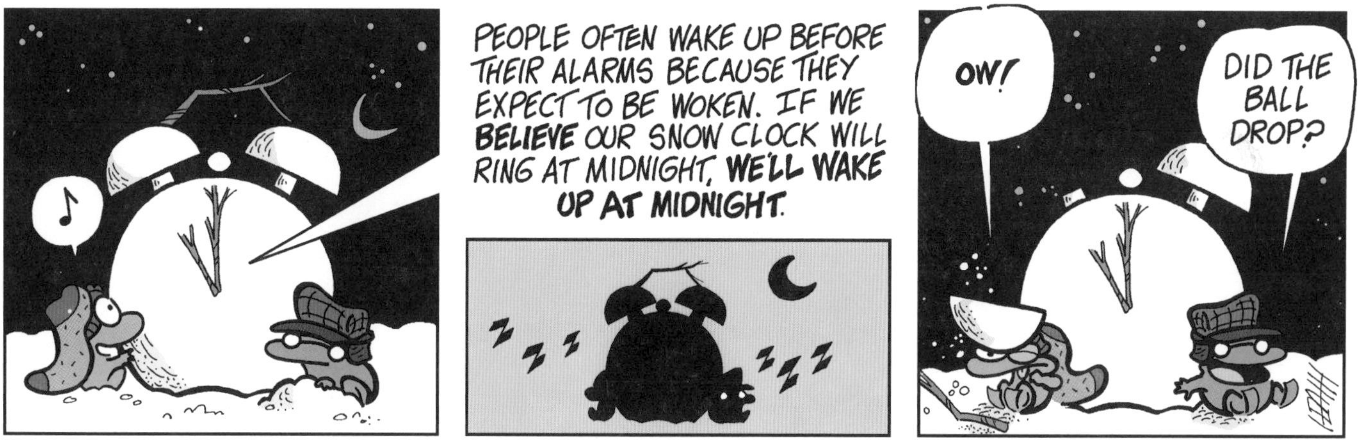
PEOPLE OFTEN WAKE UP BEFORE THEIR ALARMS BECAUSE THEY EXPECT TO BE WOKEN. IF WE **BELIEVE** OUR SNOW CLOCK WILL RING AT MIDNIGHT, **WE'LL WAKE UP AT MIDNIGHT**.
Z Z Z
Z Z Z
OW!
DID THE BALL DROP?

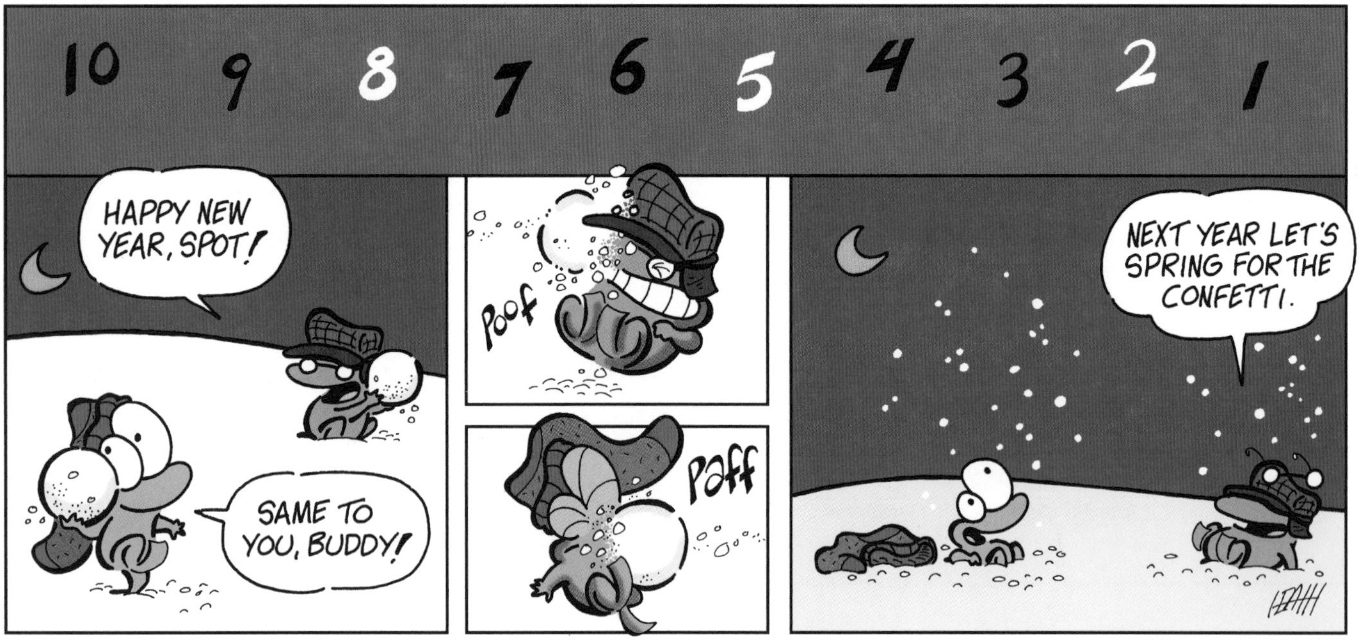
10 9 8 7 6 5 4 3 2 1
HAPPY NEW YEAR, SPOT!
SAME TO YOU, BUDDY!
Poof
Paff
NEXT YEAR LET'S SPRING FOR THE CONFETTI.

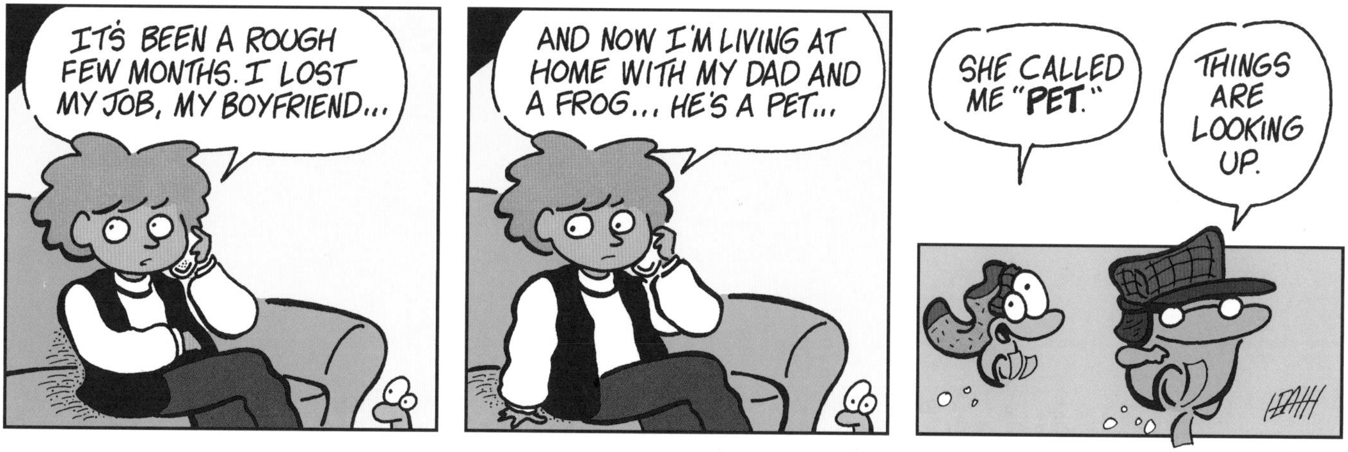
IT'S BEEN A ROUGH FEW MONTHS. I LOST MY JOB, MY BOYFRIEND...
AND NOW I'M LIVING AT HOME WITH MY DAD AND A FROG... HE'S A PET...
SHE CALLED ME "**PET**."
THINGS ARE LOOKING UP.

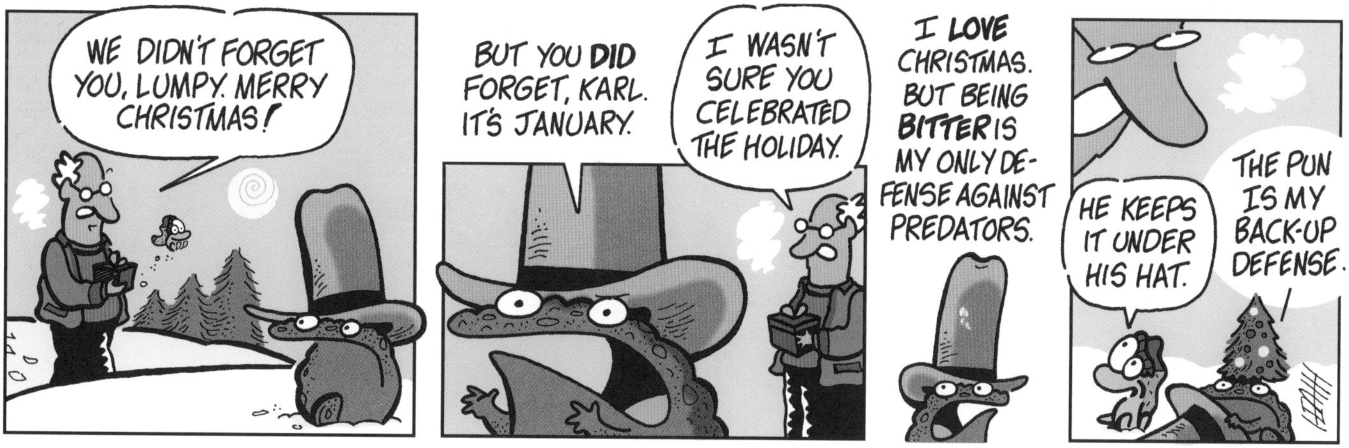
WE DIDN'T FORGET YOU, LUMPY. MERRY CHRISTMAS!
BUT YOU **DID** FORGET, KARL. IT'S JANUARY.
I WASN'T SURE YOU CELEBRATED THE HOLIDAY.
I **LOVE** CHRISTMAS. BUT BEING **BITTER** IS MY ONLY DEFENSE AGAINST PREDATORS.
HE KEEPS IT UNDER HIS HAT.
THE PUN IS MY BACK-UP DEFENSE.

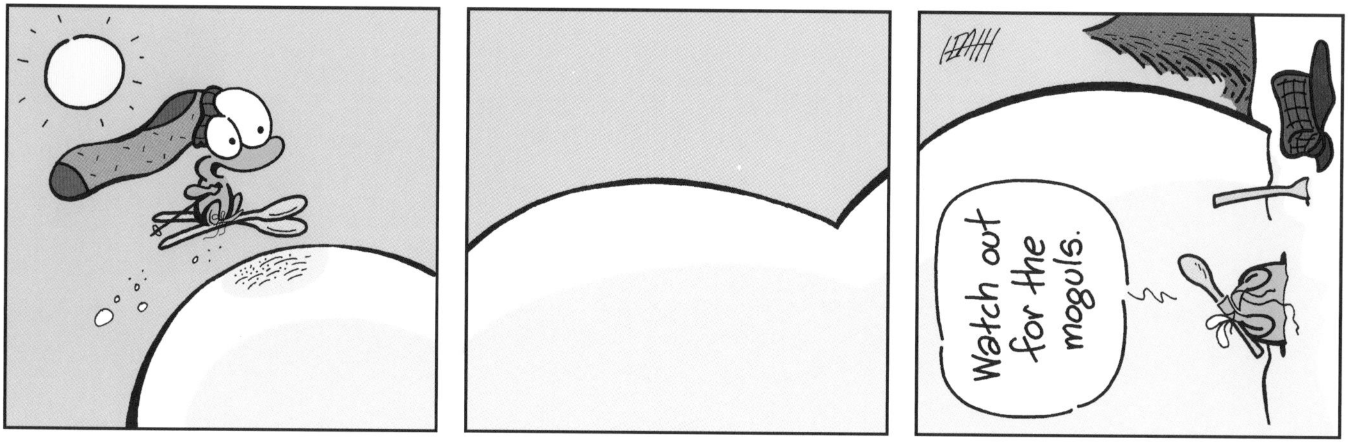
Watch out for the moguls.

Polar Distress:
A Holiday Tale for Cold-Blooded Readers

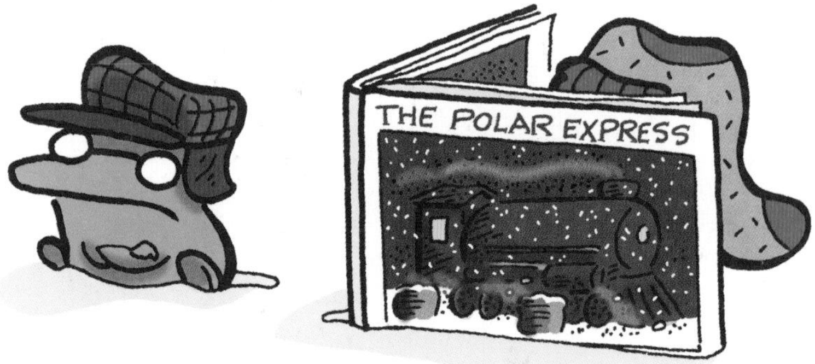
THE POLAR EXPRESS

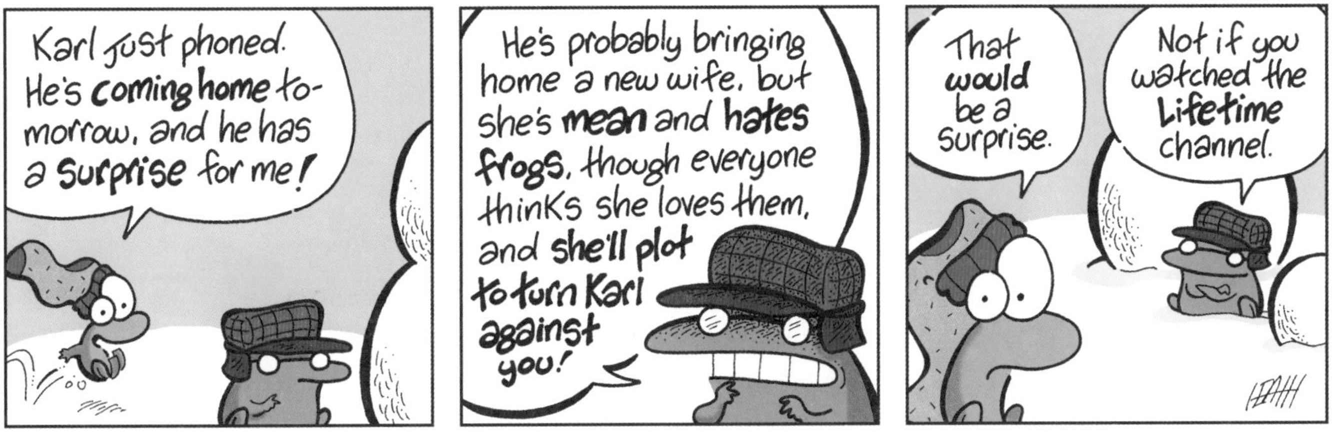
Karl just phoned. He's coming home tomorrow, and he has a surprise for me!
He's probably bringing home a new wife, but she's mean and hates frogs, though everyone thinks she loves them, and she'll plot to turn Karl against you!
That would be a surprise.
Not if you watched the Lifetime channel.

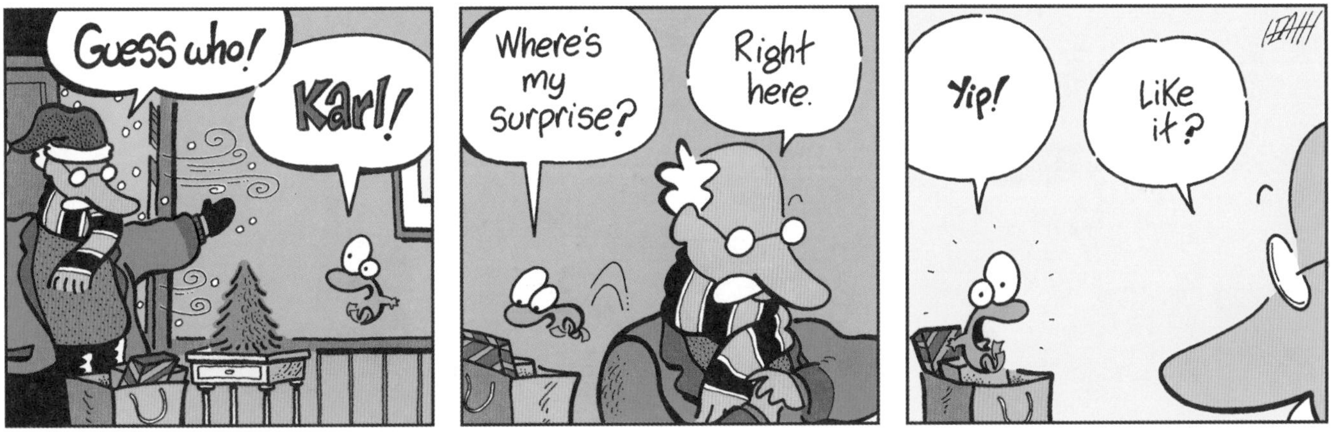
Guess who!
Karl!
Where's my surprise?
Right here.
Yip!
Like it?

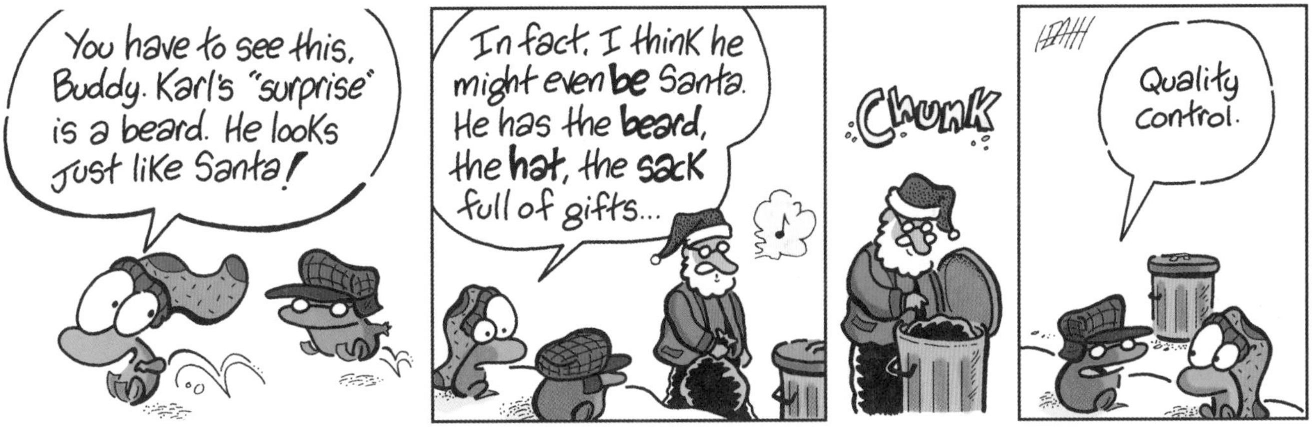
You have to see this, Buddy. Karl's "surprise" is a beard. He looks just like Santa!
In fact, I think he might even be Santa. He has the beard, the hat, the sack full of gifts...
Chunk
Quality control.

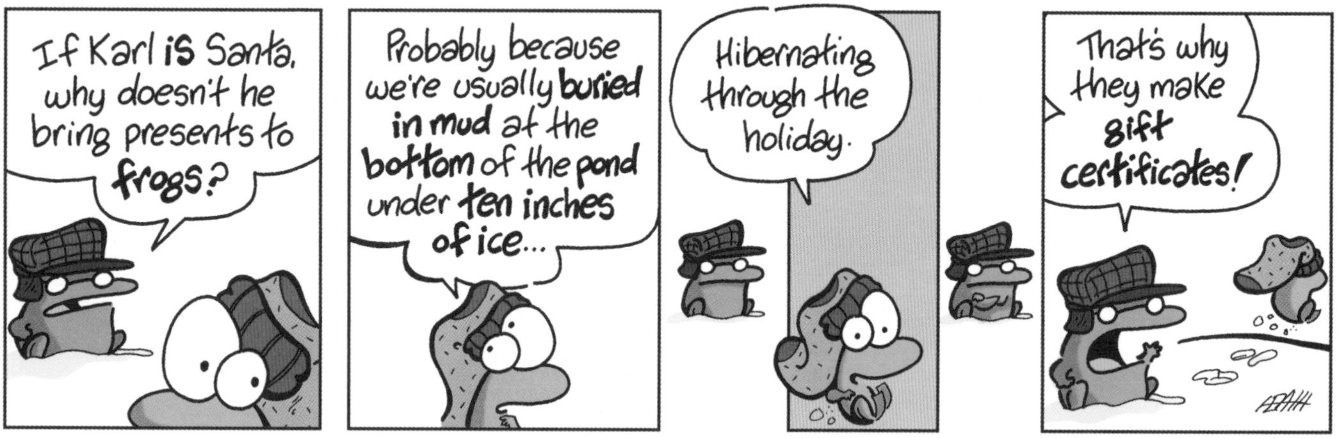
If Karl **is** Santa, why doesn't he bring presents to **frogs?**
Probably because we're usually **buried in mud** at the **bottom** of the **pond** under **ten inches of ice...**
Hibernating through the holiday.
That's why they make **gift certificates!**

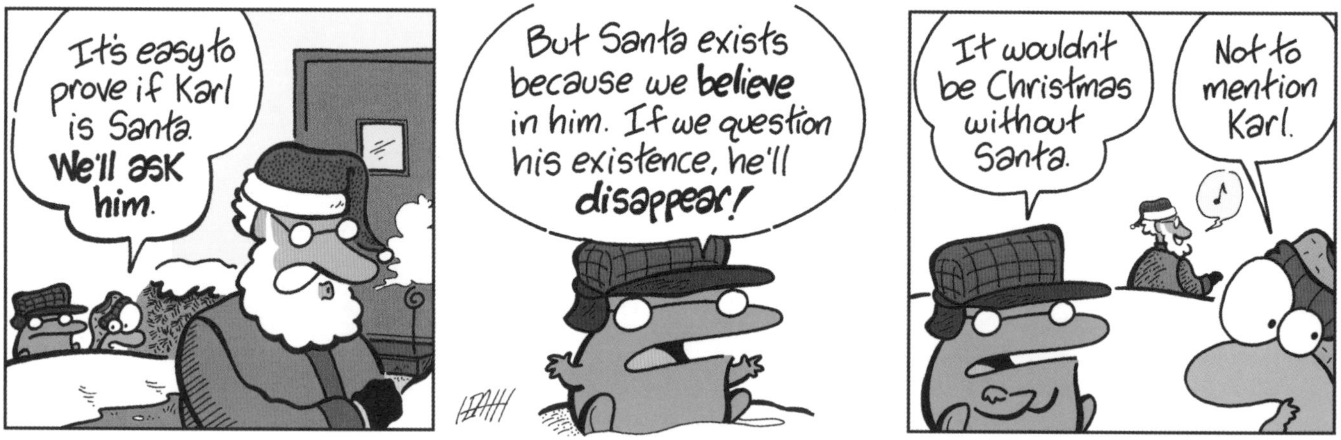
It's easy to prove if Karl is Santa. **We'll ask him.**
But Santa exists because we **believe** in him. If we question his existence, he'll **disappear!**
It wouldn't be Christmas without Santa.
Not to mention Karl.

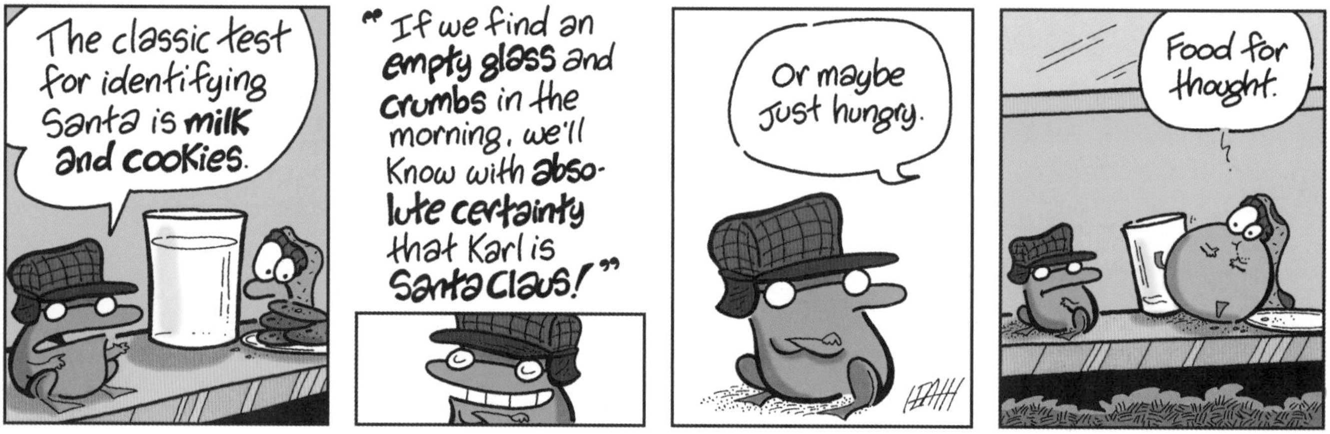
The classic test for identifying Santa is **milk and cookies.**
"If we find an **empty glass** and **crumbs** in the morning, we'll know with **absolute certainty** that Karl is **Santa Claus!**"
Or maybe just hungry.
Food for thought.

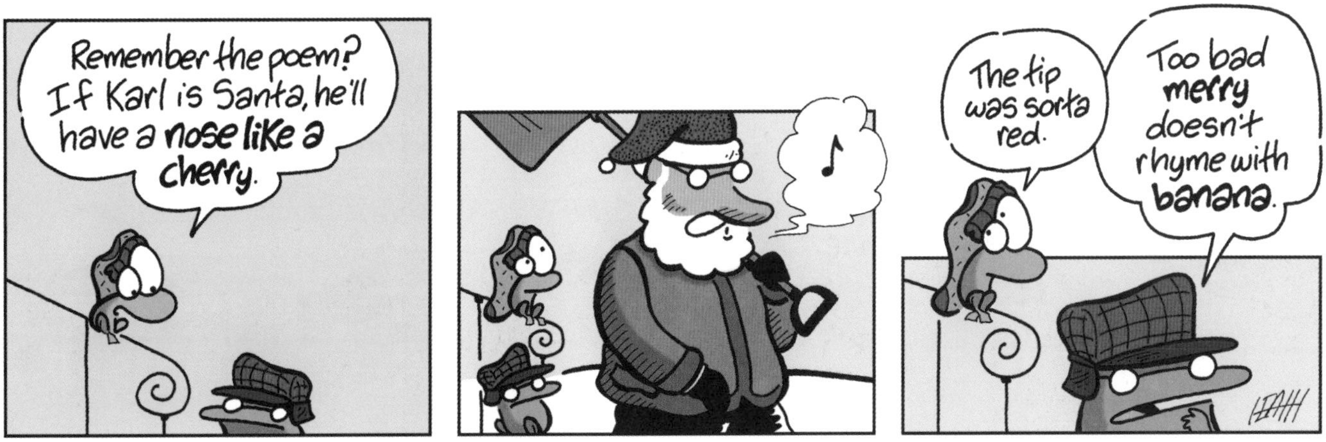
Remember the poem? If Karl is Santa, he'll have a **nose like a cherry**.
The tip was sorta red.
Too bad **merry** doesn't rhyme with **banana**.

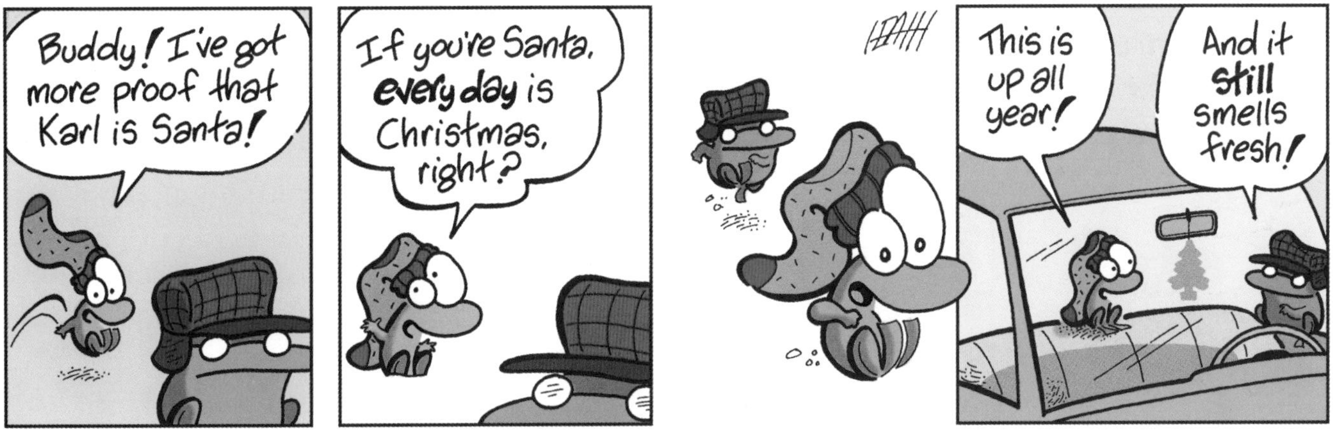
Buddy! I've got more proof that Karl is Santa!
If you're Santa, **every day** is Christmas, right?
This is up all year!
And it **still** smells fresh!

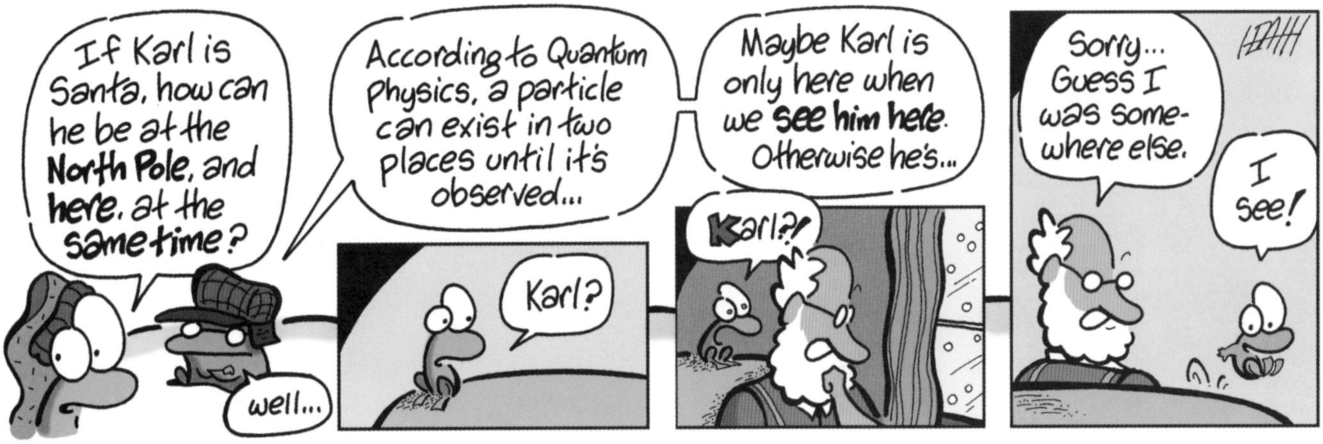
If Karl is Santa, how can he be at the **North Pole**, and **here**, at the **same time**?
well...
According to Quantum physics, a particle can exist in two places until it's observed...
Karl?
Maybe Karl is only here when we **see him here**. Otherwise he's...
Karl?!
Sorry... Guess I was somewhere else.
I see!

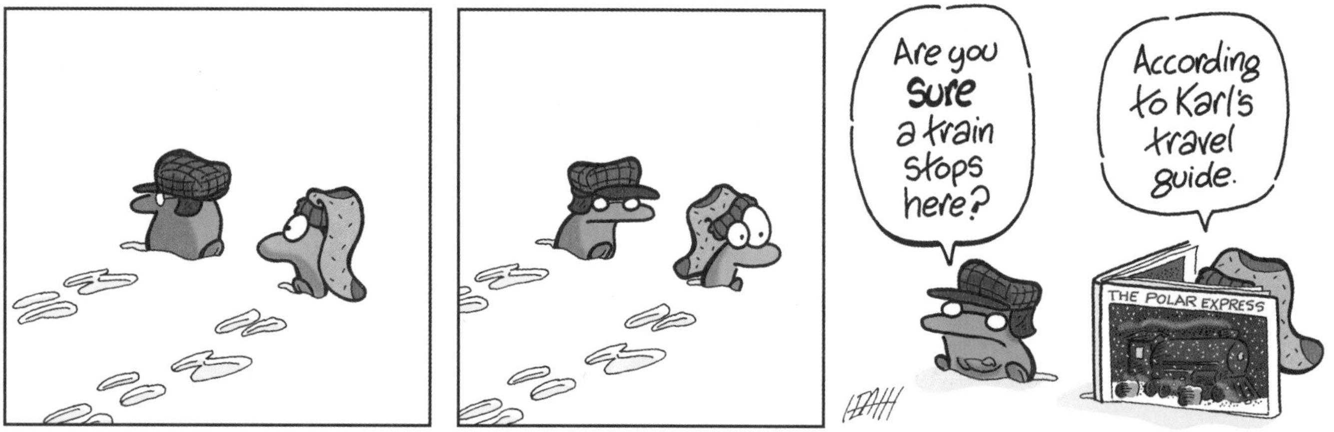
Are you sure a train stops here?
According to Karl's travel guide.
THE POLAR EXPRESS

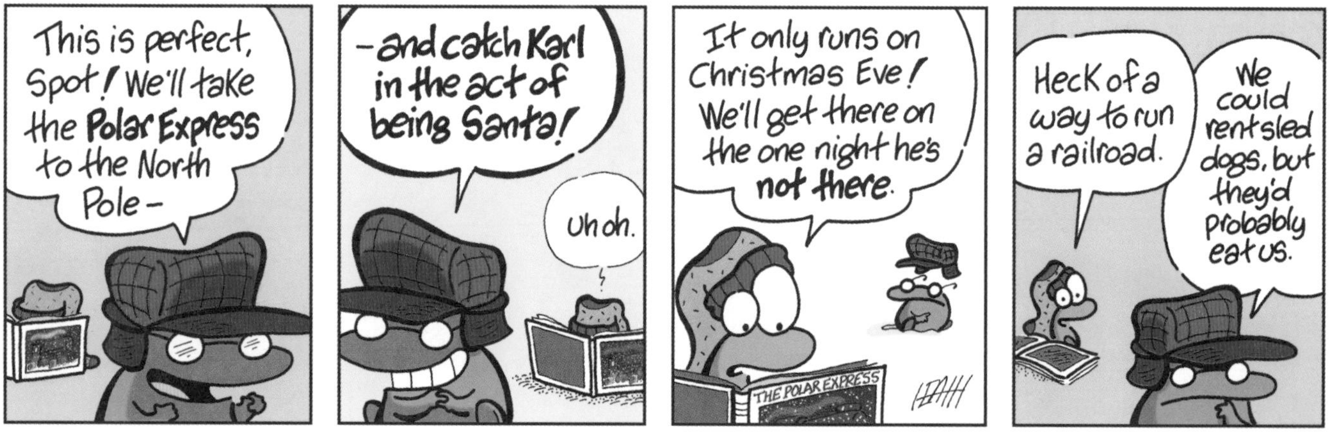
This is perfect, Spot! We'll take the Polar Express to the North Pole –
– and catch Karl in the act of being Santa!
Uh oh.
It only runs on Christmas Eve! We'll get there on the one night he's not there.
THE POLAR EXPRESS
Heck of a way to run a railroad.
We could rent sled dogs, but they'd probably eat us.

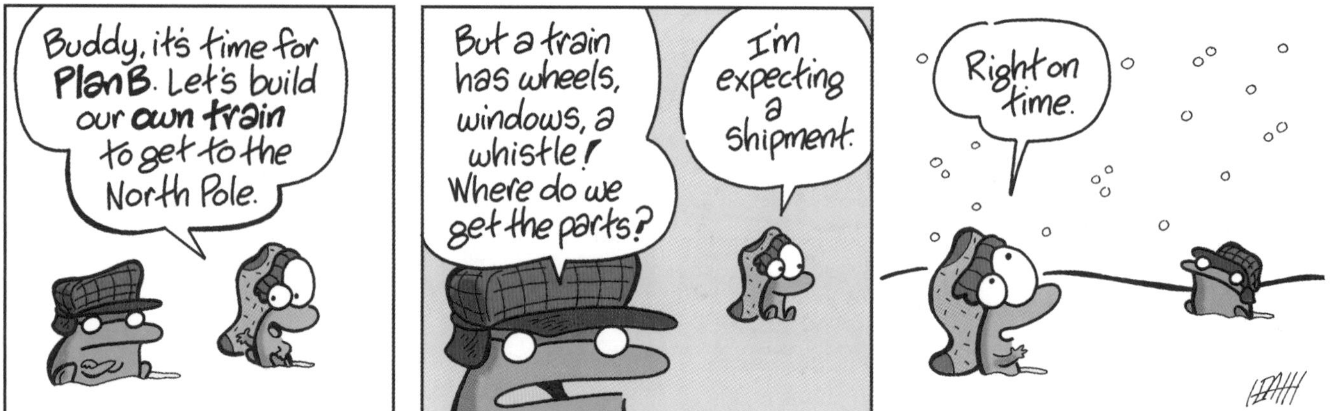
Buddy, it's time for Plan B. Let's build our own train to get to the North Pole.
But a train has wheels, windows, a whistle! Where do we get the parts?
I'm expecting a shipment.
Right on time.

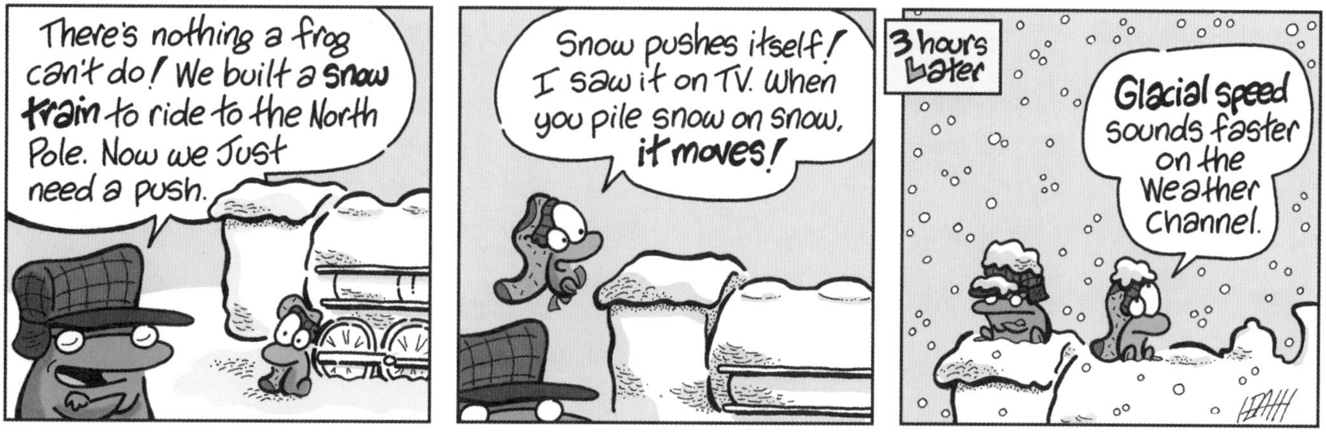
There's nothing a frog can't do! We built a **snow train** to ride to the North Pole. Now we just need a push.
Snow pushes itself! I saw it on TV. When you pile snow on snow, **it moves!**
3 hours later
Glacial speed sounds faster on the Weather Channel.

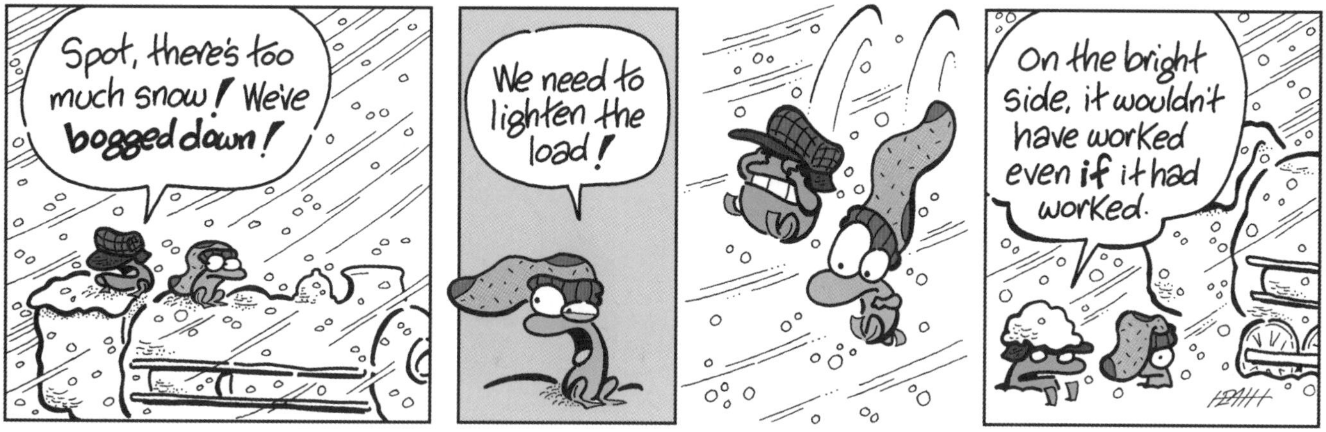
Spot, there's too much snow! We've **bogged down!**
We need to lighten the load!
On the bright side, it wouldn't have worked even **if** it had worked.

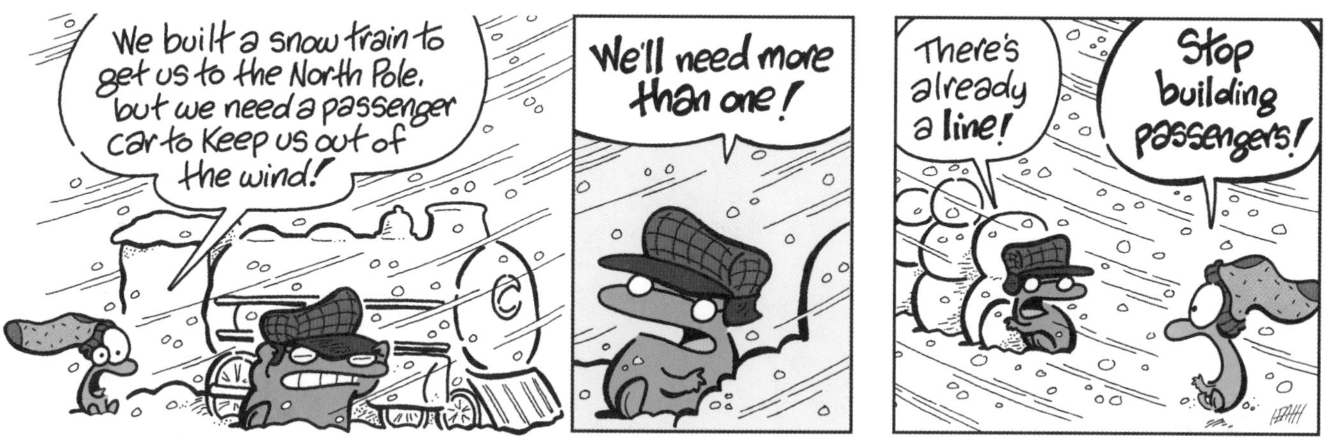
We built a snow train to get us to the North Pole, but we need a passenger car to keep us out of the wind!
We'll need more than one!
There's already a **line!**
Stop building passengers!

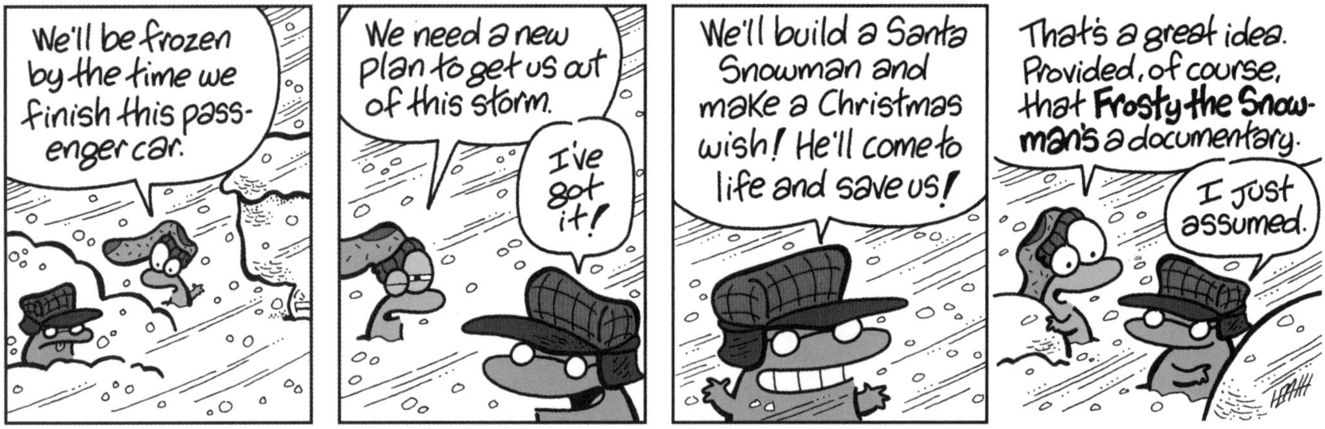
We'll be frozen by the time we finish this passenger car.
We need a new plan to get us out of this storm.
I've got it!
We'll build a Santa Snowman and make a Christmas wish! He'll come to life and save us!
That's a great idea. Provided, of course, that **Frosty the Snowman's** a documentary.
I just assumed.

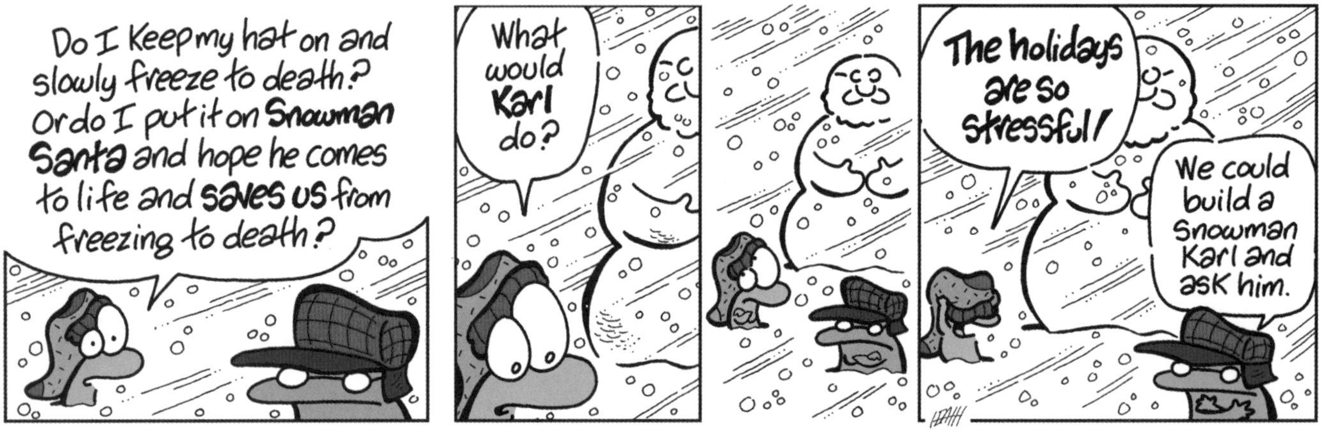
Do I keep my hat on and slowly freeze to death? Or do I put it on **Snowman Santa** and hope he comes to life and **saves us** from freezing to death?
What would **Karl** do?
The holidays are so stressful!
We could build a Snowman Karl and ask him.

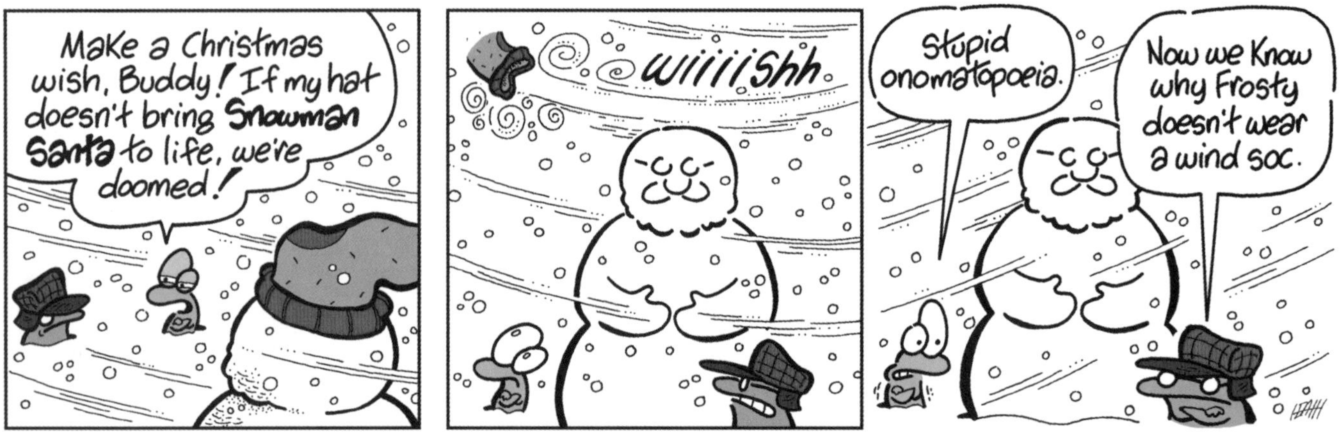
Make a Christmas wish, Buddy! If my hat doesn't bring **Snowman Santa** to life, we're doomed!
wiiiishh
Stupid onomatopoeia.
Now we know why Frosty doesn't wear a wind soc.

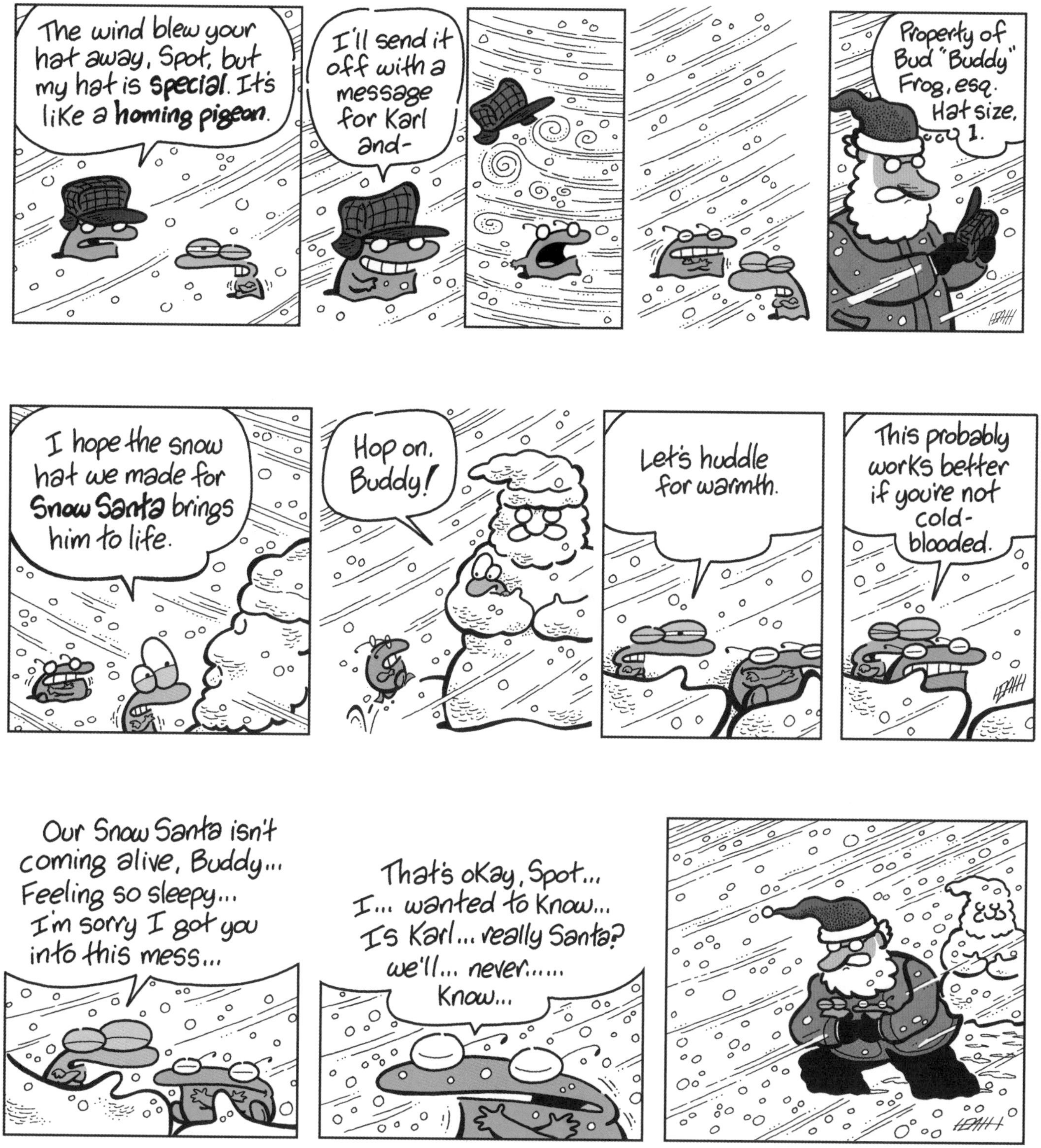
The wind blew your hat away, Spot, but my hat is **special**. It's like a **homing pigeon**.
I'll send it off with a message for Karl and-
Property of Bud "Buddy" Frog, esq. Hat size, 1.
I hope the snow hat we made for **Snow Santa** brings him to life.
Hop on, Buddy!
Let's huddle for warmth.
This probably works better if you're not cold-blooded.
Our Snow Santa isn't coming alive, Buddy... Feeling so sleepy... I'm sorry I got you into this mess...
That's okay, Spot... I... wanted to know... Is Karl... really Santa? we'll... never...... know...

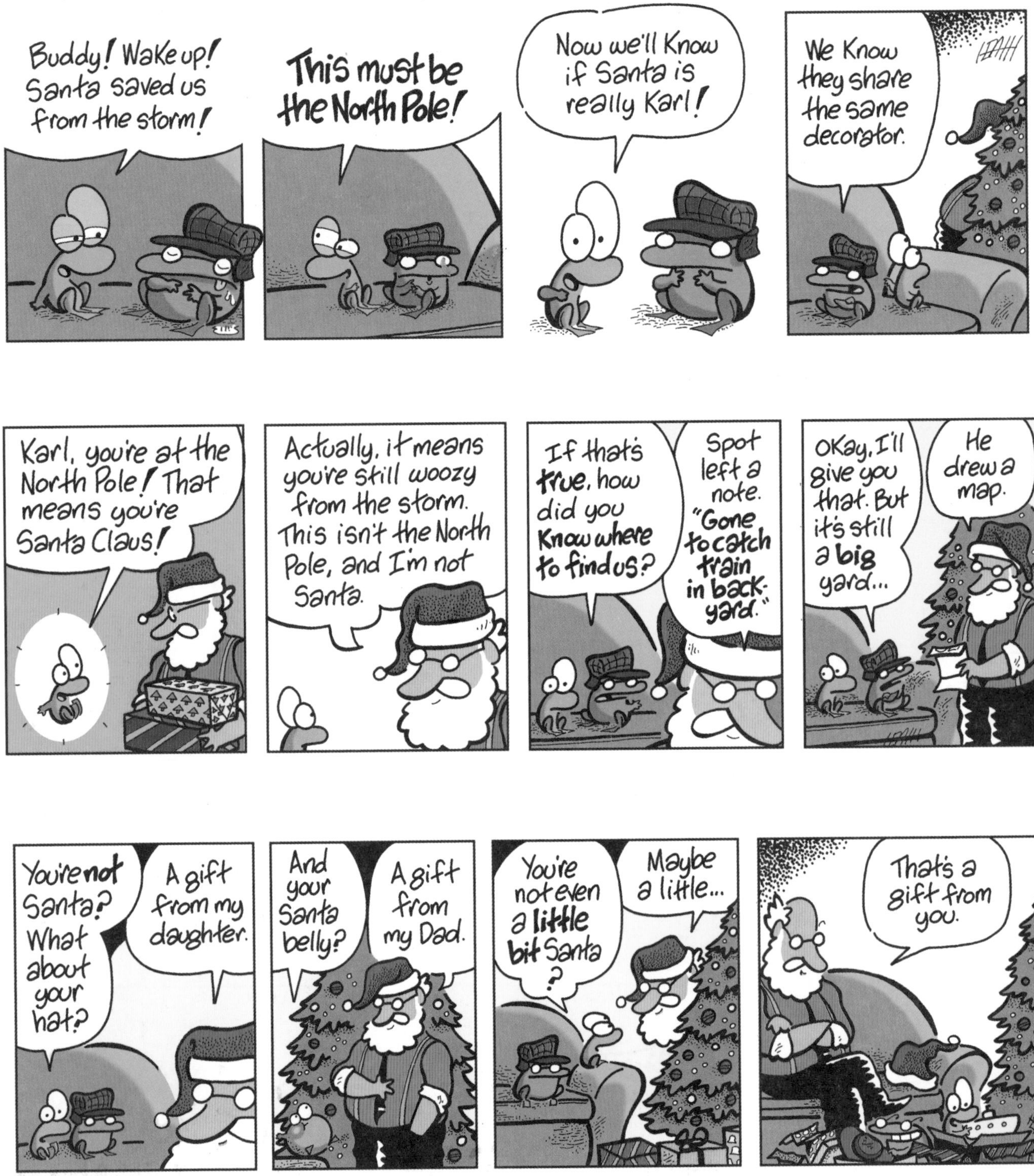

Buddy! Wake up! Santa saved us from the storm!
This must be the North Pole!
Now we'll Know if Santa is really Karl!
We Know they share the same decorator.
Karl, you're at the North Pole! That means you're Santa Claus!
Actually, it means you're still woozy from the storm. This isn't the North Pole, and I'm not Santa.
If that's **true**, how did you **know where to find us?**
Spot left a note. **"Gone to catch train in back-yard."**
OKay, I'll give you that. But it's still a **big** yard...
He drew a map.
You're **not** Santa? What about your hat?
A gift from my daughter.
And your Santa belly?
A gift from my Dad.
You're not even a **little bit** Santa?
Maybe a little...
That's a gift from you.